Extreme Situations

Now our children are in the world
Everything could be theirs –
Every harm could hurt them,
Every joy can make them laugh or run.
They could have stood in the queues at Buchenwald.
They can brown in the sun.
They can grow on into the years
When the torturers' prisons crumble into the past
And peace is breathed, unthinkingly,
By every single man.

Extreme Situations

Literature and Crisis
from the Great War to
the Atom Bomb

DAVID CRAIG
and
MICHAEL EGAN

BARNES & NOBLE
BOOKS
10 East 53d St., New York 10022
(a division of Harper & Row Publishers, Inc.)

First published in Great Britain 1979 by
The Macmillan Press Ltd

Published in the U.S.A. 1979 by
HARPER & ROW PUBLISHERS, INC.
BARNES & NOBLE IMPORT DIVISION

Printed in Great Britain

British Library Cataloguing in Publication Data

Craig, David, b.1932
    Extreme situations.
    1. Politics and literature
    2. Literature, Modern – 20th century – History
    and criticism
    I. Title   II. Egan, Michael
    809'.04   PN51

    Macmillan ISBN 0–333–24579–2
    Macmillan ISBN 0–333–24580–6 Pbk

Barnes & Noble ISBN 0–06–491305–8
Library of Congress Catalog Number: 79–54651

Contents

ACKNOWLEDGEMENTS   vi

1   Literature and Crisis   1

2   Total War   12

3   The Russian Revolution and Stalinism   65

4   Decadence and Crack-up   117

5   The Nullity of the Slump   138

6   Social Tragedy   153

7   Thwarted Revolutionaries   187

8   The Literature of Unfreedom   210

9   Artists and the Ominous   235

10   Spain: Life Against Death   253

11   Collapse and Survival   276

REFERENCES   288

INDEX   304

Acknowledgements

Acknowledgements are made to the editors of journals in which parts of this book have been published, sometimes in a different form: *Comparison; Continuum; The Journal of Peasant Studies; The Minnesota Review; Praxis; The Radical Reader.*

The authors and publishers wish to thank the following who have kindly given permission for the use of copyright material: Curtis Brown Ltd and Viking Press Inc. for extracts from *The Grapes of Wrath*, © 1939, © renewed 1967, by John Steinbeck; Jonathan Cape Ltd for extracts from *Fontamara* by Ignazio Silone (translated by Gwenda David and Eric Mosbacher); Jonathan Cape Ltd and Delacorte Press/Seymour Lawrence for extracts from *Slaughterhouse-Five* by Kurt Vonnegut Jr.; Andre Deutsch Ltd for extracts from *The Naked and the Dead* by Norman Mailer; Hamish Hamilton Ltd and Editions du Seuil for extracts from *The Case of Comrade Tulayev* by Viktor Serge (translated by W. R. Trask); Hamish Hamilton Ltd and Editions Gallimard for extracts from *Man's Estate* by André Malraux (translated by Alastair Macdonald).

Every effort has been made to trace all the copyright holders, but if any have been inadvertently overlooked the publishers will be pleased to make the necessary arrangement at the first opportunity.

The authors and publishers are grateful to the following for permission to reproduce illustrations:
1. Associated Press
2. John Hillelson Agency/Magnum Photos and the Estate of Robert Capa
3. (cover illustration) and 4. Galerie Klihm, Munich; and Frau Martha Dix
5. Grove Press, Inc. and the Estate of George Grosz, Princeton, N.J., USA

6. Deutsche Fotothek Dresden and Staatliche Kunstsammlungen, Dresden
7. © by SPADEM, Paris, 1979 Collection; on extended loan to the Museum of Modern Art, New York, from the artist's estate
8. from *The Russian War 1941–45* edited by Daniela Mrazkova and Vladimir Remes; © 1975 by Daniela Mrazkova and Vladimir Remes. Publisher: Elsevier Dutton, New York.

List of Plates

1. *Planting the Stars and Stripes atop Mount Suribachi on Iwo Jima Island 1945* – Photograph: Joe Rosenthal
2. *The Last Man to Die* (Berlin, 7 May 1945) – Photograph: Robert Capa
3. *Nächtliche Begegnung mit einem Irrsinnigen* (Night time meeting with a mad man) by Otto Dix, from *Der Krieg* (1924)
4. *Durch Fliegerbomben zerstörtes Haus* (House destroyed by flying bombs) by Otto Dix (Tournai) from *Der Krieg* (1924)
5. *Cross Section* (1920) by George Grosz
6. *Vision einer brenningden Stadt* (1936) (Vision of a burning city) by Hans Grundig
7. *Guernica* (1937) by Pablo Picasso
8. *Searching for Loved Ones at Kerch* (1942) – Photograph: Dmitri Baltermants

Certainly a special effort is needed today in order to write in a popular way. But at the same time it has become easier: easier and more urgent. The people has clearly separated from its top layer; its oppressors and exploiters have parted company with it and become involved in a bloody war against it which can no longer be overlooked. It has become easier to take sides. Open warfare has, as it were, broken out among the 'audience'.

Nor can the demand for a realist way of writing any longer be so easily overlooked. It has become more or less self-evident. The ruling strata are using lies more openly than before, and the lies are bigger. Telling the truth seems increasingly urgent. The sufferings are greater and the number of sufferers has grown. Compared with the vast sufferings of the masses it seems trivial and even despicable to worry about petty difficulties and the difficulties of petty groups.

There is only one ally against the growth of barbarism: the people on whom it imposes these sufferings. Only the people offer any prospects. Thus it is natural to turn to them, and more necessary than ever to speak their language.

– Brecht, 'The Popular and the Realistic'

1. Literature and Crisis

This book discusses the literature produced in many countries during the age that has experienced the two World Wars, the Russian, Chinese, and other revolutions, and the rise and collapse of Fascism. Our aim has been to find out how people's way of seeing life has changed and how their way of expressing their view has evolved in response to historical pressures that were at work over most of the world. This already picks out certain trends and makes less of others. It emphasises storm centres, crises, the front line of events. For in our time it has come about that not just special groups are involved, but the whole species tends to be embroiled in the worst upheavals. It has been said of Ludendorff's *Der Totale Krieg* (published in Munich in 1936) that 'the most brilliant strategist produced by modern imperialism demonstrates that the next war will be a war for the extermination of whole peoples, and that therefore the entire activities and every waking moment of every man, woman and child must henceforth be directed and organised in preparation for this'. This forecast was right. In the First World War, 5 per cent of the fatal casualties were civilian; in the second, 44 per cent; in the Korean War, 88 per cent; and in the war in Vietnam, 91 per cent.[1]

The writers fully alive in this age have naturally tended to create a literature of crisis, and our first impulse in studying it has not been academic. In the ghetto in Warsaw in 1941, Ludwik Hirszfeld asked a little girl, 'What would you like to be?' She answered, 'A dog, because the sentries like dogs.' In another ghetto, in Rovno, when the Germans were evacuating it by force in 1942, Friedrich Graebe saw children 'hauling and dragging their dead parents by the arms and legs through the streets to the train'.[2] Much more recently, much nearer home, John Heilpern spoke to children in the streets of Londonderry:

Fourteen-year-old boy: 'I shake for about 10 minutes after the explosions. I can't stop this shaking . . .' Fifteen-year-old girl: 'I've seen about five riots. I wasn't exactly horrified. I was ashamed.' Eleven-year-old boy, after thinking for several minutes: 'I'm just terrified.' Two-and-a-half-year-old, talking to himself: 'Don't let the Army shoot me, no. Don't let the Army shoot me, no.'[3]

And in Vietnam in the spring of 1969 Richard West went to see what it was like in a provincial capital, My Tho, in the Mekong delta:

American tanks – I saw three named Alcatraz, Assassin and Amputator – grind down the streets between monstrous hedgerows of rusty barbed-wire. An old hunchback, less than a yard high, begs for cigarettes in GI bars, mouthing 'Okay! Number One!' through wet, toothless gums. A café loudspeaker blares out a popular song, set to the accompaniment of revolver shots. Real shots echo the gramophone record. A child is run over and killed by a US truck, and when the Vietnamese MPs arrive they arrest the mother for causing a nuisance.[4]

Nearly every day this century things of that kind have been there for the observing, the reporting, the recreating in art. They are unbearable, they are being endured. They are unthinkable, they must be understood. It has come to pass that a typical witness of our time (not average, but typical) is the man who can write:

For my part, I have undergone a little over ten years of various forms of captivity, agitated in seven countries, and written twenty books. I own nothing. On several occasions a Press with a vast circulation has hurled filth at me because I spoke the truth. Behind us lies a victorious revolution gone astray, several abortive attempts at revolution, and massacres in so great number as to inspire a certain dizziness. And to think that it is not over yet. Let me be done with this digression; those were the only roads possible for us.[5]

When Serge began to be active politically, as an anarchist in

Paris sixty years ago, his kind of experience was still special. He was 'asking for it'. He was living what was in many ways the life of an outlaw – in literary terms, the life of the hero in a thriller. Since then, terror and the worst suffering, manhunts, amazing escapes, and shocking violent deaths have become usual. In the First World War, 41,435,000 people were killed, or one in forty of the people in the world. From the United Kingdom, 9 per cent of men aged between twenty-five and forty were killed, plus seventeen million wounded. In the Second World War, fifty-five million people were killed *excluding* Burma, Japan, China, and 'other Eastern nations whose records do not exist' – and in which the deathrolls were in fact huge. In February 1945 the Allies inflicted on Dresden the biggest massacre in history. At least 202,040 people were killed in a night.[6] And in Indonesia in 1965 there took place an event which most people in this country are surprised to be reminded of, or told about, the biggest massacre ever in time of peace – the anti-Communist *putsch* whose death-roll will never be known but almost certainly reached a quarter of a million. Mankind is now armed to the teeth, both with the small-arms that are convenient for things like urban guerrilla warfare and assassination, and with the vast systems that could wipe out the species. There are 750 million rifles and pistols in working order, or one for every adult male in the world; and as for the big systems, they read like the imaginings of those writers who have been marrying black satire to sci-fi:

> Then Mr Nixon flew off to Chequers in his helicopter, AP-One, with thirteen fellow-passengers. Besides Mr Heath and an American and British security man there were Secretary of State William Rogers, the President's national security adviser, Dr Henry Kissinger, and the American Ambassador, Mr Walter Annenburg. Also on board was Mr Nixon's personal physician, Dr Walter Tkach – and Brigadier General James Hughes, in charge of the 'Doomsday Box' containing the code by which the President can activate a nuclear 'strike' at a moment's notice. General Hughes accompanies the President wherever he goes.[7]

Such is the equipment of the world which had seen fifty-five wars between 'the last war' and 1969.[8] Such is the behaviour of its rulers.

It is almost a mark of a major writer or thinker in recent times that he is saturated in such materials and particularly concerned with the dilemmas that flow from them. Gorky remembers Lenin responding to Beethoven:

> I know nothing that is greater than the *Appassionata*; I'd like to listen to it every day. It is marvellous superhuman music ...' Then screwing up his eyes and smiling, he added, rather sadly: 'But I can't listen to music too often. It affects your nerves, makes you want to say stupid nice things and stroke the heads of people who create such beauty while living in this vile hell. And now you musn't stroke anyone's head – you might get your hand bitten off. You have to hit them on the head, without any mercy, although our ideal is not to use force against anyone. Hm, hm, our duty is infernally hard.[9]

This is very close to one of the deepest passages in Simone de Beauvoir's autobiography, the late volume called *Force of Circumstance*, in which she reaches her most final thoughts about her life amongst the arts:

> Reality still interests me, but it no longer reveals itself like an awful lightning flash. Beauty yes, beauty remains; even though it no longer stuns me with its revelations, even though most of its secrets have gone flat, there are still moments when it can make time stop. But often I loathe it too. The evening after a massacre, I was listening to a Beethoven *andante* and stopped the record halfway in anger: all the pain of the world was there, but so magnificently sublimated and controlled that it seemed justified. Almost all beautiful works have been created for the privileged and by privileged people who, even if they have suffered, have always had the possibility of expressing their sufferings; they are disguising the horror of misery in its nakedness. Another evening, after another massacre – there have been so many – I longed for all such lying beauty to be utterly destroyed. Today, that feeling of horror has died down. I can listen to Beethoven. But neither he nor anyone else will ever again be able to give me that feeling I used to have of having reached some absolute.[10]

Living in such a world, we would be guilty of bad faith if we did not put such views and concerns at the centre of our taste, our methods, our ideas. The writers themselves have affirmed this time and again. We will never know what course Keats might have followed as a poet if he had lived long enough for his imagination to be steeped in the Industrial Revolution and the fierce class struggle that was launched by Peterloo in 1819. But in his important unfinished poem *Hyperion* he wrote that the only person who could reach the height of creativity was

> . . . he to whom the miseries of the world
> Are misery, and will not let them rest . . .

Wilfred Owen wrote in the last year of the First World War (and of his own life), 'All a poet can do today is warn'. Recently, from another storm centre, Solzhenitsyn wrote, in his open letter to the Fourth Soviet Writers' Congress in 1967:

> Literature that is not the breath of contemporary society, that dares not transmit the pains and fears of that society, that does not warn in time against threatening moral and social dangers – such literature does not deserve the name of literature; it is only a façade. Such literature loses the confidence of its own people, and its published works are used as wastepaper instead of being read.[11]

The taste, methods, and ideas that flow from such views and concerns will show themselves more satisfactorily in practice – in the body of this book – than they could in any attempt to write them out in advance as a unified theory. But the reader will know better what to expect if we at least sketch some general features. For example, the writers have had to become expert at quickly transmuting the rawest materials from public life, from the headlines and front pages, into sufficiently subtle or inward art: think of Malraux' handling of the 1927 Shanghai massacre in *La Condition Humaine*, or Arthur Koestler's handling of the Moscow 'Show Trials' in *Darkness at Noon*. Again, the writers have managed to treat burning issues with ample stylistic resource that takes nothing away from the harshness of the original: think of how counter-revolutionary terror is treated as 'timeless' fable or folk-tale in Silone's novel *Fontamara* or Lu Hsun's story 'Medicine'. At the same time the writers, theatre directors, and filmmakers have not flinched from abandoning the elegant rearrangements of full-blown art and allowing the facts to reveal themselves unprocessed: think of the back-projected photographs in the theatre of Piscator and Brecht, or the periodic showing of the latest casualty figures throughout Theatre Workshop's *Oh What a Lovely War*.* In our world the facts are so starkly striking that they can express and dramatise themselves with the least help from the artist. So documentary becomes a major form. John Hersey's *Hiroshima* is one of the most necessary books to have been written since the war. It is as necessary to read Nadezhda Mandelstam's *Hope Against Hope* and Evgenia Ginzburg's *Into the Whirlwind* as it is to read Solzhenitsyn's *One Day in the Life of Ivan Denisovich*, if we wish to fathom some of the most extreme experiences undergone by the people of Europe in our time. We feel Graham Greene to have concentrated as much creative effort into the writing of 'travel books' like *Journey Without Maps* and *The Lawless Roads* as into novels like *The Heart of the Matter* and *The Power and the Glory*. Serge's *Memoirs* have the same moral depth and seriousness as his best creative work, *The Case of Comrade Tulayev*. Covering an event for a paper turns naturally into treating it with the fullness of classic fiction, as when Steinbeck set out to write a feature on migrant workers for *Life* and it turned into *The Grapes of Wrath*. The examples are endless. What such works have in common is so urgent a concern to bring a real state of affairs home to readers, that the original texture of it (its language, its sights and motifs) is as far as possible allowed to come through unaltered.

A similarly direct application to actuality is at work in the field of thought. The nineteenth-century sociologist, a Herbert Spencer or a J. S. Mill, tended to aspire to a System in which all data, at least in principle, could be schematised. The sociologist or psychologist or historian in our age is more likely to study a single burning phenomenon. Sorel wrote on violence, Durkheim on suicide. A generation ago, the psychiatrist Bruno Bettelheim had no sooner undergone the experience of Dachau than he saw

---

* This is discussed with many examples in chapter 14 of David Craig's *The Real Foundations* (1973).

that the concentration camp could be an analytic model of totally industrialised society: hence his book *The Informed Heart* (1961). Perhaps the classic case of such thinking through involvement is Reich's work on the 'pathology of civilised societies' in Germany and Austria just before the Fascists took power. In July 1927 in Vienna 100 people were killed and 1000 injured when police and militia shot into a crowd of socialist demonstrators. Reich at once joined the 'Workers' Help', a medical group affiliated to the Austrian Communist Party, and went on to carry out during protest marches and mass meetings the 'sociological field work' which presently issued in *The Mass Psychology of Fascism*.[12] More recently, the American psychologist Robert Jay Lifton has helped found a new discipline, the study of 'psycho-historical process', which uses psychoanalytic methods to investigate mass experiences, in the first place the experience of being bombed in Hiroshima: 'My emphasis is upon shared psychological and historical themes, but these themes express themselves through, and are inseparable from, individual psychological experience. In themselves they are neither pathological nor "normal".' Here is one argument of the present book, that the 'public' and the 'personal' are not opposed to but continuous with each other; and here, too, is our sense that the extreme is no longer special but typical. Lifton also stresses the 'significance of the investigator's relationship to the environment in which he has chosen to work'. Most recently he has taken this a long way in his therapeutic and research work with Vietnam veterans, work which he has found he cannot do except in 'a kind of anti-war community' which is participatory and egalitarian, in which the 'patients' continually question and evaluate the 'therapists'.[13]

So in our time, action and thought incessantly flow together and fuse. The thinker and the writer can no longer function from the armchair, but must get into the thick of practice. As Lenin wrote in a postscript to his unfinished *The State and Revolution* (we presume with some irony), 'It is more pleasant and useful to go through the "experience of revolution" than to write about it.'

The sort of approach to literature that arises from such concerns may be put in a question: What image of things have artists been moved to create as they strove to cope, imaginatively and practically, with life as they found it? This stresses the use of artistic imagination as a means of personal development and sanity. It also treats the products of that imagination as valuable in themselves. The writers living at the storm centres have been moulded in intimate ways by the forces raging round them. As a simple fact, many of those who bulk large in this book have used pen-names. Lu Hsun's real name was Chou Shu-jen, Serge's was Kibachich. Anna Seghers's is Netty Radvanyi, Silone's is Secondo Tranquilli. In China, Russia, Germany, Italy, it has been so dangerous to bear witness that writers have had to disguise themselves. Sometimes in the style of their work they have been cryptic to creative effect: in *Conversation in Sicily* (1941) Elio Vittorini had to dip deep into the wells of folk myth (ghosts, furies, a mysterious wayfarer) to figure the struggle between Fascists and socialists obliquely enough to pass the censor (they still imprisoned him). Sometimes even lying low or refraining has been to no avail, as when Isaac Babel was driven to 'perfect the genre of silence' and yet died in an unknown labour camp. In such conditions it takes extraordinary nerve, bravery, and stamina if literature is not to shrivel into the condition of the 'Writers' Circle' described by Silone in the first version of *Bread and Wine* (1937). It devoted itself to producing one work – 'Don Benedetto Was Poisoned' – scribbled on walls at dead of night. Nor does literary criticism escape. Those teaching it peacefully in universities and colleges today should ask themselves whether or not they would have carried out the one useful job the Nazis found for scholars of modern literature – identifying the authors of anonymous pamphlets against the régime.

Many writers and thinkers managed to escape at the last moment as the terror closed in. That is why, in addition to the abundant 'literature of unfreedom' (which we discuss in Chapter 8), there is so much work about the take-off into exile: for example, Anna Seghers's *Transit Visa*, Serge's *The Long Dusk* (especially its final chapter), and Koestler's *Scum of the Earth* and *Arrival and Departure*. In Russian such experience even threw up a special word to describe 'one who dies on the move' – *dokhodiaga*.[14] It was typical of Brecht's prescient sense of his epoch that as early as the middle Twenties he was already figuring the typical person of the age as a migrant, in the sequence written in 1926–7 called 'A Reader for Those Who Live in Cities':

Part from your friends at the station
Enter the city in the morning with your coat buttoned up
Look for a room, and when your friend knocks:
Do not, o do not, open the door
But
Cover your tracks.

If you meet your parents in Hamburg or elsewhere
Pass them like strangers, turn the corner, don't
              recognise them
Pull the hat they gave you over your face, and
Do not, o do not, show your face
But
Cover your tracks . . .

Whatever you say, don't say it twice
If you find your ideas in anyone else, disown them.
The man who hasn't signed anything, who has left
              no picture
Who was not there, who said nothing:
How can they catch him?
Cover your tracks . . .[15]

This theme is so strong among black South African writers that it is almost a genre in itself. Almost always their novels are disguised third-person autobiographies, like Ezekiel Mphahlele's *Down Second Avenue*, Alex La Guma's *A Walk in the Night*, or Peter Abrahams' *Tell Freedom*. Almost always the novel is 'resolved' by escape from the racist trap as the aeroplane lifts off for New York, London, elsewhere in Africa. Other studies on the same theme and with a similar pattern have been overtly documentary, for example Lewis Nkosi's collection of essays, *Home and Exile*, and Bloke Modisane's *Blame Me on History*. The cruel irony of this situation is that as soon as these writers have found a haven somewhere else, their work has tended to deteriorate. They cannot work in South Africa, they cannot write outside it. This has led some of them to opt for the ultimate exile: like Nat Nkasa they have killed themselves. Others (like Babel in the Soviet Union) have stopped writing.

Such people are 'neither pathological nor "normal"'. Their

condition and their feelings are only an intensification of the general truth that a writer is, inevitably, situated – is more or less bound by his place and time. However 'inspired' he is, however independent of or out of step with his age he feels himself to be, he cannot in practice create at his own sweet will and his work is bound to be, whether directly or not, evidence for what has been happening in our time.

This book is not a history of socialist literature from 1914 to 1945 – we are not aiming at that sort of completeness; nor is it chapters from a treatise on 'literature and society' – we are not attempting to develop a systematic theory. Our aim is to throw as strong and clear a light as possible on those writers who have lived through or close to the most extreme of modern situations and whose work is the most needful for us to know because it offers the most feeling, observant, and unforgettable a view of what it was like to be alive at this time of crisis and struggle. Our effort has been to work in the spirit recently defined by Milan Kundera, the Czech novelist who now lives in France and whose books are banned in his own country:

> If you cannot view the art that comes to you from Prague, Budapest, or Warsaw in any other way than by means of this wretched political code [which views all East European work as either 'dissident' or not], you murder it, no less brutally than the worst of the Stalinist dogmatists. And you are quite unable to hear its true voice. The importance of this art does not lie in the fact that it pillories this or that political regime but that, on the strength of social and human experience of a kind people here in the West cannot even imagine, it offers new testimony about mankind.[16]

Readers will no doubt feel that there are good witnesses to the age whom we have 'missed out'. Why, for example, is Arthur Koestler's *Darkness at Noon* (1940) not among the books we discuss in the chapter on the Russian Revolution and Stalinism? We chose, instead, to concentrate on Victor Serge's *The Case of Comrade Tulayev* (along with Solzhenitsyn's *First Circle* and Fedin's trilogy) because we think that it deals, quite as authoritatively as Koestler, with the essential dilemma of conscience faced by Communists who succumbed in the Show Trials, while also presenting in rich and coherent detail an area that Koestler does not attempt – the daily life of the society which engendered that travesty of justice. But it is Koestler's novel and not Serge's which is famous, and this is typical of the age as we see it: the most telling witnesses were the most likely to be ignored, forgotten, or silenced. They fell foul of both Establishments, the Stalinist and the conservative or 'apolitical'. We hope that readers of this book will come to share our view that the writers we discuss deserve to be, but for historical reasons have often failed to become, modern classics.

2. *Total War*

The 'Great War' imprinted itself so deeply in our culture that it remains perhaps the most distinct collective image that we have. We can all see 'the trenches' plainly in the mind's eye. Muddy slots in the ground – parapets – soldiers with rifles going over the top led by a lieutenant with a revolver – craters – flares exploding in the sky – the bristling coils of wire – duck-boards and mud and corpses lying brokenly . . . What are the sources of this collective image? The experiences and the memories of thousands of men, passed through to us by pictures in old magazines, a sentence or two spoken by a schoolfriend's father, some poems by Siegfried Sassoon in a thirties anthology, and now – for most people – the *Great War* series on BBC-TV and the film of the Theatre Workshop play, *Oh What a Lovely War.*

No other war compares with the First World War in the distinct-ness of its image. Earlier wars left their mark: Waterloo survives in folksong as imagery of red blood and amputated legs, the Crimea likewise as imagery of hurtling iron, suffering amidst cold and shortages, and of course the senseless bravery of the Light Brigade. The Second World War by contrast is a conglomerate of things from widely scattered places, not so much because it is too recent to have knit together as because it was waged all round the globe: Dunkirk, Warsaw, Monte Cassino, the Western Desert, the Burma Road, Iwo Jima, Stalingrad, Hiroshima. Each of these places (and Berlin, and the Arctic convoys, and Pearl Harbor) has its cluster of potent associations or images but none typifies 'the war' as does, for example, the Somme of the 'trench poets'. The *meaning* of that churned and shattered landscape in the north of France and of the figures that people it – men running, cowering, labouring in a frenzy – can perhaps be put in a phrase, the obliteration of humanity. Millions were killed outright, millions had bits burnt and torn off their bodies, the destruction of flesh and grass and trees amassed itself, on a scale industrial in its precision and its continuous outflow, over the days, months, and years of fighting. In one day on the Somme, 1 July 1916, 60,000 British men were killed. The next day in *The Times* Philip Gibbs reported: 'It is, on balance, a good day for England and France.' The same day in the *Manchester Guardian* the Press Association man admitted that 'One almost shrinks from recording it, so heavy is the toll.' By 6 September the *Daily Mail* was offering postcards titled 'The Glorious First of July 1916'.

Values were bound to be obliterated along with people. Robert Graves, speaking at first hand in his autobiography, has this to say:

> Patriotism. There was no patriotism in the trenches . . . The nation included not only the trench-soldiers themselves and those who had gone home wounded, but the staff, the Army Service Corps, lines of communication troops, base units, home-service units, and then civilians down to the detested grades of journalists, profiteers, 'starred' men exempted from enlistment, conscientious objectors, members of the Government . . .
>
> Religion. It was said that not one soldier in a hundred was inspired by religious feeling of even the crudest kind. It would have been difficult to remain religious in the trenches though one had survived the irreligion of the training battalion at home.[1]

The most accessible record of the massive obliteration (given that most of us do not have video-tape of films and television ready to hand) remains the poetry, the anonymous soldiers' songs as well as Sassoon, Owen, Rosenberg, and Edward Thomas, and it is a record which is unprecedented in its honesty. The filth, terror, and injuries of war had, since prehistoric times, been glorified out of recognition by the chroniclers and bards, because of the psycho-social need to repress traumas and keep morale well-tempered (and also because of the hardihood of people inured to primitive conditions: survivors of Culloden who had lost legs cauterised their own stumps with swords heated in the campfire).

Thomas Hardy and others tried to keep up the traditional style but the best new writers were turning to a man against the waging of the war and so brought down on themselves the abuse and persecution of the Establishment. In the autumn of 1915 Lawrence published *The Rainbow*, with its slur on Gordon's Sudan campaign a generation before. The magistrates had the book destroyed (ostensibly for a sexual scene between two women) and J. C. Squire, 'himself a poet', suggested that Lawrence must be 'under the spell of German psychologists'. Augustine Birrell, 'himself a writer', in his capacity as Chief Secretary for Ireland said in a speech that he would 'forbid the use, during war, of poetry'. In America the *New York Times* denounced critics of the war after the publication of John Dos Passos's very compassionate and moving novel, *Three Soldiers*, about an artist destroyed by army service.[2]

The poetry which both the authorities and the mass of readers really wanted, and at first got, was high-minded rhetoric which focused nothing and implied that everything was for the best. To name an example almost at random, we have a copy of a poetry best-seller called *Bees in Amber* (1913, 1916) by John Oxenham, bound in limp purple suede. Oxenham's view of life is expressed with evangelical verve in verses like

> So – Ho for the Pilot's orders,
> Whatever course He makes!
> For He sees beyond the sky-line,
> And He never makes mistakes.

Specifically on war, Oxenham writes, in a poem called 'For the Men at the Front':

> Lord God of Hosts, whose mighty hand
> Dominion holds on sea and land,
> In Peace and War Thy Will we see
> Shaping the larger liberty.
>   Nations may rise and nations fall,
>   Thy changeless Purpose rules them all.

The sales of this book accelerated markedly as the war went on. By the eve of the Glorious First of July 1916 it had sold

95,000 copies – far more than Sassoon ever reached. In the late autumn of 1914, as fighting got under way, Rupert Brooke was serving his country by telling it why it should be thankful for this splendid new war:

> Now, God be thanked Who has matched us with His hour,
>   And caught our youth, and wakened us from sleeping,
> With hand made sure, clear eye, and sharpened power,
>   To turn, as swimmers into cleanness leaping,
>
> Glad from a world grown old and cold and weary,
>   Leave the sick hearts that honour could not move,
> And half-men, and their dirty songs and dreary,
>   And all the little emptiness of love![3]

This so struck the note that the 'God be thanked' sentence was used as a recruiting slogan. In 1916 the line about 'dirty songs and dreary' was taken out of context by *The Review* to use against the new anti-war poetry. Brooke was not actually giving a lead. On 8 August 1914, four days after the state of war with Germany was proclaimed, the *Daily Mail* announced that the country had 'passed from the twilight of sloth and indulgence into the clear day of action and self-sacrifice'.

This view, which had the state and the mass newspapers on its side, gave way only slowly before a disabused and clear-eyed realisation of what was happening. All the classic poets we go to for true images of the war had begun by justifying it. For Sassoon in 1915,

> War is our scourge; yet war has made us wise,
> And, fighting for our freedom, we are free.

For Owen in the same year, the war was a force of nature, necessary and fertilising:

> But now, for us, wild Winter, and the need
> Of sowings for new Spring, and blood for seed.

For Rosenberg in 1916, the twentieth-century soldier was a Titan who had 'outgrown the pallid days' when he 'slept like Circe's swine'.[4] In Rosenberg's imagination the destroying force of war remained to the end (he was killed in May 1918) a part of the vitality of nature. Yet in 'Dead Man's Dump' he wrote the supreme passage in our language about the moment of dying, seen as an utter end, not at all blurred or explained away:

Here is one not long dead;
His dark hearing caught our far wheels,
And the choked soul stretched weak hands
To reach the living word the far wheels said,
The blood-dazed intelligence beating for light,
Crying through the suspense of the far torturing wheels
Swift for the end to break
Or the wheels to break,
Cried as the tide of the world broke over his sight . . .

So we crashed round the bend,
We heard his weak scream,
We heard his very last sound,
And our wheels grazed his dead face.[5]

Sassoon did not work at that depth but his poetry was indispensable for its straightforward showing of combat as it was – his words feel like physical things as he labours to get his unforgettable memories onto the page:

. . . green clumsy legs
High-booted, sprawled and grovelled along the saps
And trunks, face downward, in the sucking mud,
Wallowed like trodden sand-bags loosely filled;
And naked sodden buttocks, mats of hair,
Bulged, clotted heads slept in the plastering slime . . .[6]

It is at this point, in the *Counter-Attack* volume, that the making of war by our species at last emerged into the light of complete realisation. Eight years later Lawrence was to write: 'There's nothing else for it. Take the foul rotten spirit of mankind, full of the running sores of the war, to our bosom, and cleanse it there. Cleanse it not with blind love: ah no, that won't help. But with bitter and wincing realisation.'[7] What the soldier poets

and singers did was to put it permanently in the record – for
the work of Owen and Sassoon and the *Lovely War* songs on
disc and film have now, at last, outstayed the glory-and-honour
school in living currency – that war consists of cowardice, fear,
panic, guilt, resentment, discomfort, agony, and sadism as well
as selfless courage, endurance, and skill. The poems and songs
are wholly candid, they leave nothing covered up. Sassoon writes
about suicide in the trenches:

> In winter trenches, cowed and glum,
> With crumps and lice and lack of rum,
> He put a bullet through his brain.
> No one spoke of him again.[8]

Owen writes about a doctor's reaction to a soldier demoralised
to the point of madness:

> We sent him down at last, out of the way.
> Unwounded; – stout lad, too, before that strafe.
> Malingering? Stretcher-bearers winked, 'Not half!'
>
> Next day I heard the Doc's well-whiskied laugh:
> 'That scum you sent last night soon died. Hooray.'[9]

In a trench-song (in its day 'one of the most famous of war
songs') a soldier sang about his dearest wish:

> I want to go home,
> I want to go home,
> I don't want to go in the trenches no more,
> Where whizz-bangs and shrapnel they whistle and roar.
> Take me over the sea
> Where the Alleyman can't get at me.
> Oh my,
> I don't want to die,
> I want to go home.

A great strength of the trench-songs is that the person whose
voice we hear is himself owning to his fear and cowardice and
his wish that someone *else* will get hit – the degrading effect

of combat is not confined to the exceptional few who killed
themselves or shot their own foot off to get sent home. A parody
of the 1914 music-hall hit 'I'll make a man of you' has these
lines:

> I don't want to be a soldier,
> I don't want to go to war.
> I'd rather stay at home,
> Around the streets to roam,
> And live on the earnings of a well-paid whore.
> I don't want a bayonet up my arse-hole,
> I don't want my ballocks shot away.
> I'd rather stay in England,
> In merry, merry England,
> And fornicate my bloody life away.[10]

The 'collapse of values', whether we call the value in question
respect or deference, comes out in Sassoon's readiness, as a junior
officer, to identify with and express what the rank and file were
coming to feel about the Higher Command:

> 'Good-morning; good-morning!' the General said
> When we met him last week on the way to the line.
> Now the soldiers he smiled at are most of 'em dead,
> And we're cursing his staff for incompetent swine.
> 'He's a cheery old card,' grunted Harry to Jack
> As they slogged up to Arras with rifle and pack.
>
>   . . .
>
> But he did for them both by his plan of attack.[11]

The troops' own counterpart would be the following utterly rude
and resentful quatrain about an NCO:

> You've got a kind face, you old bastard,
> You ought to be bloodywell shot:
> You ought to be tied to a gun-wheel,
> And left there to bloodywell rot.[12]

While the *War Illustrated* regaled its readers with paintings of kilted soldiers dashing into the attack, with teeth bared and eyes alight for blood, and quoted a French eye-witness who is supposed to have said, 'Never have I beheld faces so lit up with enthusiasm as were those of the Scottish at the tragic moment when, in the dawn of the battle, they leaped from their trenches' (9 June 1917), Owen was carefully detailing how soldiers looked as they retreated,

Bent double, like old beggars under sacks,
Knock-kneed, coughing like hags, we cursed through sludge,

or kept watch:

Our brains ache, in the merciless iced east winds that
   knive us . . .
Wearied we keep awake because the night is silent . . .
Low, drooping flares confuse the memory of the salient . . .
Worried by silence, sentries whisper, curious, nervous,
   But nothing happens.

Watching, we hear the mad gusts tugging on the wire,
Like twitching agonies of men among its brambles.
Northward, incessantly, the flickering gunnery rumbles,
Far off, like a dull rumour of some other war.
   What are we doing here?[13]

The soldiers were singing for each other, relieving their feelings by sharing them. The poets were driven by an urge to tear off the old masks and veils and shove the hideous face of war under the eyes of the people at home who allowed themselves to be duped. Owen wrote: 'I wish the Bosche would have the pluck to come right in & make a clean sweep of the Pleasure Boats, and the promenaders on the Spa, and all the stinking Leeds & Bradford War-profiteers now reading *John Bull* on Scarborough Sands.'[14]

Presently, ignorance of the real conditions in France, whether it was a callous or a sentimental ignorance, came to be typified by women, since they were bound to be non-combatants. In 1917 'A Little Mother' had written a letter to the *Morning Post* which so struck the note that it sold 75,000 copies in a week in pamphlet form. It glories in the womanly act of sacrificing sons on the altar of victory for 'the British race' and sums up its standpoint in the sentence, 'Women are created for the purpose of giving life, and men to take it.' Against this attitude Sassoon wrote his 'Glory of Women':

> You love us when we're heroes, home on leave,
> Or wounded in a mentionable place . . .
> You make us shells. You listen with delight,
> By tales of dirt and danger fondly thrilled . . .
> You can't believe that British troops 'retire'
> When hell's last horror breaks them, and they run . . .
>   O German mother dreaming by the fire,
>   While you are knitting socks to send your son
>   His face is trodden deeper in the mud.[15]

What the poets and singers were finding was that they were in the most extreme situations conceivable – the worst of filth, pain, and uncertainty had become the norm – and to communicate this experience they had to find phrases that ran against the grain of the culture with its deeply escapist habits. The soldiers were expressing a widespread frame of mind when they used the tune of a smoochy pop song, 'They Wouldn't Believe Me' (1915), to hit off the wish to forget, gloss over, and cover up:

> And when they ask us how dangerous it was,
> Oh, we'll never tell them, no, we'll never tell them:
> We spent our pay in some café,
> And fought wild women night and day,
> 'Twas the cushiest job we ever had.
>
> And when they ask us, and they're certainly going to ask us,
> The reason why we didn't win the Croix de Guerre,
> Oh, we'll never tell them, no, we'll never tell them,
> There was a front, but damned if we knew where.[16]

This style looks ahead to the crooning which was to bulk large in pop for decades to come, with its slides, its soft-shoe shuffle, its droop of self-pity. It is an idiom which signals that the effort of facing reality is felt to be too much. The complex motives behind this evasion are caught in a Salford man's reminiscence of how his mother, in 1917, refused to let her daughter sing and play 'Oh, oh, oh it's a lovely war' from a new sheet of music on the piano:

> 'I won't have it,' she said quietly, 'not in this house – such carnage! And people sing "it's a lovely war"!'
> 'Don't you see?' said my father. 'It's skitting! It's ridicule! "Up to the waist in water!"' he sang. '"Up to the eyes in slush!" . . .'
> 'I see well enough,' she said, 'but some things are too terrible for ridicule.'
> My sister got up, tossed the music on top of the piano and flounced out.[17]

How else were the terrible things to be expressed? In the vehement, heartfelt, and grimly serious manner of the art-poets. But their work was in effect not available to most people, who never handled new and relatively expensive hard-backed books, and until recently could get no nearer the war experience *via* literature than, say, the 'Anthem for Doomed Youth' in a rather rare type of anthology for schools.

We implied already that the evasion of war was a long-standing thing when we said that the trench songs and trench poetry made up a record unprecedented in its honesty. This has to be tested against a standard: for example, the very large and well-documented sample of 'Soldiers' Songs from Agincourt to Ulster' which Karl Dallas has compiled under the title *The Cruel Wars*. Although a reading and hearing of these confirms our idea that total realisation of war had not sunk in before 1916, Dallas did find one song that insists on the sludge and 'crumps and lice and lack of rum' – a broadside song, with no tune named, called 'The Battle of Sebastopol' (in the Crimea). One verse goes:

> They all turned dizzy, some spewed and some spit,
> And the Russian commander in his breeches did shit,
> For he had got the skitters with Johnny Bull's pills,
> Our shot is the doctors that find out their ills.[18]

We cannot thing of a like candour about cowardice in any other war literature until the scene of the Americans landing on a beach in the Solomon Islands at the start of Norman Mailer's *The Naked and the Dead* (1949). The raw soldier Hennessey panics under mortar fire, shits in his trousers, jumps dementedly out of his bolt-hole, and has his head torn in half by shrapnel. Of course there is no telling how much in this vein has been lost. But if it did exist and has been lost, this is itself evidence of those blinkers and taboos which have worn thinner and thinner under the attacks of experience in the twentieth century. People struggle to keep *the bad thing* out of their awareness. A Crimean War veteran who had taken to singing and selling song-sheets for a living would know he risked lowering the popularity of his wares if he sold too much in the vein of 'The Battle of Sebastopol'.

Even so, the folk tradition faced the reality of war with a fairly steady gaze. According to a Dublin veteran, the most popular marching song of the Irish Volunteers in 1913–16 was 'Mrs McGrath':

> Then up comes Ted without any legs
> And in their place he has two wooden pegs.
> She kissed him a dozen times or so,
> Saying surely to Jesus it can't be you?
>
> Oh then were you drunk or were you blind
> That you left your two fine legs behind?
> Or was it walking upon the sea
> Wore your two fine legs from the knees away?
>
> No I wasn't drunk and I wasn't blind
> But I left my two fine legs behind,
> For a cannon ball on the fifth of May
> Took my two fine legs from the knees away.
>
> Oh then Teddy boy, the widow cried,
> Your two fine legs were your mammy's pride.
> Them stumps of trees wouldn't do at all.
> Why didn't you run from the big cannonball?[19]

The extraordinary flavour of this arises from the mixture of the vigorous and blithe rhythms with the brute impact of injury and its results. This is exactly the spirit of 'Johnny I Hardly Knew Ye'. A man we know remembers his father telling him how the regimental band *greeted them* by playing the tune of it as they staggered back to base from the front line in Flanders:

> Ye haven't an arm and ye haven't a leg,
> Ye're an eyeless, chickenless, noseless egg,
> Ye'll have to be put in a bowl to beg,
> Och Johnny, I hardly knew ye . . .

The English songs, however, especially the older ones, have a way of dissolving the worst shocks of war into a high-minded convention which does not protest against bloodshed, or question the function of war in human affairs. This vein at its best produced 'General Wolfe',* which is at the far end of the gamut from *Counter-Attack* in that a commander is virtually worshipped, as a father- and saviour-figure:

> Then the very first volley that the French gave us
> Wounded our general in his right breast.
> Then out of his breast living blood did flow,
> Like any fountain, like any fountain,
> Till all his men were filled with woe.
>
> Here's a hundred guineas all in bright gold,
> Take it and part it, for my blood runs cold,
> Take it and part it, General Wolfe did say,
> For you lads of honour, you lads of honour,
> Have shown the French such gallant play.[20]

Wolfe is here assimilated to a kind of cult which must draw at several removes on the idea of a feudal chief as an all-providing fountainhead for his people. Wolfe in fact served as an officer in Cumberland's army, which killed off the feudal system at Culloden (and the search-and-destroy policy that followed it). The old kind of leader cult was bound to wane as warfare moved onto a scale where commanders like Wellington, with enormous

---

* Superbly sung by the Watersons of Hull on *The Watersons* (1966) side 1, track 3. Their harmonies and slow tempo bring out the unalloyed nobility of the song.

powers (and enormous post-war payments from the grateful state), controlled from a lengthening distance their massive armies with a high proportion of pressed men. In the songs, Nelson and Collingwood, the admirals, are still cult figures in the Wolfe tradition, but they were living close to their crews in small floating communities. By the time the Crimean War is acting as a kind of distant trailer for the Great War with its trenches, prolonged bombardment, long-distance supply problems, and the madly wasteful tactics of general caught between the age of the horse and the age of the mechanised gun, the figure of the good leader has gone for ever.

The classic song of the immediately pre-modern phase in warfare is 'The Kerry Recruit', from the Crimea, and it says nothing at all about generals. The only superior with whom the man has a relationship is the sergeant who 'shoved the bob in me fist' at the recruiting. The mode in which the fighting is presented is perfectly lifelike. There is no cult of anything – neither is there any note of suggestion that such things need not or should not be. Everything is specified in a practical way, with a salt of humour that comes from making the best of things:

When at Balaclava we landed quite sound,
Both cold, wet and hungry we lay on the ground.
Next morning for action the bugle did call
And we had a hot breakfast of powder and ball . . .

'Twas there we lay bleeding, stretched on the cold ground,
Where heads, legs and arms were scattered around.
Says I to myself, If my father were nigh,
He'd bury me decent just in case I should die.

But a surgeon was called and he soon staunched my blood,
And he gave me an elegant leg made of wood.
And they gave me a pension of tenpence a day,
Contented with Sheila, I'll live on half pay.[21]

This song differs from all the kindred ones that went before it (even the best Scots ballads of feudal warfare, such as 'The Battle of Harlaw') in that it details the whole situation of an ordinary fighting man, from the hardship that drives him to enlist, to the rough deal he settles for in the end. It differs from what came after it, the songs from France in 1916-18 and the much thinner crop from the Second World War and Korea, in that the singer does not mock his own lyric medium, his tone is perfectly straight. By the time of the Great War, the songs are all parodies. The people's own making of songs had so given way before the supply of songs by the capitalist network, that the medium itself was almost as alien – fair game for mockery – as the farcical carryings-on of generals, politicians, and army chaplains.

When such a twist of obliqueness enters into a major medium in a culture, it suggests that the main energies and feelings of the society are no longer flowing wholeheartedly into the activity concerned. Whether it is warfare or worship or government, it is ceasing to be felt as so 'natural', so necessary, that people can easily identify with it.

The implications of this help to explain the great gap there is in variety and power between the First World War poetry (and song, and fiction) and the Second – so far as Britain is concerned. On the face of it, it might seem that people could have identified more easily with the social effort of the Second World War because it was so glaringly needful. Unless the army fought the toughest of rearguard actions as they retreated through France to Dunkirk – unless the little boats brought thousands of soldiers back to England – unless the Spitfires shot the Messerschmidts and the bomber squadrons out of the sky in the summer of 1940 . . . unless this and more was done, Hitler's armed forces would invade and slavery, torture, and extermination would overwhelm us. What shows in the literary record is neither the hatred and antagonism we felt for the Fascist enemy nor very much about the dangerous and exhausting work it took to hold him off and destroy him. The quintessential war poetry (the best of Keith Douglas and of Alun Lewis, a few pieces by Henry Reed and Sidney Keyes) has the air of people going through the motions and looking on at themselves doing so. There is little of Owen's total exposure, through senses and nerves, to the scenes of war, and nothing of Sassoon's vehement protest (the object for this would have been the Nazi cruelties). The songs (and again they are mostly from the ranks, the poetry is from the officer class) share this unanimity of detachment, whether it is the mundane complaint of

> Seven years in the sand,
>> Seems a long time somehow.
> Never mind, tosh, you'll soon be dead –
>> A hundred years from now,

or the ashy nostalgia between battles of

> The pipie is dozey, the pipie is fae,
> He winna be roon for his vino the day,
> The skies owre Messina are unco an grey
>> An a' the bricht chaumers are eerie,

or (later, in Korea) the resentful helplessness of men who feel marooned:

> Down there with the snakes and the lizards,
>> Down where a swaddie is blue,
> Right in the middle of nowhere,
>> And thousands of miles from you.

> Living on photos an mem'ries,
>> Thinking sometimes of our gals,
> Hoping that while we have been away,
>> They have not married our pals.[22]

Before looking into this work further to try and understand what lay behind it, we should contrast the British work in a general way with what other cultures produced. The Americans had been embroiled in the First World War only in a small way and there is no concerted literature of description and protest to match the English, although there is a fine small group of novels which show people caught up physically in the war while their main feelings lie elsewhere: Dos Passos's *Three Soldiers* and sequences from *Nineteen Nineteen*, Hemingway's *A Farewell to Arms*. In the Second World War the case is nearly opposite. Both immediately after peace had come and periodically ever since, American writers have been able to create major pieces which represent something like the totality of total war – immense outpourings of materials, extremes of ruin, agony, and mess, the sense that the whole gamut of human nature in the culture has been present in the warfare. The major books are *The Naked and the Dead, Catch 22* (1961), and *Slaughterhouse-Five* (1969). Their styles could not vary more. Each springs from an extraordinary effort to encompass enormity. No British work even attempts this scale.

Another national literature, the French, helps to extend the range of expectations we can bring to the expression of the war experience. The French response was far from null, but it never mustered the large energies palpable in the Americans. There is the genuinely noble rhetoric of Aragon's and Eluard's patriotic poems; there is the effort made by Vercors in *Le Silence de la Mer* (1942) to keep open a channel of humane understanding between the French and their German conquerors; and there are (what seem to us much the best French work from that time) the novels in which Sartre and Camus painfully digested the experience of capitulation, *Iron in the Soul* and *The Plague*. The point here is that both these writers entered the war with nearly-formed philosophies that enabled them to conceive of it as an intensification of the human condition at large. They already thought of life as a matter of creating something authentic in the face of the 'absurd' flux of unrelieved existence, they were already anguished at the provisional character of such strivings. The war did not burst on them. This it had done for Britain in 1914 (or 1916), and for the Americans at Pearl Harbor and Dresden. Our suggestion at this stage is that it is the first shocks of realisation which are most likely to fire a literature specifically of war, and that these shocks are unrepeatable. Vietnam seems not to have fired a body of major work, although it is really too early yet to say,[23] and this could be because it is for the Americans the second (or third) war. These notions must now be tested against a more detailed view of the work that sprang from 1939–45.

Sampling it is difficult, for in the nature of the case there are few pieces which would be recognised by 'everyone' as typical.[24] We suggested already that the writers tended to be going through the motions and looking on at themselves doing so. Their experiences were hardly intense enough to burn away awareness of being in a role. The role expected of the writer (for example by the Ministry of Information) was to affirm our decency and humanity in face of Nazi atrocity. For a talent best at delicate individual perceptions, such as Sidney Keyes, this could seem overbearing. In 'War Poet' he wrote:

> I am the man who looked for peace and found
> My own eyes barbed.
> I am the man who groped for words and found
> An arrow in my hand . . .[25]

The war was not bound to quell words, it was (in common with all other human experiences) expressible. But the words found even by the talent into whom the war sank most deeply, Keith Douglas, have the air of not being linked to combat by a direct circuit. Douglas's 'Landscape with Figures' and Owen's 'The Show' contrast strikingly despite their likeness. Both portray the battlefield as a huge, spreadeagled, writhing mass, as though a family of monsters was being dismembered. Owen's 'soul', along with Death, looks down from a height and sees this:

> Across its beard, that horror of harsh wire,
> There moved thin caterpillars, slowly uncoiled . . .
>
> On dithering feet upgathered, more and more,
> Brown strings, towards strings of grey, with bristling spines,
> All migrants from green fields, intent on mire.
>
> Those that were grey, of more abundant spawns,
> Ramped on the rest and ate them and were eaten.
>
> I saw their bitten backs curve, loop, and straighten,
> I watched those agonies curl, lift, and flatten . . .[26]

Thus the 'show' of the title turns out to be one only in the Great War slang sense of a campaign or 'push'. It is no mime, it is organic, fleshly, and appallingly revolting. Douglas sees the

thing, in his imagination, from so far away that it is impalpable
– just a tableau:

> Perched on a great fall of air
> a pilot or angel looking down
> on some eccentric chart, a plain
> dotted with useless furniture,
> discerns dying on the sand vehicles
> squashed dead or still entire, stunned
> like beetles: scattered wingcases and
> legs, heads, appear when the dust settles . . .

> On sand and scrub the dead men wriggle
> in their dowdy clothes. They are mimes
> who express silence and futile aims
> enacting this prone and motionless struggle
> at a queer angle to the scenery . . .[27]

No emotion is allowed to gather. The freedom of free verse
is used to place words at points in the line where they will
check the flow ('discerns dying on the sand vehicles') so that
no momentum, no rhythmic grandeur, will develop. The poem
seems to have been written as an 'answer' to Owen's – each
poet starts by positioning himself on high, each ends by writing
himself into the scene, and it is here that the contrast is sharpest.
Owen feels in his senses his full complicity in the death-struggle:
God picks up one worm from the mass and

> Showed me its feet, the feet of many men,
> And the fresh-severed head of it, my head.

Douglas is at a remove, apparently at war while feeling unreal,
not there:

> A yard more and my little fiinger
> could trace the maquillage of these stony actors:
> I am the figure writhing on the backcloth.

This poem was written in Wadi Zem Zem, in northern Tunisia. In Douglas's prose book, *From Alamein to Zem Zem* (1946), it is plain from moment after moment that the weird detachment of 'Landscape with Figures' (and 'How to Kill' and 'Aristocrats') is a kind of aesthete's counterpart of the cool style which combatants used as a defence against unbearable trauma:

> The greater part of the shells had apparently landed among the infantry vehicles and heavy tanks at the back of the leaguer. 'My tank is not a dressing station,' he said in a mock-serious voice which, so carefully did he maintain it, made it clear that it was an insurance against real seriousness . . .
>
> The great thing, said my mind, is not to flap. I involuntarily said, 'Take your time' aloud about twice, and touched the Corporal, who was still peering through his glasses at the green patch. 'That chap is a Jerry in a Mk III,' I said. 'I should quite like to shoot him up before he sees us . . .' My stomach was turning over inside me. 'King Five,' Piccadilly Jim answered before Edward could acknowledge my message. 'Give the bugger hell,' with a kind of refined emphasis quite divorced from the words.
>
> The pain in my foot, which Bert had tied up very tightly to stop it bleeding, was increasing. I said to Bert: 'Don't take any notice if I moan. I like moaning,' and with this excuse began to moan in a jerky way, dependent on the bumps. It was a way of taking my mind off the foot.[28]

This state of mind can be called, approximately, detachment. It includes the cool, the blasé, the browned-off. It can also deepen to a view of fatality poised between anguish and numbness. Alun Lewis's 'Song' and 'Dawn on the East Coast', which seem to us among the dozen permanent poems of the Second World War, both view death obliquely, for all their poignancy. The killing does not burst violently in. 'Song' is sub-titled 'On seeing dead bodies floating off the Cape' – the death does not happen in the poem. The focus is on the bereaved sweetheart left at home:

> But oh! the drag and dullness of my Self;
> The turning seasons wither in my head;
> All this slowness, all this hardness,

The nearness that is waiting in my bed,
The gradual self-effacement of the dead.

In 'Dawn on the East Coast' the death is a bad dream in the
head of a cold, bored soldier keeping watch:

The light assails him from a flank,
Two carbons touching in his brain
Crumple the cellophane lantern of his dream.

And then the day, grown feminine and kind,
Stoops with the gulfing motion of the tide
And pours his ashes in a tiny urn.

From Orford Ness to Shingle Street
The grey disturbance lifts its head
And one by one, reluctantly,
The living come back slowly from the dead.[29]

This was written in 1940 and could be said to typify the unreal-feel-
ing stagnation of the Phoney War. Yet its subdued and unviolent
way with death is akin to Douglas's and he was in the midst
of landmines and blazing tanks.

Why, then, did the writers tend to hold themselves back from
total embroilment in the war? The motives must be a whole
syndrome of feelings, since we are speaking about the reaction,
part collective and part individual, of millions of people. The
historian who records that 'The house of commons forced war
on a reluctant British government' says it is 'impossible to tell'
whether or not 'The British people' welcomed the war or 'would
have preferred some other outcome.'[30] It is true that there is
no statistically valid coverage of the matter, but there are some
opinions on record which there is little reason to think were
not shared by thousands in addition to those whose words we
do have.

First, it is often said that people could not feel the same outrage,
the same direct and whole-hearted emotions, the second time
round – they had 'seen it all before'. It is true that millions
of people still alive knew war only too well, and would never
again experience it as a revelation. Six days after war was declared,
Stephen Spender records that people in the London streets could

be heard saying: 'They're singing now, but they won't be singing
for long. Hearing 'em sing reminds me of when I went out to
fight in them trenches. We went out singing, but we didn't sing
for long.' And again, on meeting five Frenchmen carrying the
tricolor and singing the 'Marseillaise': 'They won't be doing that
for long.'[31] Too much cannot be built on this, since these were
veterans talking, the younger people *were* singing and flag-waving,
their revelations were still to come. But many younger people
were already estranged from the 'war effort'. Spender records
his own scepticism at broadcasts by Cabinet ministers the day
after war was declared in which they 'talked about gallant Poland,
our liberties, democracy, etc.' 'I dislike all the talk about God
defending the right. God has always defended the right, and
after such a long experience, he of all people should realise the
utter futility of it.'[32] This is in keeping with Cecil Day Lewis's
'Where Are the War Poets?' of 1940:

> They who in panic or mere greed
> Enslaved religion, markets, laws,
> Borrow our language now and bid
> Us to speak up in freedom's cause.
>
> It is the logic of our times,
> No subject for immortal verse,
> That we who lived by honest dreams
> Defend the bad against the worse.[33]

Spender and Day Lewis were both, as Communists, exceptionally
sceptical about the value of what the Allies were fighting to
defend. But T. S. Eliot, on the other wing politically, was of
a like mind. 'He said, "I think it's very important that as many
writers as possible should remain detached, and not have any
official position"', and he suggested writing about, not public
events, but 'a smaller theme – perhaps family life – which had
all the implications of what is going on in the world outside.'[34]
Keith Douglas had had little option but to deal with public
events, once he was at war (he had enlisted voluntarily) – yet he
started his war book by disclaiming any commitment to national
goals:

The dates have slipped away, the tactical lessons have been learnt by someone else . . . Against a backcloth of indeterminate landscapes of moods and smells, dance the black and bright incidents . . . We talk in the evening, after fighting, about the great and rich men who cause and conduct wars. They have so many reasons of their own that they can afford to lend us some of them. There is nothing odd about their attitude. They are out for something they want, or their Governments want, and they are using us to get it for them. Anyone can understand that: there is nothing unusual or humanly exciting at that end of the war. I mean there may be things to excite financiers and parliamentarians – but not to excite a poet or a painter or a doctor.[35]

★

The apparent perversity of so detached an attitude can be under-lined by means of a reminiscence by one of us (D.C.). As a boy of nearly eight when the war broke out in 1939, I had no reason at all to doubt that we were fighting for our 'liberties'. War was declared on 3 September. On Friday 1 September the evacuation of children and the blacking-out of windows had begun, as soon as news came that Germany had invaded Poland. Towards the end of that morning our teacher tried to explain to us that Europe was at war, and I walked home along a street full of copper beeches and weeping willows, roses and chrysanthe-mums, in a kind of waking nightmare. Soldiers in grey with funny-looking square steel helmets would suddenly appear in the street outside our nursery window, they would take our parents away for ever, we would be sent in rags to some ghastly place between an orphanage and a camp. In the evening there began the pinning up of opaque black cloth to stop any light showing from the windows – our bedroom window had an unusual curved top which was difficult to screen, and the cloth had to be cut specially to fit it. From that night on, the sky after dark was a menacing cave from which the *bad thing* would come at us, and we listened in a sweat, after the rising and falling howl of the air-raid sirens, as the low noise of an aero-engine with a throb instead of a continuous drone told us that German aircraft were overhead. After two years of this the menace became real when for some reason a few planes bothered to bomb Aberdeen, one bomb knocked down half a church 150 yards from our house, and for an hour I had my only experience of prolonged, squirming terror as we crouched in the basement behind a small protective angle in the kitchen wall, the great vibrating bangs seemed to force our heads into our shoulders, and I said to myself over and over again: 'God' – this was a prayer, not a swear-word – 'make it stop, I can't stand this, make it stop, I can't stand this.'

The war as something to be kept at bay was as real as a beast coming at us, and Hitler to us was Satan. In the basement room that was converted into a safe bedroom for my brother and me, two-by-two timbers were fitted to prop up and strengthen the ceiling. We drew Hitler's face on a timber with a pencil, in the likeness of a rotten egg, with his toothbrush moustache and combed-down forelock, and fumes coming out at the top, which we drew like a broken eggshell, and we threw our penknives at it like darts at a board. (Our mother had told us how towards the end of the Great War you could hammer nails for a halfpenny a time into a wooden Hindenburg which was wheeled through the streets.) When the war in Europe ended on VE Day, 8 May 1945, our relief was so acute that we rushed out shouting into the garden and hung paper lanterns all over the ash tree which had been the base for our Robin Hood and Tarzan games.

*

If millions felt something like that, how typical were the writers who repeatedly endorsed Forster's statement of 1939, in *What I Believe*: 'I hate the idea of a cause, and if I had to choose between betraying my country and betraying my friend, I hope I should have the guts to betray my country'?[36] The answer seems to be that though the war was something most people buckled down to as an obviously needful task, it could not seem a crusade, it could not stir and rouse emotion as the Great War had done (though then the gains for most people had been a mirage). The reasons are ones we will go into later, under 'The Nullity of the Slump', but here we can make the point that life in the thirties had felt too shabby for any good thing to be vividly present in people's minds as something to fight for. The economic depression had worked also as a depression in a psycho-social sense. Feelings were low. In September 1939,

> All commentators marvelled at the contrast between the hys-
> teria of August 1914 and the absence of hatred and high spirits
> now. This time, there was no stoning of dachshunds in the
> streets. But a holocaust of pets occurred as homes were dis-
> rupted; outside vets' surgeries 'the slain lay in heaps.'[37]

Different classes experienced the onset of danger and upheaval
in different ways. The socially specific thing about the Great
War was that it was the first to suck in the middle class
in a significant proportion, and it was from this class that the
war poets mostly came. Owen was a pupil-teacher and the son
of a railway supervisor. Robert Graves's father was an inspector
of schools. Rosenberg left school at fourteen, became an apprentice
engraver and then an art student. Edward Thomas was a poorly-off
freelance writer. Sassoon was the most comfortably off, he lived
with an aunt who had private means, he was taught about horses
by the groom and rode to hounds. In previous ages when there
was a small standing army officered by younger sons of landed
families, and the ranks were filled with labourers (some enlisted
by force), the middle-class man was precisely the one least likely
to experience war at first hand. Unlike an unskilled worker on
the edge of destitution, he had a lot to lose by going to war,
and nothing to gain (as had the upper class) in the way of a
top military career or company directorships and other large post-
war perks. After the first self-deluding flush of excitement, he
had no reason not to see the fruitless carnage for what it was.
This is still not the whole explanation of why the trench war
came as so brutal a shock, for the working-people felt it too:
the evidence is in their songs. A further key thing which would
have sharpened the shock of that war whatever the prior social
conditioning of the combatants was the scale of the destruction.
On the Somme 400,000 casualties were spent to gain three miles
of ground. At Passchendaele a quarter of a million were spent
to gain five miles and 75,000 were killed, missing, or destroyed
as persons mentally and physically. Bombardment was tremendously heavy: a hundred million shells were fired. The aerial
photos of the village itself among its fields and roads, or of
key points like Polygon Wood, show that the ground was totally

denatured – pocked like wood that woodworm has turned to crumbs, the highways, hollows, and earth banks surviving as the faintest traces, like the 'canals' on Mars seen through a telescope.[38] By the Second World War firepower had of course grown greatly, but the usual style of battle involved no such systematic mincing-up of fighting men because the front moved more quickly, owing to mechanisation. At Passchendaele there were 32,000 casualties in two days; at El Alamein there were 13,560 in a battle that lasted a week. When the Second World War ran to the worst peaks of destruction, it outdid the First World War by far, because machines had become so much more powerful, and in these cases a new kind of writing was engendered – the literature of atrocity.

Civilian massacre in conditions of nearly unimaginable extremity – heat-flash and firestorm of unprecedented power – is imaged in Hersey's *Hiroshima* and Vonnegut's *Slaughterhouse-Five* (1969), common-or-garden butchery in A. Anatoli's *Babi-Yar* (1966), the highly-organised sadism of the death camps in Bruno Apitz's *Naked Among Wolves* (1968). The unheard-of ferocity of these events made them half incredible. To bring them into forms of art, writers were to need techniques from two extremes of the gamut. At one end we have actuality as little changed as possible. John Hersey's *Hiroshima*, which began life as a complete issue of the *New Yorker*, for August 1946, presents with only the barest comment the experiences of six people who were at varying distances from the flash-point of the first atomic bomb. That is in the mode of news reporting; at the same time the book is now permanently in print, as a modern classic, and deserves to be because it does what is at least part of the work of novels, plays, and poems – it makes available the undiluted essence of an experience. We can presume that *Hiroshima* sold a quarter of a million in a month as soon as it came out in book form because English-speaking readers badly wanted to know what 'their' governments had done to the Japanese, in the name of ending the war. It also turns out that to pass on urgent news is not at all the only function of this reportage or unaltered-actuality mode. Peter Weiss's play *The Investigation* (1965) is called an 'oratorio' in '11 Cantos'. None of the words are the author's – he picked them out and arranged them from the transcripts of the trial at Frankfurt of staff from the Auschwitz concentration camp who had recently been traced and arrested. In his prefatory

'Remarks' Weiss calls his play 'the central core of the evidence', a strikingly literal instance of the idea of literature as evidence which underlies this book. This in no way precludes utterance so enhanced by rhythm, repetition, and even rhyme that it becomes as memorable as poetry. In Canto 1, Female Witness 4 says:

> I came into a barracks
> that was full of bodies
> Suddenly I saw
> something moving among the dead
> It was a young girl
> I took her out into the street
> and asked her
> Who are you
> How long have you been here
> I don't know
> she said
> Why are you lying here among the dead
> I asked
> And she said
> I can no longer be among the living
> In the evening she was dead[39]

If this had been invented, it might well have struck us as a remarkable fable about the irreducible essence of what it is to be mortal. As it is, it is an extreme situation turning spontaneously into words.

At the other end of the gamut are the books which turn war experience into comedy, fantasy, science-fiction, satire, and other modes which so rearrange and 'exaggerate' that we are no longer on the plane of what could literally happen. It is natural that such work should come out well after a war, since seemingly playful style could look like an affront to the sufferers. E. E. Cummings's *The Enormous Room* came out in 1928. Heller started *Catch 22* in 1953 and finished it in 1961. Vonnegut's *Slaughterhouse-Five* did not come out till 1969 and its first chapter wonderfully evokes the zigzags of an artist's mind as he swerves away from, then irresistibly comes back onto *the worst thing*. In contrast, Mailer's *The Naked and the Dead* was finished just three years after the end of the war in the Pacific, or five years after the battle for Guadalcanal in the Solomon Islands which is the nearest original for the events on Mailer's fictional island of Anopopei. It is the counterpart, in the shocking directness of its look at combat, of Sassoon's *Counter-Attack*, with the great difference that by the 1940s a writer had no longer to slough off bad old habits of high-mindedness or ornamental stylishness before he got through to life and to idioms that spring naturally from it.

The Naked and the Dead is a classic because it presents war whole – evoked so sensuously that it feels as though it dirties and burns your skin, analysed with an intellectual thoroughness that is never in the least danger either of separating itself out into philosophy, like Tolstoy's essay on history in the middle of *War and Peace*, or of sinking from the felt and dramatised into bookish military history, like the more laboured parts of Solzhenitsyn's *August 1914*. War, in Mailer's novel, is seen to consist of terror, danger, pain, and the utmost mental and physical efforts that people could well make. At the core, for most people in war, are the danger, fear, and toil. In the work of art they must be there, equally they must not bulk so large that they nourish sado-masochism or drive readers to switch off mentally. Peaks, or even simmerings, of terror are rare in Mailer's novel – on the beach at the start, later in the jungle, and finally up on the mountain – but they are so placed and evoked with so much power that they are felt to lurk at the edges of the calmer sequences too. The gun battle across the river (section 2, part 5) so rises to its subject that it should be recognised as that which war had been demanding from artists since *The Red Badge of Courage* (1895) but had never quite got, not even in the previous masterpieces of battle writing, the Borodinó sequence in *War and Peace* or Grigory Melekhov's first cavalry charge in 'Sholokhov's' *The Quiet Don*.[40]

> Someone called from across the river, 'Yank, Yank!' Croft sat numb. The voice was thin and high-pitched, hideous in a whisper. 'That's a Jap,' Croft told himself. He was incapable of moving for that instant.
>
>   'Yank!' It was calling to him. 'Yank. We you coming-to-get, Yank.'
>
>   The night lay like a heavy stifling mat over the river. Croft tried to breathe.

'*We you coming-to-get, Yank.*'

Croft felt as if a hand had suddenly clapped against his
back, traveled up his spine over his skull to clutch at the
hair on his forehead. 'Coming to get you, Yank,' he heard
himself whisper. He had the agonizing frustration of a man
in a nightmare who wants to scream and cannot utter a sound.
'We you *coming-to-get*, Yank'

He shivered terribly for a moment, and his hands seemed
congealed on the machine-gun. He could not bear the intense
pressure in his head.

'We you coming-to-get, Yank,' the voice screamed.

'COME AND GET ME, YOU SONSOFBITCHES,' Croft roared. He
shouted with every fibre of his body as though he plunged
at an oaken door.

There was no sound at all for perhaps ten seconds, nothing
but the moonlight on the river and the taut rapt buzzing of
the crickets. Then the voice spoke again. 'Oh, we come, Yank,
we come.'

Croft pulled back the bolt on his machine-gun, and rammed
it home. His heart was still beating with frenzy 'Recon . . .
RECON, UP ON THE LINE,' he shouted with all his strength.

A machine-gun lashed at him from across the river, and
he ducked in his hole. In the darkness, it spat a vindictive
white light like an acetylene torch, and its sound was terrifying.
Croft was holding himself together by the force of his will.
He pressed the trigger of his gun and it leapt and bucked
under his hand. The tracers spewed wildly into the jungle on
the other side of the river.

But the noise, the vibration of his gun, calmed him. He
directed it to where he had seen the Japanese gunfire and
loosed a volley. The handle pounded against his fist, and he
had to steady it with both hands. The hot metallic smell of
the barrel eddied back to him, made what he was doing real
again. He ducked in his hole waiting for the reply and winced
involuntarily as the bullets whipped past.

BEE-YOWWWW! . . . BEE-YOOWWWW! Some dirt snapped at
his face from the ricochets. Croft was not conscious of feeling
it. He had the surface numbness a man has in a fight. He
flinched at sounds, his mouth tightened and loosened, his eyes
stared, but he was oblivious to his body.

Croft fired the gun again, held it for a long vicious burst, and then ducked in his hole. An awful scream singed the night, and for an instant Croft grinned weakly. Got him he thought. He saw the metal burning through flesh, shattering the bones in its path . . . 'AHYOHHHH.' The scream froze him again, and for an odd disconnected instant he experienced again the whole complex of sounds and smells and sights when a calf was branded. 'RECON, UP . . . UP!' he shouted furiously and fired steadily for ten seconds to cover their advance. As he paused he could hear some men crawling behind him, and he whispered, 'Recon?'

'Yeah.' Gallagher dropped into the hole with him. 'Mother of Mary,' he muttered. Croft could feel him shaking beside him.

'Stop it!' he gripped his arm tensely. 'The other men up?'
'Yeah.'

Croft looked across the river again. Everything was silent, and the disconnected abrupt spurts of fire were forgotten like vanished sparks from a grindstone. Now that he was no longer alone, Croft was able to plan. The fact that men were up with him, were scattered in the brush along the bank between their two machine-guns, recovered his sense of command. 'They're going to attack soon,' he whispered hoarsely in Gallagher's ear.

Gallagher trembled again. 'Ohh. No way to wake up,' he tried to say, but his voice kept lapsing.

'Look,' Croft whispered. 'Creep along the line and tell them to hold fire until the Japs start to cross the river.'

'I can't, I can't,' Gallagher whispered.

Croft felt like striking him. 'Go!' he whispered.
—'I can't.'

The Jap machine-gun lashed at them from across the river. The bullets went singing into the jungle behind them, ripping at leaves. The tracers looked like red splints of lightning as they flattened into the jungle. A thousand rifles seemed to be firing at them from across the river, and the two men pressed themselves against the bottom of the hole. The sounds cracked against their eardrums. Croft's head ached. Firing the machine-gun had partially deafened him. BEE-YOWWWW! A ricochet slapped some more dirt on top of them. Croft felt it pattering on his back this time. He was trying to sense the moment when he would have to raise his head and fire the gun. The firing seemed to slacken, and he lifted up his eyes cautiously. BEE-YOWWWW, BEE-YOWWWW! He dropped in the hole again. The Japanese machine-gun raked through the brush at them.

There was a shrill screaming sound, and the men covered their heads with their arms. BAA-ROWWMM, BAA-ROWWMM, ROWWMM, ROWWMM. The mortars exploded all about them, and something picked Gallagher up, shook him, and then released him. 'O God,' he cried. A clod of dirt stung his neck. BAA-ROWWMM, BAA-ROWWMM. . . .[41]

The art of such a scene is to avoid any overloading or overdoing yet not to damp down the appalling din and jolt and panic of the original. Mailer knows the physical processes exactly, he is fully inward with the emotions weltering in his characters, and no false notions about what is 'crude' inhibit him from using, when it's needed, the idiom of the comic strip. 'BAA-ROWWMM' and 'AHYOHHHH' are not so unlike the 'POW . . . ZAP . . . AARGH' of the shoddiest war comics, with the difference that what Mailer puts on the page comes as near as letters well could to sounds that are nearly beyond language. For hundreds of thousands of readers, touches like that will have made the novel feel part of their familiar culture. Proof of this (apart from sales) came in a comic form at the Democratic Convention in Chicago in 1968. Mailer was covering it for *Harper's Magazine*. At one point he was nearly arrested for going too close to one of Mayor Daly's armoured police jeeps: ' "What sort of material do you write . . . ?"

"Officer," said his friend, "this man wrote *The Naked and the Dead*."

"Brother, does *that* have bad language in it," stated Commander Lyons with a happy face.'[42]

In scenes like those Mailer puts into words what is sometimes called the 'unspeakable', what George Steiner in *Language and Silence* (1967) alleges to be beyond expressing (and, as such, typical of our epoch). This is simply a mistake. The hideous pain of torture is expressed in Apitz's *Naked Among Wolves* (1958), in the passage about the prisoner in Buchenwald who has his head crushed in a vice. Utter terror is expressed in Anatoli's *Babi-Yar*, in the passage about a girl who jumps into a quarry of fresh corpses swimming in blood to avoid being massacred herself.[43] To deny or overlook such cases is both defeatist and mystifying, for it implies that there can be things in human experience which finally baffle analysis, which we have not the nerve or the resources to recreate. Against this view we would adapt a famous idea of Marx and say that man only sets himself such experiences as he can express.[44]

The situation of the Americans on Anopopei is many-sided in its extremity. One sort of intense stress interlocks with another. The pain and terror in that gunfight is at least short-lived. The carrying of Wilson in a litter down the mountain with his stomach burst by a bullet, dying of thirst and loss of blood yet so wounded in the gut that a drink would kill him, is more like a prolonged crucifixion. But it is only a minority who are hit by bullets and mortar shells. For most of the soldiers, extremity comes in some such form as the manhandling of the anti-tank guns along the muddy trail through humid jungle darkness. The men are totally gruelled. Their fears, their wishfulness, their co-ordination, orientation, and sense of time are more or less wiped out. They are in the state of the dockers in Hong Kong who carry hundredweight sacks up narrow gang-planks all day in tropical heat and only go on because they are dazed by their permitted smoke of opium in the morning, dinner-break, and evening.

That passage in *The Naked and the Dead* is a classic sequence about unskilled manual work, and this is only one of many ways in which Mailer shows the war, not as a freak or bolt from the blue, but as an intensification of peace-time industrial society: that is, a society marked by divided labour, the socialisation of work into large units, gross inequalities in material rewards and comfort and in personal freedom, the closely calculated management of people by means that include promotion from one subclass to another. At mealtimes, the men (the workers) queue in the open, and their cook's motto is 'When it's smokin', it's cookin'. When it's burnin', it's done.' The officers in the mess tent (the board of directors) are served a meal of several courses at long tables, as though they were dons in khaki inside an Oxbridge college made of canvas. The relation between the managing director – General Cummings – and his favourite executive

– Lieut. Hearn – is done with an analytic care which shows how conscious Mailer is of his managerial theme. Before moving to that, it should be noted that he is equally concerned to proportion the classes correctly. The officers are a minority of the characters, and they do not dominate the drama. Most of the characters are workers, whether blue-collar or white-collar, and the 'Time Machine' sequences (modelled on the condensed biographies in Dos Passos's *USA*) key each man into the civilian life that has shaped him, whether he has put his hunter's marksmanship to Fascist uses as a member of the National Guard, as Croft has done, or drifted via precinct politics into smouldering semi-Fascism, like Gallagher, or gone on the bum like Red, who has spent 'Puberty in the coal dust' and escapes from the coalfield when the mines stop work two years after the Wall Street Crash. This historical and literary kinship of Mailer's with the thirties has led critics to patronise him as one who, at that time anyway, had not followed the proper trend past naturalism to modernism. To us it is impressive evidence that he was at home in his own society and knew its basis.

General Cummings is dramatised as a member of what we now call top management, in every aspect of his being from the most public side of his functioning to the most intimate. The public and the intimate fuse in his acutely uneasy relationship with his aide, Lieut. Hearn. As a very vain, lonely, and talented man, Cummings preens himself on his strategic and tactical mastery. This hinges, for such a man, on his having an aloof contempt for the 'human material' (to use a standard Fascist expression)[45] that he orders about, inspects, sends into the jungle to kill or be killed. Because he is human himself, he has to relate and confide. Because his ego is so armoured in rank and consciously acquired manner, he can never be at ease. For him, to talk to someone is to put his talents on display, like a woman turning a diamond on her finger, admiring herself for owning such a thing, admiring herself for being admired. Because he is homosexual by nature, yet is absolutely blocked by his profession from living this out, every relationship he has, every move he makes, is in some way a substitute for the fullness of living he can never break through to. The growth of all this is given with rich detail in the condensed biography called 'A Peculiarly American Statement' which comes in the middle of the novel. Long before that point it has been shown in action, dramatised, in the terribly fraught and wary interactions with Hearn. Cummings wants to confide in him, and invites him across, disguising it as an order: ' "Sir?" "I need you" ', and the general goes briskly out of Recreation and across to his tent. They touch in the doorway and Hearn's bodily intuition senses the other man's buried desire. The general's tent is perfectly ordered – a desk with nothing on it, a map, a cot that looks unslept in, a chair at right angles to the lockers. It is the military, under-canvas counterpart of a bank manager's office with its bare desk, its seemingly unused presentation ball-pen in a special stand, its uncrumpled copy of the *Financial Times*. Cummings favours Hearn (who is Leftish in a sceptical, rich-college-boy way) with his theories on how to deploy and dominate the human material at his disposal:

'I don't care what kind of man you give me, if I have him long enough I'll make him afraid. Every time there's what you call an Army injustice, the enlisted man involved is confirmed a little more in the idea of his own inferiority.' He smoothed the hair over his temple. 'I happen to know of an American prison camp in England which'll be a terror once we invade Europe. The methods used will be brutal, and it's going to cause a stink eventually, but it happens to be necessary. In our own back yard we have a particular replacement depot where an attempt was actually made to kill the Colonel in command.* You aren't capable of understanding it, but I can tell you, Robert, that to make an Army work you have to have every man in it fitted into a fear ladder. Men in prison camps, deserters, or men in replacement camps are in the backwaters of the Army and the discipline has to be proportionately more powerful. The Army functions best when you're frightened of the man above you, and contemptuous of your subordinates.'

'Where do I fit into this?' Hearn asked.

'You don't yet. There are such things as papal dispensations.' The General grinned at him, lit another cigarette.[46]

Cummings is in good form because a few days earlier he has

---

* This sort of thing reached its terrible extreme towards the end of the Vietnam war when the favourite sport in some parts of down-town Saigon among GIs was fragging – throwing hand-grenades at officers.[47]

had a tactical success and defeated General Toyaku after 500 Japanese troops with tanks had for a time penetrated the American lines. On that occasion Cummings had summed things up with what should be known as Fascist wit: ' "This kind of thing is what I call my dinner-table tactics. I'm the little lady who allows the lecher beside me to get his hand way up under my dress before I cut off his wrist." ' The note struck here – the sadism inside the studied cleverness – is typical of what we know about Nazi style, for example Goebbels: 'difficulties invariably stem from second-class personalities . . . The smaller the brain, the bigger the appetite.' Or Himmler: 'every SS man should have a child before he dies in battle. If this increases the total number of children, I accept the runts – in breeder's parlance – that will occur in the mass.' Or Hans Frank, the Nazi Governor-General of Poland: 'We too find the Jews exceptionally troublesome animals . . . If I wanted to put up a poster for every seven Poles shot, all the forests of Poland would not be able to produce enough paper.'[48]

Presently Cummings challenges Hearn to a game of chess, which serves him as a substitute for anything heart to heart or man to man. When the general has duly defeated his subordinate, he calls chess 'a concentration of life' and in particular of war. Hearn's reply asserts the need to see war as human behaviour, Cummings is provoked to confide his hatred for his wife (whom he has made use of, and who has 'let him down'), Hearn sees the beseeching in his eyes, recoils from it, and has a vision of the general, paralysed by repression, as 'a large and petrified bird, waiting . . . waiting for what must be indefinable'.

The significance of this sequence is the image it creates of the manager, or ruler, as isolated.[49] Technically (managerially, strategically, politically) he interlocks with great numbers of fellow humans. Mentally he wants to deny this – he cannot admit either the flesh-and-blood changeableness or the fallibility of the 'human material' he needs for his purposes. In the name of efficiency he makes the sort of practical blunder (relying absolutely on what Intelligence tells him) which could be prevented only if he worked to the human scale – if he were part of a community and not a system. Cummings is being a general in the south Pacific partly because the Japanese imperialist megalomania has overstretched that country as much as Hitler's had overstretched

the *Wehrmacht*, or Napoleon's the *Grande Armée*. The macro-plan-
ners – the dealers in overkill and megadeaths – set themselves
goals which are in the mind only and cannot ever actually happen.
The first clear sight of this in literature is in *Hard Times* (1854),
where Dickens shows the self-defeating nature of the Utilitarian
cult of planning. The next case, and one immediately relevant
to Mailer, is in *War and Peace* (1865–9). Tolstoy shows us Napoleon committed to throwing ever huger reserves into the battle
for Moscow at Borodinó and then, at the day's end, going back
to his tent nauseated by the realisation that the events he is
embroiled in *will* surge forwards, largely regardless of his ideas
and directives: 'And he fell back into that artificial realm of
imaginary greatness, and again – as a horse walking a treadmill
thinks it is doing something for itself – he submissively fulfilled
the cruel, sad, gloomy, and inhuman role predestined for him.'[50]

By the end of *The Naked and the Dead*, Cummings has passed
through two stages of realisation: first, that 'his' men have lost
momentum, got bogged down, have not the unified driving purpose
that his leader's megalomania has projected onto them; and
secondly, that he himself is dominated and outmatched by the
macro-system he would have liked to master. His standing as
a general has not been high enough to bring him the naval support
he needs for a quick success, the overrunning of Toyaku's forces
has happened almost accidentally, with the nominal supervision
of a not very bright subordinate, he has left in charge, while he
himself goes off to headquarters to bargain for reinforcements.
'He allowed himself this thought, brought it almost to the point
of words and then forced it back. But it caused him deep depression.' And he consoles himself with obsessionally overseeing the
details of the mopping-up on the island, and with a reversion
to his pre-war dream of moving into right-wing politics.

Mailer works throughout at remarkable depth in our psycho-social natures. This comes out in the truth of his insight that warfare
is a function or special case of large-scale industry, and in the
accuracy of his novel if you treat it as a forecast. When Cummings
goes to visit a gun emplacement, his behaviour – putting in an
appearance, professionally alert, actually bored and estranged –
is just that of a company director whose only effective contact
with the concern is through the balance-sheet. The only point
when Cummings is *in* the experience with the whole of himself

is when he decides actually to fire a gun – to abolish the gap between himself and the point of production (or in this case, destruction). Mailer manages this scene so well that it envisages Cummings's repressed sexuality as inseparable from his class position on the estranged managerial plane.

The knob of the lanyard hefted pleasantly in the General's palm. He stared at the complicated obscured mechanism of the breech and the carriage springs, his mind hovering delicately between anxiety and excitement. Automatically he had posed his body in a relaxed confident posture; it was instinctive with him to appear unconcerned whenever he was doing something unfamiliar. The mass of the gun, however, troubled him; he had not fired an artillery piece since West Point, and he was remembering not the noise nor the concussion, but a time in World War I when he had been under an artillery barrage for two hours. It had been the most powerful single fear of his life, and an echo of it now was rebounding through his mind. Just before he fired he could see it all, the sharp detumescent roar of the gun, the long soaring plunge of the shell through the night sky, its downward whistle, and the moments of complete and primordial terror for the Japanese at the other end when it landed. An odd ecstasy stirred his limbs for a moment, was gone before he was quite aware of it.

The General pulled the lanyard.

The muzzle blast deafened him momentarily, left him shaken and numb by its unaccustomed force. He felt rather than saw the great twenty-foot flambeau of flame that discharged from the muzzle, heard dumbly the long billowing murmurs of the discharge through the dark closeted aisles of the jungle. The balloon tires, the trails were still vibrating gently from the recoil.

It had taken a fraction of a second. Even the backward blast of wind had passed him, roiled his hair and closed his eyes before he was conscious of it. The General was recovering his sense-impressions by degrees, clutching at them in the wake of the explosion like a man chasing a hat in a gale. He took a breath, smiled, heard himself say in an even voice, 'I wouldn't like to be at the other end.' He noticed the cannoneers, the Captain, after he spoke. He had said it because a part of

his mind always considered the objective situation; consciously
he had been unaware of the men about him as he talked.
He strode away slowly, drawing the Captain with him.

'Artillery is a bit more impressive at night,' he murmured.
His poise was addled slightly. He would not have said this
to a stranger if he were still not absorbed in the impact of
firing the howitzer.

'I know what you mean, sir. I always get a kick out of
firing the battery at night.'

Then it was all right. Cummings realized he had almost
made a slip. 'Your battery seems in good order, Captain.'

'Thank you, sir.'

But he was not listening. The General was paying attention
to the silent rhapsodic swoop of the shell, was following it
in his mind's eye. How long did it take? Perhaps half a minute?
His ears were alerted for the sound of its explosion.

'I never quite get over it, sir. It must be bloody hell at
the other end.'

Cummings was listening to the dull muted tones of the explosion miles away in the jungle. He saw in his mind the bright
destroying bouquet of flame, the screams and the rent iron
singing through the air. I wonder if it killed anyone? he thought.
He realized the tenseness with which he had been waiting for
the shell to land by the weak absorptive relief that washed
through his body. All his senses felt gratified, exhausted. The
war, or rather *war*, was odd, he told himself a little inanely.
But he knew what it meant. It was all covered with tedium
and routine, regulations and procedure, and yet there was a
naked quivering heart to it which involved you deeply when
you were thrust into it. All the deep dark urges of man, the
sacrifices on the hilltop, and the churning lusts of the night
and sleep, weren't all of them contained in the shattering screaming burst of a shell, the man-made thunder and light? He
did not think these things coherently but traces of them, their
emotional equivalents, pictures and sensations, moved him into
a state of acute sensitivity. He felt cleaned in an acid bath,
and all of him, even his fingertips, was prepared to grasp
the knowledge behind all this. He dwelt pleasurably in many-
webbed layers of complexity. The troops out in the jungle were
disposed from the patterns in his mind, and yet at this moment

he was living on many levels at once; in firing the gun he was a part of himself. All the roaring complex of odors and sounds and sights, multiplied and remultiplied by all the guns of the division, was contained in a few cells of his head, the faintest crease of his brain. All of it, all the violence, the dark coordination had sprung from his mind. In the night, at that moment, he felt such power that it was beyond joy; he was calm and sober.[51]

An over-psychological analysis might decide that firing the gun is, for Cummings, 'really' an orgasm. An over-sociological analysis might interpret the scene as 'really' a comment on the division of labour in managerial society. In our view this type of split denatures experience, which is always a matter of personal traits and emotions working themselves out in shared or social conditions. To explain a Cummings (or any other boss who fulfils himself through domineering), the sort of theory we need is Reich's. As a doctor treating disturbed patients, he formed the view that people have three layers in their characters: the 'biologic core', which is co-operative and loving under favourable social conditions; the surface layer, on which the average person is 'reserved, polite, compassionate, responsible, conscientious'; and an intermediate layer which consists of 'cruel, sadistic, lascivious, rapacious, and envious impulses'. He saw what he called 'social tragedy' as springing from the fact that our impulses, before they come out in behaviour, have to pass through the layer of perverse drives.

When sexuality is prevented from attaining natural gratification, owing to the process of sexual repression, what happens is that it seeks various kinds of substitute gratifications. Thus, for instance, natural aggression is distorted into brutal sadism, which constitutes an essential part of the mass-psychological basis of those imperialistic wars that are instigated by a few ... The sexual effect of a uniform, the erotically provocative effect of rhythmically executed goose-stepping, the exhibitionistic nature of militaristic procedures, have been more practically comprehended by a salesgirl or average secretary than by our most erudite politicians.[52]

Theory so large and deep is always disputable, but in our view nothing less large and deep could account for the conniving at or the actual taking part in large-scale cruelty which has become objectively possible for humanity in our time because machines are so efficient and which is subjectively possible when people allow themselves to use the machines or be used by them. As R. D. Laing remarks, after citing Stanley Milgram's experiments at Yale in how much pain people let themselves be ordered to inflict on others: 'My guess is that *most* people feel guilty at *not* doing what they are told, even though they think it is wrong, and even though they mistrust those who give the orders. They feel guilty at mistrusting their own mistrust.' And he quotes a remark of Julian Huxley's (very close to Reich's affirmation of 'natural rebellion') that 'the most dangerous link in the chain was *obedience*'.[53]

We said that Mailer's novel amounted also to a forecast. As it ends, the General is poised to become a politician, or so he hopes. Major Dalleson, military counterpart of 'middle management', has found himself in command at the moment of the Japanese collapse on Anopopei. At the end he is prefiguring post-war developments in his own kind of way. He is organising for organising's sake – turning 300 yards of jungle into a level parade ground, perfecting a gunnery training schedule, and jazzing up the map-reading class. His brain-wave is:

A full-size color photograph of Betty Grable in a bathing suit, with the co-ordinate grid system laid over it. The instructor could point to different parts of her and say, 'Give me the co-ordinates.' ... That was it. He'd write Army. And in the meantime he might send a letter to the War Department Training Aids Section. They were out for improvements like that. The Major could see every unit in the Army using his idea at last. He clenched his fists with excitement. *Hot dog*![54]

Lurid publicity and pointless technical change are fused in the one image. Educational and military 'hardware' develop hand in hand. This looks ahead to our society in which the schooling business and the weaponry business are two of the prime 'growth industries' and feed into each other, for example, the way in

which university Political Science departments were hired by the
US army to invent languages in which to sell the Vietnam war
to the public, to justify the Diem dictatorship, and even to create
for it a police force and an anti-guerrilla strategy.[55]

Our point is not the usual complaint about 'high-pressure sales-
manship'. The facts are that 'the total of post-War cases of armed
conflicts that have had a significant impact on the course of
history' number more than one per month, over the whole of
this past generation. The huge total of destruction this involves
has resulted from the activities of arms salesmen (the Dallesons
in their civilian clothes) and their employers such as Honeywell
Inc., the twentieth largest war contractor in the States. By 1972
they had made 250 million dollars out of such things as napalm-
with-polystyrene (so that it clings to the victim's skin and ensures
third-degree burns), and anti-personnel bombs which fling out
plastic fragments so hot that they vaporise bone without touching
it and which cannot be found by X-rays.[56] According to expert
opinion, the trade in arms was the immediate *cause* of the Nigerian
civil war, the Pakistan–India war, the Congo crisis, the Korean
and Vietnam wars, and 'nearly all the other wars that have occurred
since 1945', since 'Ninety-five per cent of all the post-Second
World War conflicts have been fought in the underdeveloped
areas of the world, and all have been fought with imported weapons.'[57] What the Cummingses have done is to become technical
supervisors of a programme by which America, according to its
ex-Secretary of Defence Robert McNamara, 'has devoted a higher
proportion of its gross national product to its military establishment
than any other free-world nation'. (This was before Vietnam.)
The role of the ex-generals was to direct the companies who
made the arms. 'In July 1960 . . . General Dynamics, the corpor-
ation having the largest per cent of armaments contracts (by
dollars), had 27 retired generals and admirals on its payrolls.
The *total* number of retired officers of all ranks employed by
General Dynamics, however, was about 200. Its closest competitor
was United Aircraft, with 171.' American industry, concludes
this writer, '*by its very nature . . . is in a constant state of mobilisation
for war*'[58].

It is striking to find from the standard studies of American
society that militarisation is pervasive, and not confined to a
few powerful people at the top. For example, in the fifties whole

suburbs began to be built from scratch. Clusters of 'rental garden apartments' were built round a shopping centre: 'In effect, the developers were building a city to provide a sort of captive market – a constantly replenished, non-satiable reservoir of 30,000 people, many of whom would ever be poised at that stage when families just begin to lay up possessions.' One resident described this kind of thing as 'a lay version of Army post life', and this was a natural image to use. The people who went to live there are described as 'trainees for the big corporations, research chemists with the AEC, captains and majors with the Fifth Army, airline pilots, FBI men – in total, a cross-section of almost every kind of organisation man in America'. In one year, an eighth of the couples who moved from one such suburb to another were army and navy couples assigned to new stations.[59]

Such facts justify our view that *The Naked and the Dead* and *Catch 22* are not just 'war books' – their significance does not stop short at 1943. What Mailer and Heller show, with every kind of tragic and satiric detail, is that a society makes war by the same methods as it makes things. In the extreme situation of total war, the relations between people and groups of people change little from what they were in peacetime.

Heller's novel twins naturally with Mailer's: both are massively complete and elaborate views of a massive thing (what used to be called 'the war effort'); and Heller is every bit as shrewd as Mailer in his understanding of a war as a glorified managerial opportunity and a special department of the peacetime economy. Again we see that for middle management (Colonel Cathcart, Colonel Korn) output becomes an end in itself, the number of missions flown. Initiative is passing to the whizz-kid, the emerging super-manager, Milo Minderbinder. He plays the foodstuffs market, corners whole crops (all the eggs in Malta, all the cotton in Egypt, and for that matter all the police in Rome), he controls prostitution. By the end he embodies the fusion of wholesale supplier, racketeer, and undercover political manipulator who now rules America and also operates 'transnationally': consider Milo's feat in chapter 24 where he organises both the American attack on a bridge and the German anti-aircraft defence of it. Heller confirms this view of the novel when he says that 'The book's morality is a postwar morality. Its substance is Yossarian's conflict with his own superior officers ... and they are mostly symbolic of the civilian hierarchies, political and economic, of the Cold War.'[60]

Heller's feeling for the pain, danger, and death of the war is no less than that of an Owen, Sassoon, or Mailer but it is telescoped into a small space, the recurrent-nightmare treatment of the dying rear gunner Snowden. As we said earlier, Mailer's function had been to report back to the American people on the collective experience from which they were just starting to recover, and this necessitated telling it as it was in order to supplant the cover-up and ballyhoo of the official media – the speeches by commanders-in-chief, the Atlantic Charters, the ticker-tape welcomes for victorious generals. In literary terms, Mailer was working nearly as fast as a war photographer, and we should remember that for most people *the* American war photo is the one from *Life* of four GIs raising the Stars and Stripes on the summit of the shattered Pacific island of Iwo Jima. The pose, the aura, the implicit symbol of this actual instant are identical with a thousand florid war memorials. This is in effect a con, for though it was necessary to defeat the Japanese in the Pacific, it had not been necessary to fight the war at all. The League of Nations had decided not to criticise the 'internal affairs' of a member nation when Japan invaded Chinese Manchuria in 1931. The Western powers had not invoked the Treaty of Rapallo to stop the Fascist dictators in their tracks by cutting off their oil supplies. Since war is avoidable, it is not the heroism of its survivors that we should remember it by, but rather the suffering of the victims: in photographic terms, Capa's picture of an American machine-gunner killed in Leipzig on the last day of the war, who lies, like Snowden, in a puddle of his own clotting blood.[61]

Heller telescoped such sufferings, without diminishing them, because it was possible, fifteen years after the events, to transmute or craft them into a sophisticated entertainment. The deadly meaning of the novel is unmistakable, but the immediate traumas (of casualties, of bereaved relatives) have healed enough for it to be acceptable that an artist should stand well back and see the bad historical thing as one more chronic folly of our species. Vonnegut suggests this too, in his different way – in the very short, seemingly whimsical and half fantastic *Slaughterhouse-Five*. Vonnegut had happend to be a prisoner of war, housed by the Germans in a very strong concrete meat-store in a slaughterhouse in the middle of Dresden in February 1945 when the British and American air-forces committed on that city the biggest single massacre in history. The guilt people feel about this event shows in their handling of the casualty figures. England's leading historian, A. J. P. Taylor, wrote to the *Daily Express* in the early sixties to pooh-pooh the (rather overdue) concern about Dresden (following David Irving's book about it) and said in his authoritative way that it had not been such a shambles – only 25,000 had died. The air-marshal who wrote the foreword to Irving's *Destruction of Dresden* admitted to a death-roll of 135,000.[62] Actually, by March 1945 the very efficient and reliable German police had counted 202,040 bodies, mainly of women and children. This impulse to back away from the bad thing is what Vonnegut is mimicking in the amazing form of his book: the zooms forward and back through time, the trips to another (imaginary) planet, the continual alienation-effects which remind us that his book *is* a book – a made-up thing, the result of someone using his own eyes and brain to break down an event into its parts, and not a deceptive lifelike illusion in which we can lose ourselves.

Vonnegut had taken a quarter of a century to get to writing about his experience of the shambles. This was not because he was unconcerned about what people do to people. In *Player Piano* (1952) he had written powerfully about division of labour and the rat-race; in *The Sirens of Titan* (1959) about power cults and the opiate effects of religion; in *Cat's Cradle* (1963) about the dangerous uses science is put to, and the ferocity of dictatorship; and in *God Bless You, Mr Rosewater* (1965) about the helplessness of charity to do much about the main miseries in the world. In the preface to a book of his shorter prose he tells two stories, about his brother's baby and his sister dying of cancer, and draws from them two mottoes for himself: 'Scraping the shit off of practically everything' and 'No pain'.[63] With this capacity for concern, and with the Dresden experiences in his head, Vonnegut knew very well, year after year, that his Dresden novel was demanding to be written. The reasons for the delay, and for the extraordinary obliqueness of the style he finally chose (the massacre itself takes up just six pages, one of them quoted from someone else), all come out in the first chapter of the novel – not in an apologetic preface but in a chapter which deliberately alerts the reader to the provisional and inadequate force of one novel as against the life it tries to represent:

> I would hate to tell you what this lousy little book cost me
> in money and anxiety and time. When I got home from the
> Second World War twenty-three years ago, I thought it would
> be easy for me to write about the destruction of Dresden,
> since all I would have to do would be to report what I had
> seen. And I thought, too, that it would be a masterpiece or
> at least make me a lot of money, since the subject was so
> big.

(It was then that Mailer was writing *The Naked and the Dead*
and James Jones *From Here to Eternity*.)

> But not many words about Dresden came from my mind then
> – not enough of them to make a book anyway . . .
> Over the years, people I've met have often asked me what
> I'm working on, and I've usually replied that the main thing
> was a book about Dresden.
> I said that to Harrison Starr, the movie-maker, one time,
> and he raised his eyebrows and inquired, 'Is it an anti-war
> book?'
> 'Yes,' I said, 'I guess.'
> 'You know what I say to people when I hear they're writing
> anti-war books?'
> 'No. What *do* you say, Harrison Starr?'
> 'I say, "Why don't you write an anti-*glacier* book instead?"'
> . . . It wasn't a famous air-raid back then in America. Not
> many Americans knew how much worse it had been than Hiros-
> hima, for instance. I didn't know that, either. There hadn't
> been much publicity.
> I happened to tell a University of Chicago professor at a
> cocktail party about the raid as I had seen it . . . he told
> me about the concentration camps, and about how the Germans
> had made soap and candles out of the fat of dead Jews and
> so on.
> All I could say was, 'I know, I know. I *know*.'[64]

The tension of helplessly but determinedly facing the bad thing
which we feel in that last stressed '*know*' is underlined again

and again throughout the novel by the simplest device: whenever someone's death is mentioned, the author adds the sentence 'So it goes'. This is essence of Vonnegut. His idiom or style, as well as his form, is finely adjusted to suggesting the great difficulty of dealing with the worst things. He often writes nearly basic English, repetitive, using the simplest shortest words, and though this will partly be to make himself readable by anybody and everybody, it also has rich expressive effects. It gives the feel of taking the utmost pains to focus experience – to clean off any blurs or false tints. It gives the feel of handling as carefully as possible something very dangerous and painful, like a bomb-disposal expert making his fingers work with maximum sureness while he suppresses, for the time being, the feelings which are natural but useless (fear, outrage, self-doubt). For example, Vonnegut tackles that dreadful experience, the shipping to and fro of people in cattle-trucks, which certain photos have seared onto our minds' eyes and which recurs in the literature – in *Comrade Tulayev*, for example,[65] and in the final sequence of Sartre's *Iron in the Soul*. In chapters 3 and 4 of *Slaughterhouse-Five* it comes out like this:

> Even though Billy's train wasn't moving, its boxcars were kept locked tight. Nobody was to get off until the final destination. To the guards who walked up and down outside, each car became a single organism which ate and drank and excreted through its ventilators. It talked or sometimes yelled through its ventilators, too. In went water and loaves of blackbread and sausage and cheese, and out came shit and piss and language.
>
> Human beings in there were excreting into steel helmets, which were passed to the people at the ventilators, who dumped them. Billy was a dumper. The human beings also passed canteens, which guards would fill with water. When food came in, the human beings were quiet and trusting and beautiful. They shared.
>
> Human beings in there took turns standing or lying down. The legs of those who stood were like fence posts driven into a warm, squirming, farting, sighing earth. The queer earth was a mosaic of sleepers who nestled like spoons. . . .
> Listen – on the tenth night the peg was pulled out of the hasp on Billy's boxcar door, and the door was opened. Billy

Pilgrim was lying at an angle on the corner-brace, self-crucified, holding himself there with a blue and ivory claw hooked over the sill of the ventilator. Billy coughed when the door was opened, and when he coughed he shit thin gruel. This was in accordance with the Third Law of Motion according to Sir Isaac Newton. This law tells us that for every action there is a reaction which is equal and opposite in direction.

This can be useful in rocketry.[66]

This is the opposite of taking the reader by storm. Not only the emotive but even the descriptive is pared away till nothing is left but items. Normally they would have been treated so as to arouse our horror or disgust, but our horror and disgust would fall so far short of what was there in the original that Vonnegut bypasses them – apart from the scientifically exact reminder, in that last sentence, that around and beneath the bare items, sausage and cheese and shit and piss and language, there lurks the bad thing: weapons, warfare, extermination. It is a style as far as possible from highbrow literature, it is the style of the new journalism with its dedication to telling it like it was, as in a recent story about a marine who gets shot through the spinal cord in Vietnam:

Ron pushed through the ring of marines and found a hole. No tent. Just a hole. In the bottom was something that looked like five or six bodies. They were all powder-burned and torn up. Ron reached in to find IDs and could only find Bodigga's wallet. After looking again, Sgt. Kovic realised that Bodigga was all there was in the hole ... all those pieces were just Bodigga. Ron stacked Sgt. Bodigga on a stretcher and cried. Over his shoulder, in the motor pool, someone was screaming.

'McCarthy,' they screamed. 'They got McCarthy. Those motherfuckers. Those rotten motherfuckers. They got McCarthy.'

McCarthy was from Boston and he had blue eyes. When he was laid out with the rest of the dead, stripped naked in front of the command bunker with his loose parts piled next to him, McCarthy's eyes were open and looked straight up into the rain.

Ron saw him there and wanted to kill somebody. He wanted

to kill somebody and use them to paste McCarthy and Bodigga back together.

In hospital at Da Nang:

Before the plane left Marble Mountain, a general came down the ward, distributing Purple Hearts, bed by bed. The general's shoes were shined and he had a private with him. The private carried a polaroid camera and took pictures the men could send home to their families. The general handed Ron a medal, the private took a picture and Ron put the ribbon under his pillow.

Then the general went to the bed next door. There was a 19-year-old marine in it. He'd had the top of his skull blown loose. The 19-year-old's brain was wrapped in wet towels. He babbled like a two-year-old and pissed in his sheets. Ron waited to see if the general's private would leave a picture.

He did. The private told the nurse to send it on to the marine's mom and dad.[66]

In *Slaughterhouse-Five* the raid itself is finally described in half a page, preceded by the formal phrase 'as follows':

He was down in the meat locker on the night that Dresden was destroyed. There were sounds like giant footsteps above. Those were sticks of high-explosive bombs. The giants walked and walked. The meat locker was a very safe shelter. All that happened down there was an occasional shower of calcimine. The Americans and four of their guards and a few dressed carcasses were down there, and nobody else. The rest of the guards had, before the raid began, gone to the comforts of their own homes in Dresden. They were all being killed with their families.

So it goes.

The girls that Billy had seen naked were all being killed, too, in a much shallower shelter in another part of the stock-yards.

So it goes.

A guard would go to the head of the stairs every so often to see what it was like outside, then he would come down and whisper to the other guards. There was a fire-storm out there. Dresden was one big flame. The one flame ate everything organic, everything that would burn.

It wasn't safe to come out of the shelter until noon the next day. When the Americans and their guards did come out, the sky was black with smoke. The sun was an angry little pinhead. Dresden was like the moon now, nothing but minerals. The stones were hot. Everybody else in the neighborhood was dead.

So it goes.

There is then a long interruption (a zoom forwards in time) before the hideous mess following the raid is described equally briefly:

A German soldier with a flashlight went down into the darkness, was gone a long time. When he finally came back, he told a superior on the rim of the hole that there were dozens of bodies down there. They were sitting on benches. They were unmarked.

So it goes.

The superior said that the opening in the membrane should be enlarged, and that a ladder should be put in the hole, so that the bodies could be carried out. Thus began the first corpse mine in Dresden.

There were hundreds of corpse mines operating by and by. They didn't smell bad at first, were wax museums. But then the bodies rotted and liquefied, and the stink was like roses and mustard gas.

So it goes.

The Maori Billy had worked with died of the dry heaves, after having been ordered to go down in that stink and work. He tore himself to pieces, throwing up and throwing up.

So it goes.

So a new technique was devised. Bodies weren't brought up any more. They were cremated by soldiers with flamethrowers right where they were. The soldiers stood outside the shelters, simply sent the fire in.[67]

These are not the vividly entertaining parts of *Slaughterhouse-Five* that leave us marvelling at the writer's ability to create comedy, without becoming either irrelevant or sick, out of terrible things: for example, the perfect pacifist fairy-story which spools action backwards so that bombers suck the bombs back up into their racks and the metals used to make weapons are tucked safely back into the ground.[69] The pieces we have chosen to quote are the bedrock of necessary truth which the novel was written to expose. The perfectly plain style, often devoid of even implicit comment, is akin to the numbness and detachment of the Second World War poets, and a further reason for it shows through in a remark Vonnegut plants in his description of how people began to move about again over the moon-like surface of burnt-out Dresden with its heaps of hot stone and dollops of melted glass. 'Nobody talked about much as the expedition crossed the moon. There was nothing appropriate to say.'

This detached style leads us right up to the facts of total war and makes us look at them, with not a single distraction from the kind of exaggerated effects with which artists have commonly treated the *much less extreme* situations of the past. The makings of a twilight of the gods or, better, a witches' sabbath were actually all there in Dresden on 13–14 February 1945. In the midst of the firestorm, a troupe of Arab horses from a circus stood huddled in their gaudy trappings until the flames killed them. They were torn to bits two days later by a flock of vultures from the zoo. Naked women were found lying dead on their fur coats – they had been unwilling to ruin them by soaking them in the fire-buckets as protection against the heat. Giant trees were uprooted by the updraughts, people died glued to the molten tarmac, corpses of adults were shrivelled by the heat to three-foot lengths. By March, heaps of unidentified dead had been bulldozed by the thousand into mass graves. The inner city had become a desert inhabited by nothing but horses, monkeys, a lion, and unusually big rats.[70]

Such are the facts. They could all have been *imagined* by an artist of the Ken Russell type who wanted to make a meal of his theme. That is why Vonnegut avoids them. The mother and child, killed in each other's arms by melted tar, could have made a heart-rending point – and stolen the show from the other, equally deathly deaths. The same applies to the mingling of corpses of ragged refugees and opera-goers in their finery.[71] Vonnegut has moved beyond this sort of point in order to insist, as unanswerably as possible, on the historical fact of a massacre which people committed, for which they were and are answerable, which people want to forget and try to cover up, and which cannot be undone or morally cancelled-out. The case is an intensely important one because, along with the decision to make and use the two atomic bombs, it shows us the *semi*-automatic escalation of effort inside a large system in spite of a lack of distinct human will or purpose. In this respect it is more daunting even than the death camps, since they were clearly conceived and distinctly willed and, as such, called for a convergence of factors which is likely to remain rare. Escalation, however, is not uncommon, and has recently been repeated on a large scale in Vietnam. All that escalation needs, as Dresden and the A-bombs show, are the usual habits of swollen administrative systems: cross-purposes and faulty communication between departments, the false pride that finds it impossible to back down or admit mistakes, and large expensive departments set up to concoct and broadcast false reasons, so that the people doing the jobs can hide from themselves the real horror, inhumanity, and uselessness of their acts. For example, the US air-force chief, Spaatz, said that the Americans kept strictly to their policy of bombing military targets only. The only such targets in Dresden were railway marshalling yards and factories. Although 2000 bombers dropped 3000 tons of bombs on the city, whole marshalling yards (to the south-west) were untouched; twenty-four trains and four hundred wagons and carriages were left untouched in another yard; the one key railway bridge was untouched; and a double track was working again within three days. The only factory of direct military use, a fuse factory in Dresden-Neustadt, was undamaged.

Spaatz's line about 'military targets only' was in fact a transparent bluff – by which his superiors, for example, Eisenhower, allowed themselves to be taken in.[72] This type of *bad faith* is the stigma of all such events, and in Dresden it worked also in advance. If the RAF had seriously been trying to single out military targets, they would have briefed the bomber crews by means of the usual elaborate maps of the city. For once there were none. Experts have suggested that this is evidence that the British air chief, Harris, lacked 'any fundamental desire . . . to destroy this city'.[73] Yet that is what he did. Many members of the command group in the RAF were so taken aback by the wanton thing they were about to do that they asked for confirmation of the order, and by the evening, when 6000 airmen had been briefed, dissatisfaction had 'permeated as far as the lowest levels in the Command'. The terrible human incoherence of the thing comes out acutely in an individual case. The master bomber had refused four months before to take part in the raid on Freiburg because he had studied there before the war and had many friends in the target area (around the cathedral). But since he had never been to Dresden, 'he could find no personal reason for objecting', although he 'deeply regretted' destroying so beautiful a city. So nobody 'really wanted' to burn and asphyxiate those 200,000 women and children. Yet it happened. And since air raids and other massacres are not glaciers, or avalanches, they must have motives – which show through, if we decode the false language in which they are typically couched. The British chief of air staff, Portal, had said a few months before: 'It may become desirable in the immediate future to apply the whole of the strategic bomber effort to the direct attack on German morale.' This was closely debated between Harris, Churchill, and his scientific adviser, Lord Cherwell. Its meaning was not spelt out: 'Shall we slaughter as many civilians as possible?' They could not admit to themselves or each other that they were choosing total war.

The same is true of the decision to drop the atomic bombs. The only remotely acceptable reason for killing 80,000 people in a flash would have been to save a bigger death-roll which otherwise was bound to happen. This is the stock argument (still mouthed by thousands of laymen and academics) that 'the atom-bomb ended the war in the Pacific'. Experts now agree that 'the alternatives of dropping the bomb or allowing the war to go on indefinitely did not . . . correspond with the true nature of the situation'. For example, the Japanese had nearly run out of food and fuel and their harbours were already being mined. Unfortunately the American general, Norstad (later military chief of NATO), felt such tactics to be beneath his warrior status. He 'declared, at Washington, that this blockading action was a cowardly proceeding unworthy of the Air Force. It was therefore discontinued'. Negotiations were also going on actively at top level for an end to the war. But the military man in charge of the nearly completed project to build the bomb, General Groves, 'had not been told of the Japanese peace feelers' – while at the same time the people in charge of these feelers, the US State Department, 'had been given not the slightest warning of the imminent use of the new weapon'. The Japanese could perhaps have prevented the massacre, since leaflets warning of 'total destruction' were dropped on Tokyo ten days before the raid on Hiroshima. Presumably they were not believed. And when the leading Japanese nuclear physicist was ordered to build a Japanese A-bomb as fast as possible, proved that he could not, and suggested instead that the anti-aircraft defences should shoot down *all* planes approaching Japan in case one of them was carrying a nuclear device, nobody took him seriously.[74]

The conclusions of the historians should be imprinted on all our minds:

> Most of the men who were responsible for Japan's policy had not known a fortnight before that the atom bomb was in existence. Even General MacArthur, who, more than any other man, was responsible for the overthrow of Japan, was given the information only a very brief time before the bomb was due [and] had no time to make his protest effective. Admiral William D. Leahy, the Chief-of-Staff of the President ... said, bluntly, that he thought that the use of the bomb was brutal, and served no rational end ... President Truman ... may have acted in these days very much in the dark.

(He was also reluctant to make *no* use of the already very costly project to build the bomb, since a waste of public money could be used against him in his first post-war election campaign.)

> Churchill judged it useless to press for discussion. All these statesmen suddenly found the bomb at their disposal, and they had no reasonable opportunity to think out the implications of atomic warfare, nor, it seemed, was the phenomenon of fall-out clear in their minds.[75]

On such grounds as those, Robert Jungk's chapter on the final decision to use the bombs is well named 'For They Know Not

What They Do'.[76] Our suggestion, on the basis of the novels and the history, is that total war is essentially incoherent because it can only be carried on by systems too large for humanity to manage. This does *not* mean that the resulting massacres are accidental or random. The 'Thunderclap' raids on Hamburg, Dresden, and Tokyo, the nuclear raids on Hiroshima and Nagasaki – and the raids with chemicals which have destroyed a quarter of the virgin forest in Vietnam – have indeed followed inevitably from the main technical and political trends of modern times. But they have not been *distinctly* willed or envisaged by those who give the orders, they have been among many mixed options which nobody has had the nerve or lucidity to sort out according to a norm of expediency, even, let alone of decency. It is this, along with the mammoth scale of the destruction, that gives writers and others the peculiar sense of helplessness as they strive to take in and bring home to others the actuality of the worst thing. Hot protest springs up in us, but it nearly dies in our mouths. Vonnegut catches the attitude with his usual fine idiomatic brevity:

As the Americans were waiting to move on, an altercation broke out in their rear-most ranks. An American muttered something which a guard did not like. The guard knew English, and he hauled the American out of the ranks, knocked him down.

The American was astonished. He stood up shakily, spitting blood. He'd had two teeth knocked out. He had meant no harm by what he said, evidently, had no idea that the guard would hear and understand.

'Why me?' he asked the guard.

The guard shoved him back into the ranks. 'Vy you? Vy anybody?' he said.[77]

3. *The Russian Revolution and Stalinism*

Most political analysts, of whatever allegiance, now agree that the Russian Revolution struck a sour note soon after 1917, and has been in a bad way ever since. The year of Lenin's death, 1924, is usually given as the terminus of its integrity. Even political theorists of the Right, those 'hired prize-fighters in the interests of the capitalist class', as Marx described them, will usually grant nowadays that the Old Bolsheviks, though misguided, were inspired by social ideals of a praiseworthy kind. The fact that they failed in these high aims is one more illustration of the elementary truth that you cannot change human nature . . . Moving towards the Centre, we discover that the Revolution failed because that is in the nature of revolutionary violence. Revolutions always yield dictatorships. Those which have not, for example the American revolt of 1776, or the English revolution of 1688, are not counted as 'true' revolutions at all: really they were wars of independence or necessary constitutional reform. Further to the Left we come upon several variations on the 'betrayed revolution' theme. The individual villainy of Stalin looms large here and it is common to lament the untimely death of Lenin, to refer to his dying testament suggesting Trotsky as his successor, and generally to behave in a strikingly unMarxist way by ignoring the historical forces which produced the political and economic extremes of the 1920s and 1930s. Finally, still further Left, among the Trotskyist groups, we meet an extraordinarily prickly tangle of factions and interpretations, ranging from the 'corrupt bureaucracy' view, to the 'degenerate workers' state' analysis, and the idea that the Soviet Union is 'state capitalist'. Others, like Djilas, have argued for the notion of a 'new class'. In our judgement, only two historians, Victor Serge and Isaac Deutscher, come close to an accurate view of the matter.

Before looking in more detail at Russian society after 1917, here are two quotations which are relevant to the argument. The first is from Engels, in a letter written twenty-five years before the October Revolution and thirty years after the emancipation of the serfs:

> The circumstance of Russia being the last country seized upon by the capitalist *grande industrie*, and at the same time the country with by far the largest peasant population, are such that must render the *bouleversement* caused by this economic change more acute than it has been anywhere else. The process of replacing some 50,000 landowners and some 80 million peasants by a new class of bourgeois landed proprietors cannot be carried out but under fearful sufferings and convulsions. But history is about the most cruel of all goddesses, and she leads her triumphal car over heaps of corpses, not only in war, but also in 'peaceful' economic development.[1]

Engels does not envisage for a moment that there could be an immediate movement from feudalism to the more complex structures of socialism. He understood that Russia would have to pass first through a capitalist stage before it could move on to its negation, the socialist commonwealth; and he realised that the Tsarist autocracy, representing the decisive class in the Russian economy at that time, would not give up its privileges without bloodshed.

Marx likewise saw that the working class might seize power before the objective conditions for establishing socialism were present. In that event, he predicted, the anomaly would correct itself: the workers' government would collapse under the economic pressures exerted by the bourgeois order containing it. In 1847 he wrote:

> the political domination of the bourgeois class flows from ... the existing relations of production. Therefore, if the proletariat overthrows the political domination of the bourgeoisie its victory will be only temporary, a point in the process of the bourgeois revolution itself, and will serve its cause as it did in 1794, so long as the 'movement' of history has not created the material conditions which make it necessary to abolish the bourgeois

mode of production and therewith definitely overthrow the political domination of the bourgeoisie. The 'Reign of Terror' in France therefore had to accomplish the cleansing of the surface of France from feudal ruins by its terrible hammer blows. The timid, cautious bourgeoisie would not have managed to complete this task in decades. The bloody acts of the people hence merely served to level the path for the bourgeoisie.[2]

Marx's reference to the White Terror of 1793–5, under the revolutionary dictatorship of Robespierre and others, suggests a useful analogy between the risings of 1789 and 1917. In France at the outbreak of the Revolution, as in Russia 130 years later, the working class was very small, about 3 per cent of the population or 600,000 out of twenty-five million. The middle class was even smaller; most of the people were peasants. (In Russia in 1917 there were three million workers in a peasant population of about 100 million.) Furthermore, the workers were concentrated almost wholly in the large industrial centres, such as Paris and Marseilles. Yet nearly all the decisive events of the Revolution were carried out by this small class: the storming of the Bastille, the imprisonment and execution of the king, the seizure of political power and its defence on the battlefield. It was able to do this because, allied to a revolutionary middle-class leadership, it was moving with forces of economic production which had already been transformed. What the actual struggles in the streets, monasteries, and landed estates achieved was the cancelling-out of moribund feudal institutions and their replacement by new ones that favoured, and existed in a state of symbiosis with, the emerging capitalist system.

The militant slogans of the French Revolution ended in the consolidation of power by a new ruling class. The Declaration of the Rights of Man was the banner under which the new form of exploitation was established. This shows up sharply in the difference between the draft of it and the final version. The draft says everyone can use his 'hands, work, and capital' as he thinks fit; this diplomatically vanishes into a general 'natural right' to liberty in the final version of paragraph 4.[3]

The reforms made by the new ruling class were genuinely revolutionary, for example, the abolition of feudal privileges, the confiscation of the prime source of wealth (the large church and *émigré* lands), and the introduction of bourgeois law (later codified by Napoleon). But our point is that the institutions and values of the state do not necessarily bear an obvious relation to its basic economic arrangements. The French middle class had no difficulty at all in adapting its allegiances to republican forms after the downfall of Napoleon III, the last of the emperors, in 1870. So far as the French economy was concerned, the collapse of the monarchy was irrelevant. The middle class can flourish – in their role as the owners of the means of production and therefore as the decisive class – under seemingly diverse and even contradictory political systems: a constitutional monarchy, a democratic republic, a Fascist dictatorship, a collective despotism, a racist or religious oligarchy, and so on. What is important are not the titles or forms of government and not whether, as Lenin sarcastically puts it in *The State and Revolution*, the particular member of the ruling class who happens to be in office can on this or that occasion be exchanged for another, but the property relations between people. The State itself – the means of legal enforcement, as Lenin (following Hobbes) defined it ('special bodies of armed men, prisons, etc.') – is the instrument for maintaining these basic relationships. The ferocity or subtlety with which they are enforced is almost infinitely flexible, and it depends on how seriously these relationships are challenged.

If this analysis is right, it should apply also to Russia before and after the Revolution. The years between the publication of Dostoevsky's *The Possessed* in 1871–2 and the Revolution in 1917 – which has dominated Soviet literature ever since – were years of increased industrialisation and political reaction. Industrial production trebled in the twenty years between 1877 and 1897, from 541 million roubles to 1816 million. Thousands of *versts* of railway line were built. Isaac Deutscher selects the Tiflis region of Georgia as a typical area, and shows how the national industrial revolution was transforming oriental, tribal, and feudal Russia. Within four years (1887–91) the total industrial production of Tiflis and Kutais soared from ten million to thirty-two million roubles. British and French capital was brought in to develop the oil wells at Baku and Batum (nationally, foreign investment had reached 1500 million roubles) and manganese mines were opened in Chiaturi. Tiflis became the centre of the huge railway network needed to handle all this production, and Baku and Batum were linked with the Caspian coast and the Black Sea. The railway junction and related services became the main life of the town, yet, even if we exclude rail workers from the count, the number of wage-earners virtually doubled, from 12,000 to 23,000. Again this typifies the national trend. In the ten years from 1887–97 the number of engineering workers rose by 50 per cent, from 103,000 to 153,000, while the number of textile workers doubled, from 309,000 to 642,000. As Lenin put it: 'The country, sparsely populated in the years after the Reform, inhabited by highlanders and staying aloof from the development of world economy, aloof even from history, was becoming transformed into a country of oil industrialists, wine merchants, grain and tobacco manufacturers.'[4]

In literature this time found its voice in Gorky. His stories and novels from around 1900 are filled with imagery of new and already decaying slums, dirty air, shabby crowds, and smouldering mass discontent. In *The Artamonovs* (1922) he evokes the above history in classic epitome as a story of several generations in the life of a family business. Politically it was a time of intense reaction and increasing violence. During the early 1870s the non-conspiratorial and peaceful movements of protest were crushed by state policies that flowed from the attitudes of panicky scorn and hatred for the 'mob' that are sanctioned by Dostoevsky in *The Possessed*. A reduced and hardened opposition went underground and began to promote acts of terrorism. The *Narodnaya Volya* or 'People's Will' party, with fewer than fifty members, organised itself into a grim movement of political assassins. They used to warn their victims that they were next on the list. By 1882 three high-ranking officials had been murdered and thirty-one revolutionaries had been hanged or shot.

This duel could have only one outcome for the Tsar. In 1881, after three attempts on his life, he was at last assassinated, blown to pieces by a bomb. It had been made by a relative of Serge's on his father's side who was also a leading theoretician of the *Narodnaya Volya*. He was hanged, and Serge's father, whose politics were the same, had to hide and then flee into permanent exile.[5] The next Tsar, Alexander III, retaliated by intensifying the activities of the political police. On his accession he announced that he was determined to 'preserve autocracy for the good of the people'. To this end he set up the *Okhrana*, an even more fearfully powerful police arm than the Third Section; reintroduced sweeping powers of censorship; cracked down on the peasantry to the point where, as Serge puts it, serfdom was more than half reinstated by the system of appointing heads of the village communes, with autocratic powers, from among the nobility; and restricted higher education to the ruling class. Jews were hounded out of the cities where they had settled and forced to live in miserable congestion in the districts they had come from. The aim was to divide the people and channel its aggression away from the government.

Such was the period that runs up to 1905, the year of the first Russian Revolution, and beyond it to 1917. It was a time of capitalist boom and proletarian immiseration, alongside a more and more obsolete peasant system of farming the land. Nevertheless, when the revolutions of 1917 took place, the balance of social classes was still in the main feudal. It was, as we said, nearly identical proportionately with the balance of classes in eighteenth-century France. Apart from the aristocracy, nearly 80 per cent of the people still made their living on the land and only 10 per cent from manufacturing industry, mining, and transport. The average income of people employed in Russia in 1913 was less than 80 per cent of the corresponding figure for Britain in 1688, nearly a century before our Industrial Revolution.[6]

Such figures show more clearly than anything else the ripeness of the country for a middle-class revolution. The old, wasted feudal order, with its exhausted economic, social, and political arrangements, had finally worn itself out. It could no longer grow, and it could not adapt itself to the new sort of production and the movements and relations of people springing from it. The negation of feudalism, capitalism, was poised to seize state power as the political counterpart to the economic supremacy it was now achieving. The unsuccessful rising of 1905, put down with the greatest difficulty and brutality by the waning aristocracy, was an early move in the same direction, although of course the spontaneous springing-up of workers' soviets at this time frightened many thinking members of the middle class. The period of liberal constitutionalism that followed under Stolypin was doomed to failure: Tsarism could not bring itself to give in without a struggle. By 1914 the stage was set. War – in Trotsky's phrase, the locomotive of history – was about to carry the bourgeoisie to power. Their first prime minister was Kerensky.

The Bolshevik leadership, that is, Lenin and Trotsky, were not unaware of the role they were playing in the middle-class revolution of 1917 – for such we believe it to have been. They knew Engels's sharp-edged comment of more than sixty years before:

> The worst thing that can befall a leader of an extreme party is to be compelled to take over a government in an epoch when the movement is not yet ripe for the domination of the class which he represents, and for the realisation of the measures which that domination implies. What he *can* do depends not upon his will but upon the degree of contradiction of the various classes, and upon the level of development of the material means of existence, of the conditions of production and commerce upon which class contradictions always repose ... he necessarily finds himself in an unsolvable dilemma ... he is compelled to represent not his party or his class, but the class for whose domination the movement is then ripe. In the interests of the movement he is compelled to advance the interests of an alien class, and to feed his own class with phrases and promises, and with the asseveration that the interests of that alien class are their own interests. Whoever is put into this awkward position is irrevocably lost.[7]

Lenin argued acutely that it was not the role of the working class in a socialist revolution that was at issue in 1917, but its role in a bourgeois revolution in a country that was largely peasant. He added that whoever hid the fact that the economic content of the revolution was bourgeois helped the bourgeoisie.[8] He pinned his own hopes on a successful outcome to the German revolution. As we know, its defeat in 1923 left the Soviet Union completely isolated.

Lenin, who had only a year left to live, watched developments in his Party with the greatest worry. The New Economic Policy, which he had brought in in 1922, committed the Soviets to a programme of renewed industrialisation and limited capitalism. It had been launched on the gamble that the German Socialists would take power. Justifying the NEP to the Third Congress of the Comintern, Lenin had said: 'We quite openly admit, we do not conceal the fact, that the concessions in the system of state capitalism means paying tribute to capitalism. But we gain time, and gaining time means everything, particularly in the epoch when our foreign comrades are preparing thoroughly for their revolution.'[9] It is impossible to think what else he could have done at that time. Food was scarce, industry almost non-existent, the peasantry preferred either to burn or conceal their crops (against the reintroduction of the market system) rather than give them up to government agents. This situation and Lenin's view of it confirm Engels's analysis.

In his last months Lenin realised that the battle for communism in the USSR would be long drawn out. At first he seems to have believed that the revolution was still in a critical phase; that though the period was indeed transitional, what followed could be 'either to socialism or a return backward to capitalism'. His fears deepened, however, and he wrote about the growing bureaucracy under Stalin: 'If we take that huge bureaucratic machine, that huge pile, we must ask, who is leading whom? I doubt very much whether it could be said that the Communists were guiding this pile. To tell the truth, it is not they who are leading, they are being led.'[10] Just before he was finally disabled by cerebral thrombosis he wrote a series of confidential memoranda, including the political testament which was later suppressed by Stalin. In one of these he strongly attacked the repressive brutality of the secret police under Ordjonikidze and pronounced a final, clear-eyed judgement on the new state. It had become, he wrote, 'a bourgeois czarist machine . . . barely varnished with socialism'.[11]

The best Soviet novelists of the post-Revolutionary epoch – Fedin, Serge, Solzhenitsyn, and 'Sholokhov' – have tended to confirm the uncompromising honesty of Lenin's final judgement. Their artistic integrity, usually operating in the teeth of the most terrifying deterrents to the telling of the truth, led them to put down on the page the real details of the lives they saw around them. Their views often remain implicit, especially in books which they had some hopes of publishing in Russian for Soviet readers. For example, there is a revealing moment in Fedin's *The Conflagration* which lights up much that is otherwise barely expressed in the novel. The playwright Pastukhov is being driven through town by his chauffeur Verigin, an ex-peasant who enjoys hooting at pedestrians to clear the way. Pastukhov remonstrates jovially and Verigin replies: 'You're always teasing, Alexander Vladimirovich, but you love it really . . .'

> Pastukhov did too – the trumpeting of the horn, the crepe de chine curtains on the rear window (a sign of Yulia Pavlovna's tender care), and Verigin's habit of keeping as long as possible to the central lane reserved for government cars after he had overtaken some vehicle on the road. Pastukhov pinned all the blame for this childish pretence on his driver, although it tickled his fancy to think his car was easily mistaken for a government official's.[12]

An aspect of a whole society is epitomised in this moment: one privileged individual, equipped with chauffeur and private car, whose life-style and self-image make him virtually identical with the ruling bureaucrats. There is also the telling detail of that central lane reserved for government cars, coupled with the threat like the distant crack of a whip that its exclusiveness really is preserved: Verigin stays in it only 'for as long as possible'. Fedin does not dwell on the moment, it is a fact of life, as a novelist in the West might describe the receipt of a bill. Yet it reaches to the heart of Stalin's Russia, exposing its distance from Bolshevik ideals.

This is not to say that Fedin's novels, and in places 'Sholokhov's', do not conscientiously repeat the falsehoods that Stalin required of his writers. As Deutscher says,

> Marxism had, in fact, shortened the distance between politics, philosophy, and literature. Stalin crudely oversimplified the Marxist view of their interconnections, until he degraded science, history, and art to the point where they became handmaidens of his politics. Every time he issued a new economic and political directive, the historians, the philosophers, and the writers had to check carefully whether in their latest works they were not in conflict with the leader's last word.[13]

That is well known. What has not been carefully enough noticed is the rich, if oblique, evidence offered even by novels that accommodated themselves to the Stalinist system. For Nadezhda Mandelstam, Fedin personifies the 'tribe' of hacks with fishy eyes who wrote to a regular timetable and 'went in for mahogany', that is, they filled their apartments with heavy bourgeois furniture bought with the lush proceeds of their hackwork.[14] Serge is more just in viewing Fedin as a writer of 'paralysed honesty' – one who had the tenacity to register at least some truth while conforming 'not without distress' to the enforced code of the time.[15]

Fedin was born in Saratov on the Volga in 1892 and so came to intellectual maturity at the time of the Revolution. This, together with the fact that he wrote the first two books of his trilogy during the Second World War when Stalin's personal ascendancy was at its peak, accounts for much of his willingness to go in for the required Stalinolatry. This reaches its height at the end of *No Ordinary Summer* (1948), which is about the Civil War. The hero, Kirill Izvekov, a young Bolshevik serving with the Red Army on the southern front, glimpses Stalin at a troop parade and experiences a moment of 'spiritual uplift':

> By this time the Southern front had come to associate Stalin's name with the sweeping drive launched against Denikin. This name was spoken not only at staff headquarters, but throughout the army. There were cavalrymen who remembered their first meeting with Stalin in the Salsk steppe as far back as the summer of 1918. A little more than a year had passed since Stalin smashed Krasnov's Cossacks at Tsaritsyn, and there were a great many commanders and commissars in the South who could tell the Red Army men about the revolution's early battles for the Volga. Now the name 'Stalin' had spread to all armies and all fronts. After Stalin's telegram reporting victory at Voronezh, his name resounded on every front, acquiring for the entire Red Army a new purport as the hallmark of military genius ... Most Communists, Izvekov concluded, were aware that Stalin's role in the struggle waged on the civil war fronts by no means exhausted his activities since the October Revolution.[16]

This is sheer panegyric, rising (or plunging) to the image of Stalin on the final page bathed in light streaming from a doorway. Readers may remember the Soviet film *The Fall of Berlin*, visually unforgettable in its battle scenes, then outdoing Hollywood in the vulgarity of the final shot – Stalin as God, smiling seraphically as he steps slowly down from his plane dressed in a gleaming white uniform.

The counterpart of the Stalinolatry is the running slur on Trotsky. Never named but always sneered at as 'the Commander-in-Chief' or 'the Supreme Command', the man who helped save the Bolshevik revolution from annihilation is presented as a bumbling fool, his personal role is minimised to vanishing-point, and it is repeatedly suggested that he was at loggerheads with the Central Committee. Lenin, says Fedin, was time and again forced to countermand Trotsky's asinine instructions to the Red Army in favour of the ultimately successful strategies put forward by Stalin. In fact the victorious plan for an offensive in the Donets basin during the 'extraordinary summer' of 1919 was Trotsky's.[17] Stalin supported a campaign against the Don Cossacks – in the novel, of course, Fedin has him pour scorn on this idea.

Our interest in Fedin's trilogy today, however, is not in the accuracy or otherwise of its more strictly historical parts. The fact is that Trotsky played down Stalin's role in the war when he could, and Stalin repaid the compliment: as Deutscher says, the 'whole literature' on the strategic controversies of the Civil War was 'designed mainly to promote the legends of the various claimants to power'.[18] Fedin's historical sequences are expendable, partly because they are written in a flat, almost textbook style that looks quite lifeless beside *War and Peace*, *The Quiet Don*, or *August 1914* and partly because they are separated from the main fabric of the trilogy – Fedin seems to have realised that far-flung and violent scenes were not his *métier*. Precisely his strength is his finesse in rendering the interplay between people, often in a domestic or private situation, although (like most Russian writers) he was too much a man of his epoch and his nation to forget for even a chapter that people's lives are steeped in the atmosphere and conditions of their time.

The trilogy begins with *Early Joys* (1945). It deals with the years between 1905 and 1917. *No Ordinary Summer* came out in 1948. In the following year Fedin was awarded the State Prize for Literature. Part One of *The Conflagration* (1962) deals with the outbreak of war with Germany in 1941 and, retrospectively, with the Stalinist terror of the 1930s. Discussing what he was aiming at in the trilogy, Fedin wrote:

It has always been my aim to find an image of *the times* and include it in my story on an equal and even preferential basis with the characters of the book, and this desire is stronger now than ever. In other words, I see my trilogy as a historical work.

At first sight this looks as though it clashes with another idea in the preface:

Now, when the novels have been completed and I recall the work that went into them, I see that the original idea did not perish. It underwent considerable change and remained alive as a separate theme in the life story of one of the main characters, closely linked to that of the main character. This is the story of a little girl who grows up to become an actress, it is the theme of art, of a sunny, snow-white city in which a new reality penetrates the fabric of the past, gradually destroying it.[19]

In the context of the whole work, with its crowd of characters, the long sequences devoted to the savage skirmishings of the Civil War, the analysis of the rise and decline of the Bolsheviks, and the insistent theme of how Soviet society was being transformed, Fedin is saying an extraordinary thing, as though Shakespeare had said that *Hamlet* was really about Ophelia. In terms of space and action, Anna Parabukina is not even a major character, let alone the central figure. The playwright, Pastukhov, looms far larger, and even Pyotr Ragozin, the Old Bolshevik, looks a more likely character to represent the thrust of the novel. Fedin must be pointing to something more important than mere length of time spent on stage, or before the reader's eye. Anna first appears in *Early Joys* as a little girl, the daughter of a worker, Tikhon Parabukin. She is sympathetic, quick-witted, but unimportant so far as the trend of the action is concerned. By the time of *No Ordinary Summer* she has flowered into a lovely young woman with a flair for acting. She starts to work with the theatre after the Revolution and we see her serving her apprenticeship under the actor Tsvetukhin who saunters, poses, and converses his way through the trilogy from the start till near the end (Fedin is exceptional for a Soviet writer in being able to make so many of his main characters sophisticated: his attitude to them is neither uncritical nor dogmatically and puritanically disapproving). Later, Anna marries Kirill Izvekov, a Bolshevik whose awakening to political consciousness has been given in an unforgettably fresh and vivid sequence in *Early Joys*.[20] Through this relationship she is always present at least on the fringes of the main historical trend: the Civil War, the hounding of the Old Bolsheviks by Stalin, the search by artists to take in and express these experiences. Finally, in the second half of *The Conflagration*, Fedin places her in Brest-Litovsk when the Germans invade in 1941 and this experience (the terror bombing, the mass of refugees fleeing eastwards from the German army) is mediated mainly through her consciousness.

So Anna is important but not, until the end, central. We can only understand the author's comment that the trilogy is her story if we realise what she represents, that is, how typical she is in the way the Revolution changes her life. Like Pastukhov and Tsvetukhin she is a trace element of the direction taken by Soviet society after 1917. Before the Revolution her family have been poor. In an early scene Pastukhov and Tsvetukhin, representing both the theatrical profession and the bourgeoisie, visit her home more or less at random on a slumming expedition. With the detachment of their kind, they are looking for the authentic smell and look of poverty, so that their art can become more lifelike (it is a few years after Stanislavsky had had a hit in Moscow with Gorky's *The Lower Depths*). It is a finely done scene which enables Fedin to make many points, implicit and explicit, about the dreadful inequalities of Russian society and the insolent patronage of the middle class. At the end we see Anna running off with the coin the well-off visitors leave behind as payment for their intrusion.

After the Revolution Anna is fiercely proud of her class origins. When she is about to make her name as an actress, she resists all the pressures from the old-style actors to take on the title and manner of the *prima donna*. She especially refuses to change her name with its proletarian associations to something more genteel. One old pro insists on what he calls the indispensability of a 'euphonious' stage name. '"What kind of a name is that, child: Parabukina! Just think how it will sound when they start shouting from the gallery; '. . . bu-u-u-kina!'"'' But Anna retorts tartly, on her dignity because she's secretly hurt: '"A person's deeds embellish his name."' Later, when she triumphs, she is proved right, for when someone calls out her name, 'She found the sound impressive and even musical, despite the long-drawn-out "u-u-u" in the ". . . b-u-u-kina".' One of the Fedin's themes is the emergence of a proletarian art distinct from the old bourgeois realism and he has made Anna's name a symbol of the new form. A Red cavalry detachment, delighted with her acting, make out a certificate to 'Comrade A. T. Parabukina' and invite her to the front where '"you will show us your proletarian art, and we in our turn will grind the reptile Denikin into the dust"'.[21]

In this context it is a shock to see in *The Conflagration* that Anna now styles herself 'Ulina' and behaves towards young actors and actresses like any *grande dame* of the theatre. She is losing her roots in the experience of the people she came from, her art is no longer revolutionary. The novelist notes that Anna, 'née Parabukina but generally known by her stage name Anna Ulina', likes above all to play in the theatre of the old, small towns. It was in Yaroslavl, he makes Anna remember, a provincial town famous for its ancient churches, that 'the professional Russian theatre' first took shape. What is implied is that Anna is neglecting the large urban working class and succumbing to something very like a middle-class cult of the antique. A few lines later her husband Kirill recalls '"those travelling shows [Anna] put on for the Red Army men at the fronts during the Civil War"'.[22] By this stage in the trilogy, art, and especially theatre, has become quite central enough for us to see it as typifying the hardening into conservative modes which was creeping over many areas of Soviet life.

This re-emergence of bourgeois style, even after the Revolution, is embodied throughout the trilogy in the two confrères, the playwright and the actor. Tsvetukhin has a complex personality, a mixture of hedonism and idealism. In *Early Joys* he is almost wholly distasteful, vain and egoistical, interested only in playing the Great Actor and the Great Lover, preferably (since he tends to seduce young actresses) in one. By *No Ordinary Summer* he is showing some selflessness in his project to build a travelling theatre company capable of going wherever people are: '"In factories. In homes. In villages. Out on the fields. At the market.

On public squares. At the front if a war is on. At amusement
centres in times of peace." '23 He is avowedly not a Bolshevik
but willing to carry out Bolshevik ideas. This is the essence of
his position. Really he is an opportunist. He knows when to
accept a political *fait accompli* and take advantage of it, and
the Revolution appears to offer him his great chance. 'Above
everything else he wished to be an innovator in the theatre ...
The first thunder of revolution sent Tsvetukhin's spirits soaring.
It seemed that the new epoch would do for man what had been
beyond his own poor strength. Tsvetukhin imagined that he could
immediately convert the whole theatre to his ideas.' But he declines
into routine – like most of his contemporaries, the novel implies
(though this is buried between the lines). 'His flight turned into
a run, his run into an even stride, and even this stride was
sometimes checked by indecision.' Finally his innovatory flair
gutters out and he falls back more and more on dully repeating
the stale conventions of the conventional (middle-class) stage.24
Fedin's silent comment is sharp: Tsvetukhin flourishes. When
we meet him again in *The Conflagration*, he is, like Anna, at
the top of his profession, a widely-respected Grand Old Man
of the theatre.

Tsvetukhin is almost always seen together with Pastukhov, at
a play, a meal, a social occasion, earnestly discussing the nature
of the drama. Each needs the other, and together, with Anna,
they personify the theatrical profession. The two men also personify
the middle-class intelligentsia who were never Bolsheviks, or socialists of any kind, or people who cared about the social misery
that surrounded them. They lived off the fat of the land before
1917, and learned how to play the system after the Civil War.
Fedin is expert at presenting the events of the Revolution through
the consciousness of non-political people, people who are neither
Red nor White. Pastukhov, for example, is just bewildered by
the upheavals of the Civil War, fleeing from the front lines when
he can, collaborating with whoever is in power when he has
no alternative. He could not differ more as an individual from
Grigory Melekhov, the major protagonist of *The Quiet Don*. But
the two characters are at the same point in their helpless inability
to commit themselves, to make political choices. It is a remarkable
fact that these two major fictions, so widely read and admired

in the USSR, should both have at their centre a person so different from the 'positive hero' which the 'Ministry of Truth' required of the writers.

Pastukhov is clearly shown to have a vested class-interest in the pre-revolutionary world of *Early Joys*. He agrees to Tsvetukhin's plan to go slumming in order, as Tikhon Parabukin puts it, to 'gratify your curiosity about poverty'.[25] By 1910 he is already a successful young playwright with plays running in Moscow and St Petersburg. He is career-minded, mean, self-indulgent, and indifferent to the sufferings of poor folk. The novelist reminds us several times that his father was a greedy though unsuccessful businessman who once ran for Parliament as a Cadet. Pastukhov is clearly one of the Revolution's natural opponents; it is against him and his class that, in the minds of the Bolsheviks, the Revolution was made. In *No Ordinary Summer* a young girl cracks a joke, calling the time before 1917 ' "the last century" '. Pastukhov reflects:

> Last century! The adjective stunned him as applied to a time so recent that he was accustomed to looking upon it as the present. But it had gone never to return. Was he not himself the last century? A broken bit of the cornice of some shattered edifice? A frozen phrase of a forgotten tune; a lost chord from some provincial 'Maiden's Prayer'?[26]

But Pastukhov is lucky. The action of *Early Joys* turns on the finding of a revolutionary printing press and some leaflets. As a result Pyotr Ragozin goes underground and Kirill Izvekov is sent to prison. During the investigations, Pastukhov's name is casually mentioned to the police and so he is formally questioned. Since he clearly has nothing to tell, he is of course released, but with the grinding stupidity of bureaucracy he is forbidden to leave town without permission. After the Revolution this little incident, which he forgets almost at once, becomes the token of his 'real' sympathy with the Reds. And of course he does not go out of his way to set the record straight. In *No Ordinary Summer* he tells Tsvetukhin:

> 'At present there are lots of people claiming that they too did something or other, sometime or other, for the cause of the revolution. That may be petty, but I can understand it. As

you put it – very timely. But what would you like to have
me do? Break my neck to announce I never did anything
for the revolution?'[27]

Fedin wants to show how people like Pastukhov (for example,
Tsvetukhin or the oily Oznobishin who succeeds in destroying
a damning little document about his career as an Assistant Prosecutor under the Tsars) managed to survive the Civil War and prosper
in the following years. But first they have to force their way
through the narrow jaws of the Revolution, and Pastukhov squirms
at this:

> History, the times, the calendar, the hands of the clock, all
> sentenced Pastukhov to war. Sentenced him to death. This
> was a fact.
>   How could he find a meaning in that fact? Why should
> Alexander Pastukhov perish in a war which he had not caused,
> did not want, and from which he wished to stand aloof? Sen-
> tences are pronounced for some crime. What crime had he
> committed? Of what was he guilty? He was not a Red, so
> he counted as a White. He was not a White, so he counted
> as a Red. He was sentenced because he was neither Red nor
> White. Was it possible that the whole world was either Red
> or White?[28]

Pastukhov's little piece of luck now becomes his greatest liability.
Saratov is captured by Denikin, the White general, and though
Pastukhov goes along as one of the eight-man delegation to welcome the victor, his reputation as someone who has been implicated
with the Reds is known and he is put in prison. Yet this misfortune
is turned to good account when the town is relieved by the
Red Army. The upshot of these experiences is that Pastukhov
is forced to make a choice. Being a realist, he declares himself
a Red. The flair for survival which shows in this decision is
dramatised in a discussion with his wife, Asya.

> 'What must the conclusion be,' she continued eagerly, 'if,
> regardless of whether we interpret history falsely or correctly,
> we remain its victims? Submission. That's the only conclusion.
> Am I right?'

Pastukhov replies with a forceful statement on the value of being 'pragmatic', that is, choosing the winning side and sticking to it. It is what we would expect of him and it places him as *the* embodiment of the class which not only survived the Revolution but, as we will show, inherited its fruits.

> 'There is no trick to understanding that what is happening in St Petersburg, in Saratov, in Kozlov, and I don't know where else, is part of the course of history. The trick lies in discovering the motivating force behind it all. It is necessary to identify yourself with whatever is propelling history forward ... My choice is final. Do you understand? I made it in there – in that local branch of Dante's Inferno. I resolved that if I ever got out alive, the first thing I would do would be to write a letter to Izvekov confessing to having been an ass. And to Dorogomilov too. I want them to know that I am not a Whiteguard.'[29]

In fact the first thing Pastukhov does on his return from Denikin's prison is have a bath: the novel makes no further mention of the letter. Pastukhov has made a lot of noise about using his free will on the side of history but he realises by the end of the discussion that what he is saying is only an elaborate intellectualised version of his wife's candid knuckling-under. Asya is given the last word and she finds a striking aphorism for the pragmatic cynicism of her class:

> 'That is just what I was going to say,' whispered Asya, hugging his head. 'Of course you are free in all your actions ... Like the prodigal son who came back to his father's house, you and I are free to return to the fold. With bowed heads. Bowed heads don't get chopped off.'

When we meet Pastukhov again, twenty years later, he is fatter and still more prosperous. Asya has been divorced, he has a new, prettier, younger wife. He is surrounded by friends and adulation, his plays are a success again, and at his birthday party all the prominent members of his profession come to pay their respects. His worries are small, mostly domestic, though the threat of war has clouded everyone. But Pastukhov is still very much the masterful man of the theatre, even especially when he is being a host in his own house, and Fedin again shows his true novelist's breadth of understanding in showing him to be at least a conversational match for an ardent proponent of the official view of literature. One writer is arguing hotly that his colleagues should now produce a bold, militant 'poster' type of literature to help their countrymen at war; Pastukhov is wittily defending the view that no artist can ever do other than his best in his own medium, regardless of goals or directives.[30] By showing Pastukhov as genuinely talented in his way, Fedin avoids any trace of the vulgar-Marxist view that the people have all the virtues and the bourgeoisie have none. By pitting him against people with so much less self-love and so much more humane concern (especially Kirill and Pyotr), Fedin brings out the goodness of what went into the Revolution.

When we leave Pastukhov, about halfway through *The Conflagration*, to see what has happened to Kirill, our most lasting image is of the privileged affluence epitomised in his progress through the streets in his chauffeur-driven car. He and his class are consuming the fruits of Lenin's revolution. The contrast between the blatancy of Pastukhov's success and Kirill's bitter fate is Fedin's way of showing, cautiously but definitely, how the consolidation of the revolution, after the early years of crisis (1917–21), meant a steady divergence from the policies of Lenin and Trotsky.

Between 1917 and 1921, despite the ravages of war (both civil and against the armies of intervention), the Communist Party of the Soviet Union followed a conscious policy of equal pay. In 1917 the wages of the highest paid workers were more than 320 per cent of the most poorly paid. By 1921 this had been reduced to 102 per cent. Even after the inauguration of the New Economic Policy, it was policy that no Party member be allowed to earn more than a skilled worker. With the first Five-year Plan in 1928, all this was abandoned and no further effort at egalitarianism was attempted. Stalin led the attack, declaring that *uranilovka*, his abusive term for egalitarianism, was a peasant attitude alien to Marxism. Large wage differentials were brought in and at the Seventh Congress of Soviets Molotov stated flatly: 'Bolshevik policy demands a resolute struggle against egalitarians as accomplices of the class enemy, as elements hostile to socialism.' The rule limiting the income of Party members was modified in 1929 and later, in secret, abolished altogether. By 1937, when plant engineers were earning 1500 roubles a month and factory directors 2000 roubles plus, skilled workers (at the top end) were taking home only 200–300 roubles and piece workers were earning as little as 110 roubles. In addition the management, that is, the Party members, could increase their pay through a system of bonuses and rewards. The amount depended on how far their enterprises exceeded the quotas laid down by central government. By 1948, managers, heads of department, and foremen were earning up to 30 per cent over and above their fixed salaries, sometimes for exceeding their quotas by as little as 4 per cent.[31]

Another source of income was the Director's Fund, set up in 1936. Four per cent of planned profit, and 50 per cent of all profit above this, were set aside for distribution among the senior managerial staff. In one factory, at a time when the average worker's take-home pay was 236 roubles a month, the carve-up of the Fund was: Director, 22,000 roubles; Secretary of the Party Committee, 10,000 roubles; Chief of Production, 8000 roubles; Chief Accountant, 6000 roubles; President of the Trade Union Committee, 4000 roubles; Head of the Workshop, 5000 roubles. In addition a lavish system of State Prizes ensured the further distribution of profits among the *new ruling class*. Each year as many as 1000 of these were awarded, all tax-free, and some of them as much as 300,000 roubles.[32]

This 'new class' both supported Stalin and was represented by him. Early in the thirties he called for the creation of a new 'industrial and technical intelligentsia', and new priorities to end what he called 'depersonalisation'. This would be done by showing 'the maximum care for specialists, engineers and technicians'. *Uranilovka* was condemned, and a new system of 'better pay for better work' was brought in to replace it. As the Left Oppositionist Rakovsky remarked: 'A ruling class other than the proletariat is crystallising before our eyes. The motive force of this singular class is the singular form of private property, state power.'[33]

The new class was recruited through the education system. To put the matter as concisely as possible, the best jobs went to the 'industrial and technical intelligentsia' and they were recruited from the universities. Only the children of the intelligentsia could readily get to university. In 1938, the last year for which figures are available, more than 42 per cent of all students were from white-collar homes, and this proportion must have gone on climbing: in 1958 *Pravda* quoted Khrushchev as saying that in Moscow only 30–40 per cent of students in higher education were working-class.[34]

The link between university training, managerial jobs, and Party membership can be gauged from the fact that in the late thirties only one child in twenty had completed secondary school, let alone university. Yet of just one and a half million Party members in 1939, 127,000 had received a university education. If we take this figure together with those who had completed secondary school, the proportion of delegates to the Party conferences who could be described as 'industrial and technical intelligentsia' rose from just under 18 per cent in 1924 to over 70 per cent in 1941. Similarly, there was a convergence of factory managers and Party members. In 1923 29 per cent of managers were in the Party; four years later the figure was 96.9 per cent – could anyone seriously suppose that this represented a real growth in political consciousness? By 1936 the figure had reached its obvious goal – 100 per cent. The same movement occurred among Red Army officers. Finally, if we consider that in January 1937 managerial personnel numbered just over one and three quarter million and that at least nine-tenths of these belonged to the Party, it is clear that the two groups had become more or less one. Of the non-managerial remainder, a large proportion was made up of state officials, army officers, and other functionaries. In short, about 10 per cent of the population ran the country, planned the economy, and of course reaped the rewards.[35]

Parallel with the change in social composition of the Party ran the elimination of the Old Guard – the Kirill Izvekovs, the Ryzhiks and Rublevs (to name them after the most heroic characters in Serge's *Comrade Tulayev*). Of all Party members in 1939, just over 1 per cent had been members in 1917 and just over 8 per cent since the end of the Civil War. This cannot have been due to natural causes – over half the membership was younger than twenty-nine in 1927, only twelve years earlier.[36] The period of the great purges, started by Stalin, was not simply a time of terrorism but an index of the changing social basis of the Party, the ruling class, and the government. Except for Stalin not one member of Lenin's original Cabinet survived. It was this purge that set the seal on the bourgeois revolution in Russia and marked its success. Together with the crushing of the better-off peasants, the kulaks (Serge estimates that five million people died at this time), these events constitute the Russian bourgeoisie's final rise to power – a triumph achieved, as Engels had predicted, by way of fearful convulsions, sufferings, and heaps of corpses.

Fedin's treatment of this time is ambiguous to say the least, though it took courage to touch on it at all. Nowhere does he comment directly on Stalin's dictatorship or distinctly condemn it. His attitude, shown by the direction of the plot and by hints put usually in the mouths of minor characters, is clear enough, but we have to read carefully to pick it up. Even during the political thaw, when *The Conflagration* was written, it was quite impossible to publish frontal criticism of the dictatorship except during the short spell from late in 1962 to the middle of 1963, when Khrushchev allowed the publication of a very few works such as Solzhenitsyn's *Ivan Denisovich* in an effort to strengthen his own hand against the conservatives in the government.[37] Khrushchev's 'secret' speech before the Twentieth Congress of the CPSU denounced Stalin's dictatorship as a 'cult of personality' but left his main crimes – the crushing of the kulaks, the abolition of the Soviets, and the judicial murder of the Old Bolsheviks in the purges – largely untouched. Fedin, the survivor, follows this example, criticising Stalinism clearly but implicitly and noticeably skirting the issue when dealing with such things as forced collectivisation and the destruction by bullet of the Left Opposition. By keeping his head low, he was able to remain focused on a major theme – the persistence of old ways despite the rhetoric of the new – and to give us a chilling sense of what it was like to live from day to day under Stalin, in particular for those who just managed to keep back from the brink of destruction. For the extreme form of the situation, we must go to Serge and Solzhenitsyn, since to write about it fully meant death or deportation.

The centrepiece of Fedin's critique in *The Conflagration* is the political fall of Kirill Izvekov, representative of the oldest and loyallest of the Bolshevik old guard. He is both extraordinary and typical of his generation. When his accuser at the Party Control Commission reads out the details of his career, the narrative comments:

The facts he was listening to, familiar to him down to the last detail, and the recollections that flashed across his mind at the mention of the places where he had worked, all added up to an ordinary biography of an old Party member. In another country a man could not have boasted of a biography like that, and if he did it would have been considered a miracle. But here, in this world which was made and defended by men like Izvekov, it was a very ordinary story.[38]

Kirill had begun his political life as a young revolutionary imprisoned for leafletting, served capably and heroically in the Red Army, and is now, in the 1930s, at the peak of his career: a senior official in the Department of Heavy Industry whose talents are repeatedly drawn on. Bokatov, a rather sour civil servant who has no love for him, remarks:

'When he had to he fought, traded, restored the river fleet. Who put the tugs under steam for the Nizhni-Novgorod fair? Izvekov, they say. When the time came to build factories he was right out in front. Who got the production line going at the automobile works? He managed as well as any engineer[ing] specialist. He studied, improved his qualifications. He kept awake, he didn't sleep.'[39]

Kirill's impeccable revolutionary and personal credentials are insisted on. He has been a Party member 'for well-nigh thirty years', unlike most of the new membership he is of working-class origins. He also has connections in the upper reaches of the Party: his old friend Ragozin is now a member of the Central Committee and a top official in the Military Department. With such talents and friends he might well have risen even higher but he has always willingly taken posts of the second rank, out of the limelight and away from the big rewards. Bokatov explains: '"There are people, you see, without whom you can't get a real job done, people who create the material values with their hands and feed their pride on that. People who have hands and brains of pure gold."'

It is this dedicated maker and defender of the Bolshevik revolution who is one day abruptly summoned to the Party's Control Commission, the disciplinary body, to give an account of himself. Bewildered, Kirill is interrogated by an aggressive official in a scene whose suspense and power compare with the cross-examinations in *Crime and Punishment*. Kirill is not guilty of a brutal murder. His crime is, in human and even in political terms, of the most trivial nature. Many years before he wrote a reference for a man called Gasilov, who has now defected. For this 'crime' Kirill is politically and personally ruined. He loses his job, his friends, the right to live in Moscow. He is banished to a minor administrative post in Tula.[40]

Fedin's abhorrence of such treatment is evident throughout the scene. The brute browbeats the man with 'hands and brains of pure gold', treats him like a sneak-thief, and sentences him as a major criminal. It is also stressed that Kirill had acted in good faith: Gasilov was a good worker. As Anna says later (clearly speaking for the author): '"You were deceived, Kirill, but you yourself did not deceive anyone. That's the main thing." '[41] But decency gets Kirill nowhere: by the hideous moral subversion of the time, it shows as weakness. Kirill, a man of force and backbone, 'behaves so well' under the ill-treatment that he is in effect laying his head on the block. Although Fedin could not nerve himself to mention camps beyond the Arctic Circle or bullets in the backs of skulls, Kirill *is* shown to have the emotions appropriate to the Terror. He dreads the summons, he despairs about the outcome of the interview. His friends at once put a gulf between themselves and him (the cruellest is Ragozin himself) and he is treated like a leper. As he comes out of the Control Commission, he bumps into an old friend who is at first unaware that there is now an Izvekov 'case'. Kirill is behaving like a man who is ill, the friend offers him his hand and some friendly advice on dealing with the 'flu. Before the chat is over he knows something is in the wind and 'This time he did not offer his hand to Izvekov, but rubbing it clean with a handkerchief merely nodded and walked into the building.'[42]

Ragozin has already used a striking image, one that recalls the maggot-ridden officers in Eisenstein's *Battleship Potemkin*:

1. *Planting the Stars and Stripes atop Mount Suribachi on Iwo Jima Island 1945* – Photograph: Joe Rosenthal

2. *The Last Man to Die* (Berlin, 7 May 1945) – Photograph: Robert Capa

3. *Nächtliche Begegnung mit einem Irrsinnigen* (Night time meeting with a mad man) by Otto Dix, from *Der Krieg* (1924)

4. *Durch Fliegerbomben zerstortes Haus* (House destroyed by flying bombs) Otto Dix (Tournai), from *Der Krieg* (1924)

5. *Cross Section* (1920) by George Grosz

6. *Vision einer brennenden Stadt* (1936) (Vision of a burning city) by Hans Grundig

7. *Guernica* (1937) by Pablo Picasso, Collection Museum of Modern Art, New York

8 Samburu herd boys dancing at *Orge ot Kwob* (1960). Photograph: Denise Pakenham[...]

[Ragozin] sat tapping his glasses on the stack of note-paper and staring at the blank window as if it was there that he would find the ready answers to those questions which could never before have arisen in connection with Kirill Izvekov and which were now beginning to spot him the way rain spots the clothes of a person who suddenly leaves the shelter and comes out into the open.

We have to keep reminding ourselves of the formal nature of Kirill's 'guilt'. His real crime is touched on in the conversation between the two civil service hacks, Bokatov and Pridorogin, who discuss him in private: ' "He wasn't in the opposition apparently, from what I hear," [Pridorogin] said on a low note. "It's a position that he maintains and not opposition." "A special position of one's own *is* opposition."[43] The moral and political bankruptcy of Stalinism is expressed in that one line. The slightest sign of independent thinking is treachery, a crime, and punishable by . . . but Fedin fudges this issue. Kirill is not required to pass through the charade of a show trial, a public confession that he is guilty of, say, 'Trotskyism–Bukharinism' or 'contacts with Japanese agents',[44] and, finally, the bullet behind the ear. He is merely demoted. But Fedin does venture a small, clear hint at the encircling Terror: Kirill thinks to himself, 'What would have happened if Novozhilov had not agreed to give him this job in Tula?'[45]

Kirill had first met Novozhilov in 1921, late in the Civil War, when he was unexpectedly appointed head of the Tambov district militia and Novozhilov was head of the local Cheka (political police). Mopping-up operations against small bands of White guerrillas had been going badly in the area and one group, intelligently led by a peasant called Ivan Shostak, had been especially difficult to stop. Kirill accepts the job apprehensively – the previous Red commander has been demoted for failing in it – but, by a combination of courage and skilful negotiation, he manages to contact Shostak and persuade him his struggle is hopeless. The guerrillas surrender and give up their arms, not a shot has been fired, and Kirill becomes something of a hero locally. As he leaves for another appointment, Novozhilov bids him good-bye: ' "There are two people in the world for me now in whom I believe implicitly," Novozhilov said, shaking Izvekov's hand when he was leaving." The first one is me, and the second is you."' This not only explains Novozhilov's later willingness to help Kirill in his trouble, it also suggests the weight of achievement and service to the Revolution that might have been placed in the balance against Kirill's unfortunate link with Gasilov. The fact that it is not, that it becomes the occasion for dealing with someone who has 'got too independent a mind',[46] implies many things about the treatment of some famous people – Trotsky, Bukharin, Kamenev, Zinoviev. Even Lenin might not have survived: 'If Ilyich were alive today he would be in prison,' his wife Krupskaya is reported to have said once.[47]

While the parasites flourish, people of worth suffer and fail. While Pastukhov reaches the top, Kirill is shoved into a backwater. In Pridorogin's words, he has ' "ended up where he began – a plumber!" Pridorogin grinned and suddenly slapped his friend hard on the knee.'[48] Here is the squalid underside of the apparatchik's official rectitude – the rankest snobbery. This is another of the moments in which the novelist notes that all too little has changed. ' "Money had regained its old power, and, as before, money went where money was: the rich got fatter and the poor tightened their belts," ' a peasant reflects after the introduction of the New Economic Policy. Kirill too reflects on this, in a passage where Fedin dares to be nearly explicit about the fate of the revolution. His thoughts, as he moves about the streets of Tula, are dominated by a very old water pump 'in the shape of a fat question mark with a handle that looked like a comma'. The question image looms over the city, for Kirill can see that not much has changed in it since the nineteenth century. His own view, that of the Old Bolsheviks, is clearly articulated: 'But he himself built only the newest structures, and his attitude to the old could be defined in one scathing word: survivals.'[49] His reverie, dominated by the repeated word 'survivals' and the recurring image of the question-mark, comes at last to this point, which is so unqualified, coming from so proven a person, that we must take it to be the novelist's own:

But here, in Tula, have they simply forgotten that survivals must be uprooted? They might at least have built one eight-storey apartment house so people could see which way development was heading. How could you prove anything without examples? ... He was thinking that this obsolete way of life, preserved intact by some miracle, ought to have been broken up a long time ago and replaced by a more perfect shell as required by the present age ... they had only this to love since it had not been replaced by anything better.

Fedin's note of alarm, his political comment, is characteristically placed ahead of his argument, but it is nonetheless pointed: 'Here the cosiness and attractiveness seemed to hold a startling note of warning for young Soviet Russia: unless you change the stolid old way of life, everything will remain the way it is!'[50]

That is about as far as Fedin will go. Elsewhere he shows all ranks in Russian society, from peasants to civil servants, fearfully referring to Stalin and, in one case, terrified even to whisper his name to friends.[51] It is worth having this moderate image of what it was like to live in Stalinist society, since (precisely because of the congealing and bourgeoisification we have been describing) most Russians were moderate and kept their heads down. But what they did not see, or saw and dared not express, was bound to get into the literary record sooner or later, since 'mankind only sets himself such experiences as he can express'. If we contrast the novels of Serge and Solzhenitsyn, an unmatched history of the Stalinist experience emerges, and the contrast is specially necessary because Western readers are now accustomed to treating Solzhenitsyn as gospel. He has been through the Soviet mill, he had fearless integrity in a society where millions showed themselves craven. Serge's credentials are easily as good (he risked everything to get his work published, he never failed to speak out when silence would have meant betrayal of humane and socialist values) yet his view of the Soviet tragedy comes out quite differently.

We take the core of Solzhenitsyn's work – his indispensable contribution to the human record – to be *One Day in the Life of Ivan Denisovich*, *The First Circle*, and *The Gulag Archipelago*. This was all written between the later part of 1955 and the winter of 1966–7, and in his 'Letter to the Soviet Leaders' of 1972 he wrote: 'All I had to say is now said. I too am fifty-five ...': he meant that he was as old as the Soviet Union.[52] The exposure of Stalin in general terms was done at the Twentieth

Party Congress in February 1956 and the exposure of the many crimes and sufferings in a more detailed way at the Twenty-second Congress in October 1961. In February 1957 Solzhenitsyn was cleared of the charges on which he had been imprisoned, and he had already returned from exile in Soviet Asia and settled where he wanted to be, which was the countryside of Central Russia. His best work was done, we are saying, during the heyday of Khruschev and the post-Stalin thaw, which means too that it was done when his own experiences as a victim of the Terror were what filled his mind.

With the recent publication of *August 1914* he has started out on the large historical composition he has been working towards since his teens. The comparison has to be with *The Quiet Don.* That great novel is wholly graphic, physically intense, and in touch with the whole life of the community (a Cossack village). That is, it has the specific qualities of epic – the dustjacket blurb word for *August 1914*. *August 1914* is a decent, serious book and it amounts to a telling indictment of the Tsarist blimps, which makes it all the more stupid of the Soviet bureaucrats to refuse it publication. But it is not richly imagined, too much of it is plain military history (much more than the equivalent part of Fedin's *No Ordinary Summer*), and though we should postpone our opinions until the whole work is done, it does look as though Solzhenitsyn's crucial experiences lie wholly inside the vein of what Rousset, an ex-inmate of Auschwitz, has called *l'univers concentrationnaire.*[53] *August 1914* uses this vein only in the part of Vorotyntsev, the staff officer who carries out a strange, not very convincing role of roving inspector on the Prussian battlefields. He is in effect the author – the authentic person under tyranny who chokes on the gag and craves to bear witness to what has really happened. This is strongest in the one scene where the writer seems wholly engaged, the closing one, where at last Vorotyntsev can make his report to the Higher Command, only to realise that you cannot buck the system: the military machine, the Establishment, the State has no conscience, it deals only in expediency, never in the truth.

Our opinions of Solzhenitsyn also have to be tentative because we are using English translations and there is evidence that in his case translation denatures the originals more than usual. In English he seems fairly ordinary and uninventive as a stylist.

Yet Zhores Medvedev quotes a Soviet reader: 'The richness of language, the philologists will be studying it for decades . . . When other writers write it's like bricklaying, they assemble it bit by bit. But Solzhenitsyn moulds his phrases and images in red-hot plastic material . . .' This could be the over-reaction of someone starved of vital literature. But Burg and Feifer, who read Russian, say that Ralph Parker's translation of *One Day* turns 'Solzhenitsyn's sharp, distinctive prose into a thin porridge', to say nothing of omissions 'often of the most piercing images'.[54] Since this is what we would expect of a work published in the Soviet Union (our first reading of it was in the Moscow monthly *Soviet Literature* for February 1963), and since the same diluting and pruning has been suffered by other writers who have tried to use the whole gamut of popular Soviet speech (for example, Gladkov and 'Sholokhov'), we can take it that Solzhenitsyn's fiction is better in a line-by-line way, more expressive, richer in nuance, than it seems in English.

One Day is probably not so far from the original, since it is a beautifully plain piece of writing. There is no insistent slanting or moral-pointing from the author. It is unfailingly specific about those domestic details, of food and working conditions and so on, that make life bearable or not. The prose has an abrupt, outspoken movement that keeps close to the reactions of the ordinary farm-worker that Ivan is. Tvardovsky, the remarkable poet and great editor who was the only person ever to publish Solzhenitsyn in the Soviet Union, said about the style that it was 'vivid and original by its very commonplaceness and outer unobtrusiveness'.[55] That is how the English reads. The amazing thing about the novel is that it is so unremarkable. It is written with a level-headed carefulness like that of a man crossing a temporarily stilled avalanche or scree-shoot. Not that he was afraid of consequences. In the 'Letter to the Soviet Leaders' he wrote: 'I have long since outgrown your shell . . . I set no store by material wealth and am prepared to sacrifice my life.' Our point is that Solzhenitsyn knew that the ramifications of the camp subject were endless. He could have got historical about the camps, or shrill with overt outrage, he could have written long flashbacks to explain how each named inmate came to be there. Instead he made himself concentrate, single-mindedly, on the specific emotional, industrial, and communal conditions that were average for camps outside the Arctic Circle and with a low proportion of 'common criminals'.

When he first sent the manuscript to Tvardovsky's *Novy Mir* in December 1961, he called it *SHCH-854* – the prison number of Ivan Denisovich Shukhov. The functional brevity of that would have fitted very well the method of the story, which is to let each stark item speak for itself. But the *One Day* title, still very sparse, is also more expressive; it goes with the unforgettably practical and unassuming clarity of the ending:

> Now for that slice of sausage. Into the mouth. Getting your teeth into it. Your teeth. The meaty taste. And the meaty juice, the real stuff. Down it goes, into your belly.
> Gone.
> The rest, Shukhov decided, for the morning. Before the muster.
> And he buried his head in the thin, unwashed blanket, deaf now to the crowd of zeks from the other half as they jostled between the frames, waiting to be counted.

> Shukhov went to sleep fully content. He'd had many strokes of luck that day: they hadn't put him in the cells; they hadn't sent the team to the settlement; he'd pinched a bowl of kasha at dinner; the team-leader had fixed the rates well; he'd built a wall and enjoyed doing it; he'd smuggled that bit of blade through; he'd earned something from Cesar in the evening; he'd bought that tobacco. And he hadn't fallen ill. He'd got over it.
> A day without a dark cloud. Almost a happy day.

> There were three thousand six hundred and fifty-three days like that in his stretch. From the first clang of the rail to the last clang of the rail.
> The three extra days were for leap years.[56]

This is Solzhenitsyn's most effective style – conveying what he means by pointing at things he knows to be factual, with the least possible emotional colouring or rhetorical tone or reaching inside a character to suggest his psychological reactions. This is also the style of what seems to us the most surely-written part of *The First Circle*, chapters 82–4, in which Innokenty

Volodin is processed into a prisoner:

> The naked prisoner sat down, without asking himself why. (Now that other people were doing his thinking for him, he was quickly losing the free man's habit of thinking before he acts.) The warder gripped the back of his neck and pressed a pair of clippers roughly to his temple.
>
> 'What are you doing?' Innokenty shuddered and made a weak attempt to free himself. 'You have no right! I'm not yet under arrest!' (He meant that the charge had not yet been proved.)
>
> Clutching his head as hard as ever, the barber continued to shave him in silence; Innokenty's flicker of resistance died down. The proud young diplomat who had walked with such an independent air down the gangways of international airports and glanced with such vague, *blasé* eyes at the busy daytime glitter of Europe's capitals around him, was now a drooping, raw-boned, naked man with a half-shaved head.[57]

Innokenty is stripped, searched (even under the foreskin) for any diseases or concealed possessions, he is fingerprinted, his clothes are sterilised. When there is the least chance of his seeing another prisoner in the corridor, he is hustled into a 'box' – a windowless cell with a bare light bulb and a cement floor, because 'One prisoner must never be allowed to encounter another, never be allowed to draw comfort or support from the look in his eyes.' Before his arrest he has readied himself for a duel of wits with his accusers, since that is the style of the bright young diplomat. All that happens is that he is stripped of every little comfort, every support and sign of identity, he is being reduced to the equivalent of a number (like SHCH-854), and it is done as a bored routine by the screws: 'Never had he imagined anything so simple, so dull and irresistible as the reality.'[58] This is a typically remorseless Solzhenitsyn point. The plain factuality of the sequence is so unrelieved that to read it is to feel stifled, as though your chest were being cemented over by the duress of imprisonment. There is no need for the author to spell out the point that here is a member of the Soviet ruling class, who has thrived on the bondage of others, now falling into bondage himself. And if he had spelt it out, he might have fallen into the banality of the sequences about the KGB man, Rusanov, in *Cancer Ward*. If Solzhenitsyn is Tolstoyan, as people keep claiming, it is not Tolstoy, the unerringly deep analyst of character, as in *Anna Karénina* or *War and Peace*, it is Tolstoy the anti-Tsarist publicist in the later essays and fiction where he describes, for example, the punitive detachments of troops who went through the villages publicly flogging peasants. There is no tub-thumping and very little moral-pointing, the facts speak for themselves. *One Day* is also much more than an accurate document. It conveys a particular spirit through the speaking voice that tells it, which is virtually Ivan's own, and also by means of the many skilled or crafty things he does to get through his day. The voice comes over as the blunt and canny idiom of a working man, whether country or town – practical-minded, ready with debunking witticisms and basic rules for living. The stance it implies is neither noble nor sordid, it is dogged, alert, close to the ground, able to survive. Consider the scene in which the prisoners are searched on the way out of camp to work:

> Shukhov was in regulation dress. Come on, paw me as hard as you like. There's nothing but my soul in my chest. But they made a note that Tsezar was wearing a flannel vest and Buinovsky, it seemed, had put on a waistcoat or a cummerbund or something. Buinovsky, who had been in the camp less than three months, protested. He couldn't get rid of his commander's habits.
>
> 'You have no right to strip men in the cold. You don't know Article Nine of the criminal Code.'
>
> But they did have the right. They knew the code. You, chum, are the one who doesn't know it.
>
> 'You're not behaving like Soviet people,' Buinovsky went on saying. 'You're not behaving like communists.'
>
> Volkovoi had put up with the references to the criminal code but this made him wince and, like black lightning, he flashed:
>
> 'Ten days in the cells.'
>
> And aside to the sergeant:
>
> 'Starting from this evening.'[59]

On the one hand, futile high-mindedness, on the other, a readiness to be demeaned and chivvied so long as survival is not endangered, epitomised in the seeming humility and real self-respect of the proverbial-sounding remark 'there's nothing but my soul to be found in my chest'. Self-respect, it turns out, is not to be kept up by taking a stand or shooting a line but only by incessant watchfulness and the almost domestic skill it takes to grind at a piece of scrap metal for ten days till it becomes a knife or to hide a needle so deep in your hat that you can keep it safe till it is time to tear your mattress, shove in half your bread ration, then re-sew the tear with the hidden needle at top speed while planning how best to assemble the rest of your survival kit (pair of mittens, cord belt, pair of ragged foot-cloths, pair of good foot-cloths, plus a rag with tapes at each end) before the guard forces you to fall in for the march to work ... Ivan has aches and pains and goes to the sick bay, hoping to be let off work. The scene ends:

Vdovushkin reached for the thermometer and read it.

'H'm, neither one thing nor the other. Thirty-seven point two. If it had been thirty-eight it would have been clear to everyone. I can't exempt you. Stay behind at your own risk, if you like. If after examining you the doctor considers you ill he'll exempt you, but if he finds you fit he'll refuse and then you'll be locked up. You'd do best to go to work.'

Shukhov said nothing. He did not even nod. Pulling his hat over his eyes he walked out.

How can you expect a man who is warm to understand one who is cold?

It is because the story is made up of so many hard facts, none merely atmospheric, all necessary to show how this way of life works, that seemingly elementary sentences like 'How can you expect a man who is warm to understand one who is cold?' (or 'You can push a man this way, and you can push him that way,' or 'As long as you're in a hut – praise the Lord and sit tight') take on their fundamental weight.

Solzhenitsyn has now come out not only against the Stalinist extremes in Soviet life but also against socialism as such (in the 'Letter to the Soviet Leaders': see below, p. 104). Yet his masterpiece is very much what the socialist cultures have claimed

to want from their writers: the style is grounded in common
speech, and the form is a drama of the social relations of a
team of workers on the job, with a subtle attention to the skills,
motives, and rhythms of their work which is rare in Western
literature (and forthcoming only from our best socialist writers,
for example, Robert Tressell in *The Ragged Trousered Philanthropists* and Arnold Wesker in *The Kitchen* and *I'm Talking About
Jerusalem*). To say this is another way of making our main point
about *One Day*: intrinsically, for its qualities as prose fiction,
it is unremarkable. Unless we knew its history as part of Khrushchev's campaign against his political opponents, it would be natural
to read it as a straightforward, extremely competent story about
a penal settlement something like the sort of convict camp in
America that was shown in the Paul Newman film *Cool Hand
Luke*. Of course there are touches to show that many of the
inmates are perfectly guiltless. But the only considerable piece
to that effect is the page on Ivan's conviction as a traitor because
he has been taken prisoner of war by the Germans. In his determination to convey soberly and irrefutably the common-or-garden
inhumanity of daily life in the camps, Solzhenitsyn has left out
the society that created them and which they typify. This is nearly
explicit in the comment about Ivan getting no parcels: 'He had
less and less cause to recall Temgenevo and his home there.
Camp life wore him out from reveille to evening count, leaving
him no time for idle reminiscences.'

Our suggestion is not that *One Day* ought to have brought
in the life outside the camp. Solzhenitsyn's purpose was in effect
to fill out the fairly guarded and general critique of Stalinism
that Khrushchev had made at the Twentieth Congress. Of course
many millions knew these truths already, and as the amnestied
prisoners flooded back from captivity or post-camp exile from
1956 onwards, they must have released their facts into millions
of homes. But it would not have been enough if this huge social
experience, this collective tragedy, had remained private. The function Solzhenitsyn served in publicising it imaginatively, in print,
is defined by Zhores Medvedev: he says that the earlier work
particularly was

> devoted to events which still call up a vivid and direct response
> in the minds of readers in middle life and older; events that

revive smouldering memories, stimulate a complex mixture of feelings and emotional experiences, resurrecting for some people the events of their own life, and forcing others to remember the fate of their fathers, brothers, sisters, husbands, wives and friends. Such is the history of our country that I do not know anybody who would not identify the fate of Solzhenitsyn's heroes with the fate of his nearest and dearest.[60]

This fundamental point is put with moving depth by another Soviet scholar, Venyamin Teush:

In pursuit of his goal Solzhenitsyn had to write not memoirs, not an analysis or exposé, but a poem, with a rhythmic text and structure – or, more precisely, a *folk legend* . . . and this is what he did in writing *One Day*. In this legend, the concentration camp and its evil have been set in a rhythmic pattern – an inner structural and spiritual rhythm which, with the help of a kind of resonance or induction, penetrates the inner being of, for example, a rehabilitated prisoner, warming him to the core. As if they were microwaves, these rhythms break up the stone which lies in that inner being and turn it to dust to be carried away by spiritual breezes, restoring life functions to the frozen parts of the soul – and, in particular, returning the capacity for tears and laughter.[61]

The taboo on what government by force and decree had been doing to the Soviet people was so complete, and the consequent blunting and muffling of their literature so complete too, that it did not take a writer of the very finest powers to move at one stride onto this new plane of candour and accuracy. It was enough, for the time being, to tell it like it was. We, who have not laboured under that particular gag and taboo, may well feel the need of a more complex kind of art to do justice to all that Stalinism involved. Nadezhda Mandelstam is surely implying something very like this in a profound passage from her second book of memoirs: 'The value of our main *samizdat* writer, Solzhenitsyn, is that he restores our memory of time past. This is the first step towards the recovery of one's sense of being human. Only after passing through this stage will people understand that the individual, the distinctive, stands for the whole or the general, and is a symbol of it.'[62]

Serge, in his masterpiece, *The Case of Comrade Tulayev*, which he wrote as he fled from Stalinism and Fascism through France and the Caribbean and finished in Mexico in 1942, has no sequence on the camps. They were not yet at their peak in 1937, the year of his novel, and his own experience had been of prison and exile. He nearly died in a famine-stricken town in north-east Kazakhstan[63] – the same republic in which Solzhenitsyn did his stretch. But in the chapter called 'The Brink of Nothing' Serge virtually enters *l'univers concentrationnaire*. It is about Ryzhik, an Old Bolshevik and Oppositionist, who has been in and out of prisons and the remotest Siberian exile since 1928 – the year in which Trotsky was deported to Siberia. The page evoking the start of Ryzhik's transfer back to Moscow and death can be compared with the page that ends *The First Circle*, in which Nerzhin and the others set off in the opposite direction, from the privileged prison in Moscow to the remote camps. Here is Solzhenitsyn:

The prospects that awaited them were the taiga and the tundra, the Cold Pole at Oi-Myakoi and the copper mines of Jezkazgan, kicking and shoving, starvation rations, soggy bread, hospital, death. No fate on earth could possibly be worse. Yet they were at peace within themselves. They were as fearless as men are who have lost everything they ever had – a fearlessness hard to attain but enduring once it is reached.

Buffeting its load of tightly packed bodies, the gaily painted orange and blue truck drove on through the streets, passed a railway station and stopped at a crossroads. There, halted by a red traffic-light, stood the dark-red car belonging to the Moscow correspondent of the Paris newspaper *Libération*, on his way to a hockey match at the Dynamo Stadium. On the side of the van the correspondent read the words:

МЯСО. VIANDE. FLEISCH. MEAT.

He remembered having seen several trucks like this today in various parts of Moscow. Taking out his notebook he wrote with his dark-red fountain pen:

'Now and again on the streets of Moscow you meet food delivery vans, clean, well-designed and hygienic. One must admit that the city's food supplies are admirably well organized.'[64]

Here is Serge:

Nothing but worry and work, these transfers! There are no prisons within the Arctic Circle; jails appear with civilization. District Soviets sometimes have at their disposal an abandoned house that no one wants because it has brought people bad luck or because it would need too much repairing to make it habitable. The windows are boarded up with old planks on which you can still read TAHAK-TRUST, and they let in wind, cold, dampness, the abominable blood-sucking midges. There are almost always one to two wrong letters in the chalked inscription on the door: RURAL PRISON. Sometimes the tumble-down hovel bristles with barbed wire; and when it lodges an assassin, an escaped prisoner who wears glasses and has been recaptured in the forest, a horse thief, the director of a kolkhoze the order for whose arrest came from a high source, the door is guarded by a sentry, a Young Communist of seventeen – preferably one who is good for nothing – with an old rifle slung from his shoulder – a rifle which is good for nothing either, be it understood . . . On the other hand, there are freight cars armoured with scrap iron and big nails; excrement has dribbled under the door; they are shabbily sinister; they have the look of an old, disinterred coffin . . . The extraordinary thing is that you can always hear sound coming from them – the groaning of sick men, vague moans, even songs! Are they never emptied? They never reach the end of their journey. It would take forest fires, showers of meteors, cities overthrown, to abolish their kind . . . Through a green path which the white bark of birches brightened like laughter, two naked sabres conducted Ryzhik towards one of these cars, which stood on a siding among fir trees. Ryzhik laboriously climbed in, and the rickety door was padlocked behind him. His heart was pounding from the effort he had made; the semi-darkness, the stench which was like a fox's earth, stifled him. He stumbled over bodies, groped for the opposite wall with both hands outstretched, found it by the light from a crack, through which he could see the peaceful bluish landscape of firs, stowed his sack, and crouched in stale straw. He became aware of movement around him, saw a score of young, bony faces supported by half-naked, emaciated bodies. 'Ah,' said Ryzhik, recovering his breath. 'Greetings, *chpana*! Greetings, comrade tramps!' And

he began by making a well-calculated statement of principles
to the children of the roads, the oldest of whom might be
sixteen: 'If anything disappears from my bag, I'll bloody the
noses of the first two of you I can lay my hands on. I'm
like that – nothing mean about me. Be that as it may, I have
six pounds of dry bread, three cans of meat, two smoked her-
rings, and some sugar – government rations – which we will
share fraternally but with discipline. The watchword is "conscious"!' The twenty ragged children smacked their tongues
joyously before giving a feeble 'Hurrah!' 'My last ovation,'
thought Ryzhik. 'At least it's sincere . . .'[65]

This is tremendous in its epochal intensity. What creates it are
the multiple facets of the imagery, which reflect so much life.
'Are they never emptied?' The anguished question implicates the
reader. 'They never reach the end of their journey. It would
take forest fires, showers of meteors, cities overthrown, to abolish
their kind . . .' The answer is implacable. The imagery, though
metaphorical ('showers of meteors'), is also based in the real
terrain of the novel, the cities, the forests. A rich mesh of implications grows up and out of it springs the epochal intensity –
the moment is sensuously intense, like a particular memory
('through a green path . . . two naked sabres'), but large as well.
The eye swings southwards from the Arctic Circle, many waggons
rumble on unendingly, crowds follow each other into perdition.
History stretches away on all sides like a great plain dotted with
sufferers. It is a characteristic moment of imaginative take-off
for Serge, of a kind he achieves frequently. By contrast, the
point that Solzhenitsyn plants home, with that item on the unseeing
smugness of the Moscow correspondent of *Libération*, is polemical,
a piece of showing-up and scoring-off, which is justified, but
a lesser thing, both morally and emotionally, than the Serge,
which makes us feel the pain of a whole generation.

The First Circle, written between 1955 and 1964, is the book
in which Solzhenitsyn enters into direct comparison with the masters of modern fiction: it has a large cast, several distinct veins
of prose, and a big web of ideological and historical material
such as he had left out of *One Day*. *One Day*, which he started
after *The First Circle* and then began to treat as having the
higher priority, was compressed over several years from a 'long

chronicle'.[66] This may have been the best way for Solzhenitsyn, since in his long novels he seems to allow everything that happened to him to pass through into fiction with too little transmuting, too little imaginative enrichment. Be that as it may, *The First Circle* pieces together so many episodes that ring true and amasses so many exact particulars that it belongs with *The Gulag Archipelago* as a classic record of what political policing has done to people. In chapter 4 of Serge's *Comrade Tulayev*, called 'To Build Is To Perish', we learn that in the later twenties railwaymen were shot for stealing packages from the parcel post. In chapter 39 of *The First Circle* we learn that in the later forties a factory worker was given three months in prison for over-sleeping and clocking-on late. About ten years ago Western papers copied an item from *Pravda* which said that the death sentence had been reintroduced for embezzlement and *The Gulag Archipelago* has now supplied the details of this legal reform: capital crimes in the USSR now include rape, bribery, breaking the law on foreign currency transactions, and 'threatening the lives of policemen and Communist vigilantes'.[67] In *The First Circle* we learn that research students in the forties had to go over their draft theses and cut out every named reference to a foreign scientist or other authority. Zhores Medvedev tells us that in the seventies a newspaper editor had to apply for permission to write to Solzhenitsyn – he was refused it. In Serge's novel the Central Committee man, Kondratiev, has to go and speak at an Army tank school. He is supplied with a printed outline which is 'the standard speech for Morale Office representatives with the rank of general'.[68] No doubt British generals and 'Defence' ministers all say much the same thing when they go and speak at Sandhurst or Warminster, but on pain of retirement or loss of promotion, not of Siberian exile or a bullet. And finally a society must be judged on the scale and nature of its death-roll. These things being so, Solzhenitsyn was speaking the truth when he said in a broadcast from Zurich to the Soviet Union soon after going into exile: 'serfdom reigns, not only in the camps and collective farms with their direct forced labour which is not paid for at its full value. Serfom reigns all over our country. Free citizens are not at all free. They are free neither to choose their place of employment nor to fight for a fair wage for it.'[69]

The specificity of Solzhenitsyn's evidence on these things and, with that, his unwearying way of noting how each inhuman method grinds down the human being, amounts to a permanently valuable chapter in the chronicle of man's inhumanity to man. When you read in a novel that a prisoner being admitted to jail has to sign his name on the register through a tin plate so that he cannot get even the frail support of knowing who else is in there, you know you are reading an eye-witness account which can be trusted. We also expect other things of major novelists, in particular that they understand as part of a larger process the piece of life immediately under their gaze. This seems to us not Solzhenitsyn's strength. His single-mindedness and exactitude equip him to make a moral case, about the sufferings of the unfree and the beastliness of their captors. His view of the matter is one of simple blame and what he blames is Marxism. In the 'Letter to the Soviet Leaders' he writes: 'This Ideology bears the entire responsibility for all the blood that has been shed.' He also alleges that before the fiendish Marxist subversion began, 'at the beginning of the twentieth century both the physical and the spiritual health of her [the Russian] people were still intact'.* The same *bias against Marxism* is implicit in the novels. Medvedev quotes a friend's criticism of *August 1914*: 'Lenartovich in the novel is a social-democrat and defeatist . . . Lenartovich is the only coward among the officers . . . the social-democrat is utterly unsympathetic towards the soldiers' sufferings. But a real social-democrat cannot have such a callous attitude to the fate of ordinary people.'[71] This is a case of Simone de Beauvoir's excellent test for bias in a novel: if the only Jew in it is a coward and the only coward is a Jew, the book is anti-semitic.[72] Solzhenitsyn's anti-socialist bias has not troubled readers in the West because according to the morality of the Cold War, to be *against* Stalinism is to be *for* everything that is good. Such simplifications – encouraged by Solzhenitsyn – are sadly inadequate. They see the revolution as having undone and betrayed the Russian people. They do not see that it could have been betrayed itself, that the thing was a tragedy, not a crime.

This tragedy is the heart of Serge's work – what we have of it. We do not have his novel *La Tourmente*, which was presum-

---

* From the thousands of relevant facts about the physical health of the Russian people around 1900, we have picked one at random: in the Voronezh province, one in ten peasant households were *too cold and poor to harbour cockroaches.*[70]

ably the counterpart of what Solzhenitsyn is now writing on 1916 and 1917 since Serge said that in *La Tourmente* he felt he had 'best conveyed the grandeur of the Revolution'. It was seized by the political police at the frontier when Serge was deported in 1935, although the *Glavlit*, the censorship office, had given him permission to take out all his papers.[73] In this respect Solzhenitsyn has been much luckier.

Serge understood what happened as a tragedy, not as a mere crime, in that he realised how the tyranny was spoiling and ruining the humanity of those who inflicted the suffering, as much as that of the sufferers. From a wealth of cases we will consider first the two Stalins, in *Tulayev* and *The First Circle*, and then the loyal *apparatchiki*, Makeyev and the rest in *Tulayev* and Rusanov in *Cancer Ward*.

Stalin had to be dramatised in *Comrade Tulayev* because the novel is framed to show the network of political and social control in the Soviet Union as total. Once the young clerk, almost on impulse, has shot the Central Committee member, Tulayev (like the real Kirov), everybody is in jeopardy, from the girl carrying sacks of seed-corn on a collective farm to the head of state. Careers and promotions, guilt by association, the sexual jealousy of one official's wife – every mesh in the social net begins to tighten from the murder onwards and so leads us inevitably to the hand holding the ropes, Stalin's. How to manage such scenes? how to put on stage one of the four or five most famous people who ever lived, to bring out his specialness without neglecting the ordinary gestures and phrases which will show him as a person – and yet these traits must not come out as tricks of stage business to animate an academic oil-portrait? In chapter 5, 'Journey Into Defeat', Kondratiev has to report to Stalin on his mission to Spain during the Civil War there. The imagery is of whiteness and bareness:

Kondratiev waited only a few moments in the spacious ante-room, from whose huge windows, which flooded the room with white light, he could see a Moscow boulevard, trams, a double row of trees, people, windows, roofs, a building in course of demolition, the green domes of a spared church . . . 'Go in, please . . .' A white room, bare as a cold sky, high-ceil-inged, with no decoration except a portrait of Vladimir Ilich, larger than life, wearing a cap, his hands in his pockets, standing in the Kremlin courtyard. The room was so huge that at first Kondratiev thought it empty; but behind the table at the far end of it, in the whitest, most desert, most solitary corner of that closed and naked solitude, someone rose, laid down a fountain pen, emerged from emptiness; someone crossed the carpet, which was the pale grey of shadowed snow, someone came to Kondratiev holding out both hands, someone, He, the Chief, the comrade of earlier days – was it real?

'Glad to see you, Ivan, how are you?'

Reality triumphed over the stunning effect of reality. Kondratiev pressed the two hands which were held out to him, held them, and real warm tears gathered under his eyelids, only to dry instantly, his throat contracted. The thunderbolt of a great joy electrified him:

'And you, Yossif? ... You ... How glad I am to see you ... How young you still are ...'

The novelist is not endorsing the cult of Stalin; he is showing how potent it was for those who genuinely belonged to it. Stalin and Kondratiev are old comrades with a hundred shared intimate memories of dangerous underground work together. They begin to talk, and Stalin, lonely in his autocracy, wants to confide, to justify himself:

'The situation,' Kondratiev began with a discouraged look and that gesture of the hands which seemed to let something drop, 'the situation ...'

The Chief seemed not to have heard this beginning. His head bowed, his fingers tamping tobacco into the bowl of his short pipe, he went on:

'You know, brother, veterans like you, members of the old Party, must tell me the whole truth ... the whole truth. Other-wise, who can I get it from? I need it, I sometimes feel myself stifling. Everyone lies and lies and lies! From top to bottom they all lie, it's diabolical ... Nauseating ... I live on the summit of an edifice of lies – do you know that? The statistics lie, of course. They are the sum total of the stupidities of the little officials at the base, the intrigues of the middle stratum of administrators, the imaginings, the servility, the sabotage, the immense stupidity of our directing cadres ... When they bring me those extracts of mathematics, I sometimes have to hold myself down to keep from saying, Cholera! ...'

Was he finding excuses for himself? He lighted his pipe furiously, put his hands in his pockets, squared his head and shoulders, stood firmly on the carpet in the harsh light. Kondratiev looked at him, studying him sympathetically, yet with a certain basic suspicion, considering. Should he risk it? He risked an unemphatic:

'Isn't it a little your own fault?'

The Chief shook his head; the minute wrinkles of a warm smile flickered about his nose, under his eyes ...

'I'd like to see you in my place, old man – yes, that's something I'd like to see. Old Russia is a swamp – the farther you go, the more the ground gives, you sink in just when you least expect to ... And then, the human rubbish! ... To remake the hopeless human animal will take centuries. I haven't got centuries to work with, not I ... Well, what's the latest news?'

A businesslike discussion follows, on the quality of tanks, the obsolescence of aircraft. But the interview, like all meetings in the novel, is plagued with the suspicions and fears of a society gone wrong and Stalin comes back compulsively to the troubles nearer home:

The Chief, his hands in his pockets, took him to the bay window from which there was a view of the roofs of Moscow. There was only a pane of glass between them and the city, the pale sky.

'And here at home, in this magnificent and heart-rending Moscow, what is not going right, do you think? What isn't jelling? Eh?'

'But you just said it, brother. Everyone lies and lies and lies. Servility, in short. Whence, a lack of oxygen. How build Socialism without oxygen?

The Chief smiled curiously, as if he were laughing at someone who was not present. And then, in the most natural tone:

'Do you think I have many faults, Ivan?'

They were alone in the harsh white light, with the whole city before them, though not a sound from it reached them.

In a sort of spacious courtyard below and some distance away,
between a squat church with dilapidated towers and a little
red-brick wall, Georgian horsemen were at sabre practice, gallop-
ing from one end of the courtyard to the other; about half-way
they stooped almost to the ground to impale a piece of white
cloth on their sabres . . .

'It is not for me to judge you,' said Kondratiev uncomfortably.
'You are the Party.' He observed that the phrase was well
received. 'Me, I'm only an old militant' – with a sadness that
had a shade of irony – 'one of those who need a rest . . .'

The Chief waited like an impartial judge or an indifferent
criminal. Impersonal, as real as things.

'I think,' said Kondratiev, 'that you were wrong in "liquidating" Nicolai Ivanovich.'

Liquidating: the old word that, out of both shame and cynicism, was used under the Red terror for 'execute.' The Chief
took it without flinching, his face stone.

'He was a traitor. He admitted it. Perhaps you don't believe
it?'

Silence. Whiteness.

'It is hard to believe.'

The Chief twisted his face into a mocking smile. His shoulders
hunched massively, his brow darkened, his voice became thick.

'Certainly . . We have had too many traitors . . . conscious
or unconscious . . . no time to go into the psyshology of it
. . . I'm no novelist.'

This scene and its even more powerful counterpart in the 'Road
to Gold' chapter should be read in full to get the intense oppressive-
ness of this situation where the least word is too significant and
the most significant things are unsaid, yet as though palpable
in the air between the two men. Having dramatised this, Serge
briefly analyses it: 'there began, within them and between them,
a secret dialogue, which they both followed by divination, distinctly
. . . "I'm still needed . . ." - "I pity you, Yossif . . ." ". . . I forbid
you to pity me. You are nothing . . ." They spoke none of these
words: they heard them, uttered them, only in a double *tête-à-tête*
– together corporeally and also together, incorporeally, one within
the other.'[75]

Kondratiev knows that the Tulayev affair could be an excuse

for silencing him in case he passes on his knowledge of the murderous intrigues among the Left behind the lines in Spain. He knows his file is passing from desk to desk, floating on the panic waves of scare, accusation, Terror, and power-struggle which Serge evokes in characteristic pages of historical fact which are also more than that because he so impregnates them with the fever of the time. Unable to sleep, Kondratiev walks around at night and with the intensity of a dream imagines himself challenging Stalin. His long, maddened, but lucid reverie ends like this:

When you have killed us all, brother, you will be the last, brother, the last of us all, the last for yourself, and falsehood, danger, the weight of the machine you have set up will stifle you . . .'
    The Chief raised his head slowly, because everything about him was heavy, and he was not terrifying, he was old, his hair getting white, his eyelids swollen, and he asked, simply, in a voice as heavy as the bones of his shoulders: 'What is to be done?'[76]

The imagery is of weight, Kondratiev feels Stalin as a crushing load, a shackle; and more, that he himself, Stalin, is being petrified by his own abuse of power. It is the same perception as that of Mandelstam, one of the most skilled of modern Russian poets, who was arrested (and finally sent to death in a Siberian camp) for writing the following poem:

Our lives no longer feel ground under them.
At ten paces you can't hear our words.

But whenever there's a snatch of talk
it turns to the Kremlin mountaineer,

the ten thick worms his fingers,
his words like measures of weight,

the huge laughing cockroaches on his top lip,
the glitter of his boot-rims.

Ringed with a scum of chicken-necked bosses
he toys with the tributes of half-men.

One whistles, another meouws, a third snivels.
He pokes out his finger and he alone goes boom.

He forges decrees in a line like horseshoes,
One for the groin, one the forehead, temple, eye.

He rolls the executions on his tongue like berries.
He wishes he could hug them like big friends from home.[77]

This could hardly be better in its way, but its way is that of satire, one-track antagonism, whereby every trait of the loathed object is blocked out except what it is loathed for. The same is true of Solzhenitsyn's Stalin in *The First Circle*, but here the sheer antagonism blots the work of art, since realistic fiction is too close and inward with individuals to allow of sudden gear-changes into caricature. Stalin is an animated waxwork to which are ascribed a few of the short-hand accounts of narcissism, paranoia, etc, which script-writers usually trot out when they have to do a tyrant. We first see Stalin lying down and leafing through a hack biography of himself:

> The plain, straightforward phrases had an irresistible and soothing effect on the human heart: Strategist of genius ... wise foresight ... mighty will ... iron determination ... Lenin's virtual deputy from 1918 onwards. (Well, wasn't he? ...) The revolution's greatest military leader found the front in chaos and confusion ... Frunze's operational plan was based on Stalin's orders ... (so it was ...). It was our good fortune that in the difficult years of the War for the Fatherland we were led by a wise and tested Leader – The Great Stalin (yes, they were lucky). Everybody knows the devastating force of Stalin's logic, the crystal clarity of his mind ... (without false modesty he had to admit it was true) ... his love for the people ... his great concern for human beings ... his dislike of pomp ... his astounding modesty (very true, that bit about modesty).
> Excellent. And they say it's selling well, too.[78]

Even as caricature this is blatant. It consists of what other people say about somebody, not what he 'says' to himself. Thirty pages later Solzhenitsyn's imagination has finally failed completely and all we are left with is this: 'The master of half the world in his Generalissimo's tunic, with his low receding forehead, walked slowly past the shelves and ran his claw-like hands over the ranks of his enemies.' This is no different in quality from the cartoons of Lenin and Trotsky as 'ape-men' carried by the *Daily Mail* in the twenties, or the ones of Stalin himself carried by the Hearst press in America more recently. What such work fails utterly to do, and what Serge excels at doing, is to bring out a truth crucial for our time: that the things we call monstrous (incredible, diabolical, Satanic, etc) are done not by monsters but by people.

Stalin is not integral to *The First Circle* but Rusanov the KGB man is one of the six major figures in *Cancer Ward*. He is another case of Simone de Beauvoir's test for bias. The only complete creep (the only cowardly and self-centred cancer patient in the ward) is a secret policeman and the only secret policeman is a complete creep. The only implication can be that the people who served the system of spying and denouncing which trapped everybody in that Russia were, as a mass, paltry and nasty. We know from *Hope Against Hope* and other sources that what actually happened was much more complex, more tragic. For example, if students lodged with you and the secret police were interested in you, the students would almost certainly be approached and told to eavesdrop on your social occasions, to report who met you, to invent suspicious material if there was not any available, and to do all this on pain of being expelled from their place of study. Most people, struggling to subsist, were just not able to resist such blackmail. It was not a question of being a particularly nasty piece of work. Anyone could be sucked into the machinery of denouncing and confessing, including stalwart Communists. It is this total embroilment which Serge catches, by the perfectly constructed mesh of relationships that leads to every character in turn, and which Solzhenitsyn cannot catch in his morally simplified and polemical mode of characterising and plotting.

In *Comrade Tulayev* Serge enters fully into the lives of the following people (among others): Prosecutor Rachevsky: he says when he is drunk, '"I am the beast of revolutionary duty, I am; get on, old beast"', then feels uncontrollable resentment at the friends who have heard this indiscretion. Fleischman the investigator: he cannot feel glad when his daughter kisses him because 'the ghosts of too many tortured men were astir in him'. Makeyev the Secretary of the Regional Committee: he cannot stand the thought of supervising another purge in the collective farms, with a famine on his hands, and relieves himself by virtually raping his wife: 'for a moment ... it gave him the feeling of conquering the universe'. Erchov the High Commissar for Security: his only surprise when he is arrested himself is that he cannot recognise the secret prison he is taken to, although this has been his own department. Zvyeryeva the unmarried NKVD investigator: she instantly does any humiliating job she is told to, and presently she is shown masturbating in a mirror tilted above her bed.[79] She is incapable of relating to another because she has handed herself over to the spying job – or she took that work because she could not relate – whichever way you put it, the thing is a personal tragedy. To show it as that, Serge needs his novelist's finesse at touching on intimate, as well as public, experiences.

Solzhenitsyn lacks this finesse. His ham-fistedness with purely personal relations is most disconcerting in the Nerzhin–Simochka relationship in *The First Circle* (especially the end of chapter 6). But then it was not possible for a writer brought up in the Soviet literary tradition to be in practice or at ease in presenting love affairs. More to our point is the Rusanov character in *Cancer Ward*. By that time Solzhenitsyn had grown in his ability to show intimate experience. Particularly fine, in his remorseless yet humane way, is the scene in Part 2 where Asya gets Dyoma to kiss her breast because next day it will be cut off in the operating theatre. But Solzhenitsyn still cannot bring himself to see a Stalinist as a person. For example, after his wife's visit Rusanov is brooding on the possibility that people he has denounced and had put away may come back to confront him. The style here is the barest cliché: 'The very idea of such a meeting terrified him ... Rodichev and Guzun were duly expelled as members of the same counter-revolutionary underground organisation ... This was why Rusanov was now worried about the man's ominous return ... In that excellent and honourable time, the years 1937 and 1938, the social atmosphere was noticeably cleansed and it became easier to breathe,' and so on and so forth.[80] This is the merest shorthand for someone's inner thinkings – no double feelings, no qualms of compunction angrily repressed, no self-dislike or willed compensatory self-esteem. Throughout the characterisation he shows not one contradictory or ambiguous feature. Even Nadezhda Mandelstam, most trenchant scourge of Stalinism, is sarcastically critical of people who think that 'any scoundrel, while actually engaged in doing something despicable, always thinks he is acting correctly ... remembers with deep satisfaction how he once denounced people and sighs for the good old days'.[81]

Serge grasps the tragic contradictions in the revolution as fully on the historical as on the personal plane. This comes out crucially in his treatment of the Kronstadt rising in chapter 4 of his *Memoirs*. Kronstadt was a milestone in the revolution and its implications must be faced by anyone who wants to understand how Communism turns into Stalinism. In February 1921 the Kronstadt Soviet, whose core was sailors from the Baltic fleet, led a rising with the following demands: re-election of Soviets by secret ballot; freedom of spoken and printed word for all revolutionary groups; freedom for the trade unions; release of revolutionaries being held as political prisoners; abolition of 'official propaganda'; no more food requisitions in the countryside; no more of the 'barrier-squads' who were stopping free food-marketing and food-collecting. Our immediate point is not whether these demands were possible, it is how they were dealt with. There was no negotiation, only an ultimatum: 'Surrender or be shot like rabbits.' The delegation from the Kronstadt Soviet who went to explain things to the Petrograd Soviet were imprisoned by the Cheka. The Red Army attacked the naval base over the ice, lost hundreds of men in the river, and finally seized the place. Hundreds of the rebels were then shot in small batches over a period of months. Serge got his information from eye-witnesses, including men who shared cells with the rebels waiting for death.[82]

For Serge the tragedy was double: the lying of the government and Party press, which pretended Kronstadt was 'in the hands of the Whites', and the insoluble dilemma of *what was to be done*. On the former he says in his *Memoirs*:

The worst of it all was that we were paralysed by the official falsehoods. It had never happened before that our Party should lie to us like this. 'It's necessary for the benefit of the public,' said some, who were none the less horror-stricken at it all. . . .

The truth seeped through little by little, past the smokescreen put out by the Press, which was positively beserk with lies. And this was our own Press, the Press of our revolution, the first Socialist Press, and hence the first incorruptible and unbiased press in the world! Before now it had employed a certain amount of demagogy, which was, however, passionately sincere, and some violent tactics towards its adversaries. That might be fair enough and at any rate was understandable. Now, it lied systematically.

... Throughout this tragedy, rumour played a fatal part. Since the official Press concealed everything that was not a eulogy of the régime's achievements, and the Cheka's doings were shrouded in utter mystery, disastrous rumours were generated every minute.[83]

This issue was, and remains, crucial. Who knows how many good people have been lost to socialism because they could no longer stomach having to repeat and make themselves believe what the Kronstadt sailors called 'official propaganda'? We know that Silone left the Italian Communists for this reason. He had edited a Party paper (the *Lavoratore* of Trieste) and in his masterpiece, *Fontamara*, he shows the peasants standing up for themselves for the first time. They start a newspaper, called *Che fare?* (*What is to be done?*), and their sense of its value is put in words very close to Serge's: 'This paper was to be the peasants' own paper, the first peasants' own paper, written by and for the peasants. What they might think in Rome was all the same to him.'[84] Silone's next novel, *Bread and Wine* (1937), is about a revolutionary who finds it less and less possible to be a convinced activist. One scene memorably dramatises the issue of political truth:

Bolla had a certain respect for Spina, of whom he had heard a great deal before meeting him, but he also knew that he was a little peculiar, like many intellectuals, and he wished to avoid arguing with him.

'I have prepared a small illegal paper for students, to be sent by post to about a hundred addresses,' he said.

'What does the paper say?'

'I wrote the leading article myself,' Bolla said. 'Also there's a splendid letter from a Catholic student.'

'Who wrote it?'

'I did,' said Bolla. 'There's also a short but lively letter from a nationalist student, who says he has had his eyes opened.'

'Who wrote it?'

'I did.'

'Why do you go in for stunts like that?' Spina asked.

'One must give the impression that the students are beginning to wake up,' Bolla replied.

Spina lost patience.

'We are not a party of hairdressers,' he nearly shouted. 'We are not working for appearances. The important thing for us is not to appear strong, but to be strong. The revolution is not a stunt or a conjuring trick. It's the truth, nothing but the truth!'

'And if the truth is demoralizing?'

'It is always less demoralizing than the most encouraging lie.'

Bolla did not continue the argument. He knew Spina was a good comrade, but with strange susceptibilities.[85]

The other aspect of the revolutionary tragedy was still more fundamental. Serge felt he *must* support the Bolshevik government in what it did and he held to this, but with a deep qualification, twenty-five years later:

After many hesitations, and with unutterable anguish, my Communist friends and I finally declared ourselves on the side of the Party. This is why. Kronstadt had right on its side. Kronstadt was the beginning of a fresh, liberating revolution for popular democracy: 'The Third Revolution!' it was called by certain anarchists whose heads were stuffed with infantile illusions. However, the country was absolutely exhausted, and production practically at a standstill; there were no reserves of any kind, not even reserves of stamina in the hearts of the masses. The working-class *élite* that had been moulded in the struggle against the old régime was literally decimated. The Party, swollen by the influx of power-seekers, inspired little confidence . . .

In these circumstances it was the Party's duty to make concessions, recognizing that the economic régime was intolerable, but not to abdicate from power. 'Despite its mistakes and abuses', I wrote, 'the Bolshevik Party is at present the supremely organized, intelligent and stable force which, despite everything, deserves our confidence. The Revolution has no other mainstay, and is no longer capable of any thoroughgoing regeneration.'[86]

So the Party chose the right alternative, and when a right alternative is fraught with killing, falsehood, and tyranny, then the situation is beyond facile partisanship, whether it comes from those who think the Soviet Union can do no wrong or from the anti-Marxist hacks.

4. *Decadence and Crack-up*

The twenties managed to become celebrated as bright, young, smart, jazzy, as though life at that time was all parties and holidays. Even the ten years that span the Slump, Hitler's rise to power, and the final failure to appease, let alone stop him, have been included in the 'long week-end'. Of course this is a playboy's view of social life. It has managed to become celebrated because the same 'set' owned both country houses such as Cliveden where the whooping-up went on and the newspapers which coined the images and nicknames. We cannot suppose that even, say, the merrymakers who danced the Charleston in and out of the fountains on Long Island were perfectly forgetful. Scott Fitzgerald, looking back on the twenties from 1931, recalled how his contemporaries 'had begun to disappear into the dark maw of violence':

> A classmate killed his wife and himself on Long Island, another tumbled 'accidentally' from a skyscraper in Philadelphia, another purposely from a skyscraper in New York. One was killed in a speak-easy in Chicago; another was beaten to death in a speak-easy in New York and crawled home to the Princeton Club to die; still another had his skull crushed by a maniac's axe in an insane asylum where he was confined. These are not catastrophes that I went out of my way to look for – these were my friends; moreover, these things happened not during the depression but during the boom.[1]

The style of this culture was streaked with the frantic and uneasy, it amounted to a syndrome of insecurities. What runs through it in the literary record is a feeling that some menacing, savage, or alien thing hung over or underlay the civilised and orderly, like an animal prowling in the darkness around the favoured space with its bright lights. In April 1937, Neville Chamberlain in a speech at a bankers' dinner pooh-poohed 'that fear of attack from somewhere else which is almost universal, but which may yet rest on nothing more solid than imagination'.[2] This flimsy faculty, imagination, had begun to disclose the dangers twenty years before.

In the spring of 1917, Arnold Bennett, H. G. Wells, and an American journalist called Macdonald were worrying about the likely aftermath of the fighting and the mass traumas of the War. Wells talked about 'the after-war exacerbationary reaction on nerves, which would cause rows, quarrels etc. unless it was consciously kept well in hand, and Macdonald said that a year or so after the San Francisco earthquake [1906] prominent SF men would disappear; they were in sanatoria etc. Also lifelong friends, such as business partners, would quarrel over some trifle, each go to his solicitor, and never speak to one another again.'[3] Did these forebodings of a post-war malaise come true? In such matters it is hard to generalise, or analyse, with much certainty. What would be good evidence? Numbers of patients in mental hospitals are not a proof of morale, because the policy on which people to admit or certify changes so much from age to age. The divorce rate by itself can be taken to mean either greater authenticity in personal living or more instability and a 'breakdown of values', or both together. From time to time, however, things surface to reveal forces that had been stirring amongst thousands of people and gone into the forming of their lives. Who has heard of the British race riots in the summer of 1919? Books specifically about 'immigrants' fail to mention them. Yet a writer working for television has recently recorded how angry crowds, in places several thousand strong, were 'roaming the streets of all the main seaports attacking Negroes and destroying their property'.[4] In London and Liverpool dozens of houses were smashed up. Black workers and their families were 'repatriated' by the shipload. Thousands of coloured seamen were presently made to register as aliens even though their permanent homes were in Britain. The difficulty which blacks then found in getting work made many of their children the first claimants on the meagre charity of the Public Assistance Committees when the Slump set in in 1929.

The source of these troubles lay in the aftermath of the First World War: 'White seamen and soldiers, recently discharged and unemployed, brought back a fund of resentment which began to vent itself on the blacks ... For the sex-starved, maltreated or unemployed white, the sight [of a well-dressed black man with a girl on his arm] struck at the roots of his feelings of racial and imperial superiority; and 1919 was marked by an ugly increase of hostility.' The writers chatting in the Reform Club had inclined to put the trouble down to 'nerves'. Scott Fitzgerald remarked that 'something had to be done with all the nervous energy stored up and unexpended in the War'.[5] The evidence from the back streets and docks reminds us that the forces at work were also objective and practical, a matter of people's livelihoods, though this does not mean they were any the less shot through with neurosis. Michael Phillips's insight into the emotions of the white underman – sex-starved, maltreated, and unemployed – is a complete and exact illustration of the diagnosis which Reich made of the Fascist type of violence and how it was harnessed to the military machine: 'Sexual inhibition changes the structure of economically suppressed man in such a way that he acts, feels, and thinks contrary to his own material interests.'[6]

On the part of the (largely middle-class) writers, the first premonitions were visionary – vague, even mistaken, in what they boded but true to the lurking emotions of the time. In 1919 Yeats was already writing about the second coming of an avatar which this time would be malign, not blessed. Things fall apart – mere anarchy is loosed – the best lack all conviction, while the worst are full of passionate intensity ... For thousands of people spellbound by poetry, these phrases have counted as something like a clairvoyant and authoritative forecast of 'fascism' (whether black or red). Strictly speaking, a forecast is an intuition about *present* data – seen, perhaps, as holding the embryo of what is to come. For Yeats, the menace, the rough beast slouching towards Bethlehem to be born, is coming from the tropics. 'Somewhere, in sands of the desert' a monstrous mother is moving her thighs as she readies herself to give birth. The poet seems to be haunted by some danger to the West-European leadership of world culture. A kindred notion reverberates through the fifth section of *The Waste Land* (1922). Civilisation has been turned upside down, bats harbour in the ruined cities, 'hooded hordes' stumble across the cracked earth of 'endless plains'. Eliot names the cities that have gone under (Jerusalem, Athens, Alexandria, Vienna) but the menace is featureless, it swarms 'out there'. Out there can be anywhere from the Russian steppe to the Rann of Cutch. What is clear is that Eliot's symbolic hints, while managing to avoid the more blatant sort of racism, turn us eastwards. He is dealing in the same fear of a 'Yellow Peril', of Russian soldiers 'with snow on their boots', as the halfpenny and penny papers which had been thriving on chauvinistic nightmares ever since the grab for Africa and China in the later nineteenth century.

The other major writer of that time, Lawrence, also lends himself in his best work of the early twenties to this same phantom of cultural collapse and the rampaging-in of the beast. In *St Mawr* (1924) the stallion rears as it trots along a moorland path near the Welsh border. His rider, Rico, a painter from the Smart Set, reacts with repressive brutality by pulling hard on the reins and yelling abuse at the horse. St Mawr crashes over, and as he struggles to right himself, he seems to revert through aeons of evolution: 'St Mawr gave a great curve like a fish ... He rested thus, seated with his fore-feet planted and his face in panic, almost like some terrible lizard.' Rico's leg is injured, he may be lamed for life, another young man is kicked in the face and disfigured – after coming through the war unscathed. Rico's wife Lou, who owns the horse, is at once assailed by 'a vision of evil':

All the nations, the white, the brown, the black, the yellow, all were immersed in the strange tide of evil that was subtly, irresistably rising. No one, perhaps, deliberately wished it. Nearly every individual wanted peace and a good time all round: everybody to have a good time.

But some strange thing had happened, and the vast, mysterious force of positive evil was let loose. She felt that from the core of Asia the evil welled up, as from some strange pole, and slowly was drowning earth.[7]

This is a kind of phantom that swells the more the more unspecified it is. In 1740, in the last book of *The Dunciad*, what Pope feared was the prevailing of mediocrity and dullness. But the emotion at the close is far too intense for that. We are bound to look for a hidden subject, and it seems likely that he was resurrecting the bogey of 'the mob' which had haunted the propertied classes ever since the interregnum of 1658–60, when troops had been billeted throughout the country without paying the householders, the law courts were closed, and shops put up their shutters. Not long after that, Dryden was able to deal candidly with middle-class panic: in such poems as *The Medall* and *Absalom and Achitophel*, he is quite clear about the anarchy of political and religious free-thinking which will subvert the country once it has been 'drained to the dregs of a democracy'. A century after the Civil War, this social reality has retreated beyond the fringes of Pope's consciousness, where it lurks like a repressed trauma and re-emerges disguised as something else.

In the twenties the equivalent spectre would seem to be revolution, of the kind that had just taken place in Russia. One writer has recalled that in the early thirties at Cambridge he and his friends used to go to lectures to 'catch waves' – to spot laughable instances of lecturers treating vague impulses as the cause of historical change. The Hundred Years' War, according to an eminent historian, 'was caused by a wave of cruelty that swept over Europe', the French Revolution by 'a wave of energy that flooded over Europe from the East'. 'Waves of blood and lust, again from the East, flooded the world with Communism after the October Revolution.'[8] Lawrence was in the fashion with his talk of tides of evil welling from the core of Asia. A page or two later in the story, Lou is made to think (by this time the idiom is purely the author's) that the evil is 'in socialism and bolshevism ... But bolshevism made a mess of the outside of life, so turn it down. Try fascism. Fascism would keep the surface of life intact, and carry on the undermining business all the better.' If this type of snap diagnosis were all the story had to offer, it would not help us much in the effort to gauge what exactly was stirring in this area of crack-up and collapse. But the pages on Lou's 'vision of evil' are, in their dubious rhetoric, not typical of the remarkable deep and many-sided drama that the tale creates.

The valid imagery and characterisation in *St Mawr* suggest how the uncivilised or anti-civilised was intensely potent in a double way for well-to-do Western people at that time. It caught at them both as an attraction and as a threat. We have seen already how the horse figures in the symbolism of lost control – 'that high horse riderless', as Yeats was to put it a few years later in one of his elegiac poems for the big houses, 'Coole Park and Ballylee, 1931'. That poem, like Lawrence's story, is about

the yearning, and the inability, to put down roots in a society
felt to be played-out and done for:

> We shift about – all that great glory spent –
> Like some poor Arab tribesman and his tent.

Lou is at home nowhere. Rome, Naples, fashionable London
– these are places for dabbling in being married, dabbling in
the arts, they are peopled with men and women who are tamed,
attitudinising, living from the consciousness only. Lou has left
America, touched down in England, married her Australian bar-
onet, she is 'playing at being well-bred', there is about her 'a
lurking sense of being an outsider everywhere'. She aches to belong.
It cannot come in her human-social living, since she is inextricably
of a class that has no function, whether in the production or
the management of the means of life. She can belong only in
the realm of the inhuman-organic, she heads for the wilderness,
the story ends with the possibility (which we must evaluate for
ourselves) that she will settle down in a ranch in Mexico where
man has barely scraped himself a foothold among the bristling
pine trees and electric storms and the canyons with their bears
and pack-rats. But used-up and turning inwards on herself though
she is, she must still relate, and for her the other live being
in the world is her horse. It is essential to the vision of the
story that St Mawr looks out at her from 'the inner dark'. This
is far more than the gloom of his stable in a Westminster mews.

> [It] was . . . as if the walls of her own world had suddenly
> melted away, leaving her in a great darkness, in the midst
> of which the large, brilliant eyes of that horse looked at her
> with demonish question, while his naked ears stood up like
> daggers from the naked lines of his inhuman head, and his
> great body glowed red with power . . . That black fiery flow
> in the eyes of the horse was not 'attitude'. It was something
> much more terrifying, and real, the only thing that was real.
> Gushing from the darkness in menace and question . . .

Again, the only person in the story who is not fidgetting with
dissatisfied desire for something else is Lewis, St Mawr's groom,
who stared out 'from beneath his bush of hair and his beard'

like 'an animal from the underbrush'. He only opens out and talks fluently when he is riding 'in the shadow of the wood's edge', at night with Lou's mother, as they start out on their journey over to the American wilderness.[9]

In terms of imagery, the carriers of life in the story belong to or turn to the darkness, in order to revive their non-conscious selves. They turn away from the lit-up, from the light that has been for generations a central symbol of civilisation – the known, the clearly-defined, sweetness and light, *clarté, aufklärung*. Civilisation, and particularly white civilisation, can no longer be taken for granted, and travel along the colonial and imperial trade-routes has made it easy to contrast the varieties of human life. If there is a single literary source for this vein of work, it is Conrad's 'Heart of Darkness'. This tale supplied lines for the major poem of collapsing civilisation, *The Waste Land*, and would have supplied the epigraph (" 'The horror, the horror!' ") if Ezra Pound had approved. It did supply the epigraph for Eliot's final poem of unrelieved or helpless witness to the decadence, 'The Hollow Men', 'Mistah Kurtz – he dead', and it is everywhere (sometimes explicitly cited, sometimes between the lines) in those books about actual exploration beyond the clearings of civilisation which were a dominant genre between the wars.

The writers were now travelling in a particular way. They had little or no missionary spirit. They did not wish to make respectful pilgrimages to imposing ancient sites. Often they were up and away on impulse, with the facility of the freelance who may have little solid property but always seems to have enough friends and relatives to bail him out financially or lend him a house in Greece or Mexico or Ceylon. In *St Mawr*, when Mrs Witt, Lou's mother, feels out of sorts in Paris, her natural reaction is to say, ' "For heaven's sake, Louise, let us go to Morocco or somewhere." ' Aldous Huxley undertook the journey that yielded *Beyond the Mexique Bay* because he was discussing primitive life with an English poet who happened to be the Finnish consul in Guatemala and his younger brother, Roy Fenton, who happened to have a coffee plantation on the Pacific slopes. 'On an impulse' Fenton invited him to go there. 'It was both a friendly offer and a dare', and Huxley accepted. ' "He seemed to be looking for an experience." '[10] Christopher Isherwood, who was presently to explore the decadence of Germany on the eve of

Nazi rule, recalls a moment typical of this class and the way they moved about the world. 'One evening, we left Bill's studio even more abruptly than usual. "We'll drive down to Southampton," he said, "and take a boat to Greece." But, in the Cromwell Road, we found ourselves turning north. We didn't stop again till Catterick Bridge, where we had breakfast.'[11]

The effect is of a frictionless skating over the surface of the world. Because the literary witness's presence in this or that country has no social function but is all for the sake of his own curiosity, it inclines him to pick out people and objects that correspond to his own shiftlessness. So Waugh's Guiana and Brazil, Isherwood's Berlin, and Victoria Sackville-West's Persia turn into wastelands peopled by striking oddities, the declassed and deracinated, who also fascinate the writers because they embody the blurring of cultural boundaries which was another chief preoccupation at that time. In *Passenger to Teheran* Victoria Sackville-West gives us in epitome the life of her driver on the road into Persia. He is the son of a Scottish crofter, he has served in the British Army, come through the holocaust, worked in France and Syria, and married a Persian wife who 'went mad in Bagdad'.[12] In 1932 Evelyn Waugh meets, in Boa Vista in the far north of Brazil, a German called Mr Steingler, 'part of the great exodus of disillusioned soldiers and students that followed the defeat of 1918, from Germany and the German colonies'. He is supposed to have a tiny plantation that does not pay, somewhere up-river, he is staying in a Benedictine priory, possibly to have Europeans to talk to, but 'his fluent Portuguese seemed to cause endless misunderstandings at the cafe and even his German seemed to puzzle Father Alcuin.'[13]

The world in those days was, as it is now, full of working-class emigrants and immigrants, Irishmen from Kerry toiling in Liverpool, Italians from Sicily toiling in Argentina. The English writers between the wars did not meet them. The waste land through which they roved was strictly the ruined or chaotic habitat of the affluent. Waugh's Mr Steingler is almost a stage figure of the broken-down gentleman; he wears a straw boater, no socks, home-made sandals, and he carries an ebony cane with a dented silver crook. In 1935, in Abyssinia, Waugh adds to his menagerie of types a Russian prince, 'a debonair figure, given to exotic tastes in dress', who lives in Addis Ababa running a tannery and dealing in loads of rotting cows' feet – he has tried to start a brothel but a consignment of girls ordered from Cairo has never arrived. Moving still nearer to the veritable materials of *The Waste Land*, Waugh also meets a 'monocled Latvian colonel' who is supposed to have worked as a ring-master in a German circus.[14] And Victoria Sackville-West, journeying by train through the Ukraine on her way home from Persia, is saddened to remember how she had visited this very spot before the war. She had stayed with Polish friends who kept ten thousand horses plus eighty English hunters and a pack of English hounds. There had been wild animals in a walled park, specially for hunting; Tokay of 1750 vintage was 'handed round by a giant; cigarettes [were] handed round by dwarfs in eighteenth-century liveries'. Then the estate was split by the new Polish frontier, the owner gambled away his fortune in Paris and blew his brains out.[15] Or as Eliot has it in *The Waste Land*:

> Bin gar keine Russin, stamm' aus Litauen, echt deutsch.*
> And when we were children, staying at the archduke's,
> My cousin's, he took me out on a sled,
> And I was frightened. He said, Marie,
> Marie, hold on tight. And down we went.
> In the mountains, there you feel free.
> I read, much of the night, and go south in the winter.

The writers knew that they themselves belonged to that cultural deliquescence of which they were such connoisseurs:

> I would go to the wild lands where man had deserted his post and the jungle was creeping back to its old strongholds . . . These were the years when Mr Peter Fleming went to the Gobi Desert, Mr Graham Greene to the Liberian hinterland; Robert Byron . . . to the ruins of Persia . . . there is a fascination in distant and barbarous places, and particularly in the border-lands of conflicting cultures and states of development, where ideas, uprooted from their traditions, become oddly changed in transplantation.[16]

---

* I am *not* Russian, I'm from Lithuania, I'm a genuine German.'

Greene is more drastic and black, and goes deeper, in his avowal of a kindred motive. He wanted to travel in Liberia *because* the situation there was extreme. It had been founded as an example to all Africa of a Christian and self-governing state, peopled by freed slaves. Now it was swarming with yellow fever, malaria, elephantiasis, yaws, and smallpox, and in the whole country there were six doctors. The army had been 'pacifying the interior' by burning down the banana villages, hacking children to pieces and throwing them into the burning huts.

> It really seemed as though you couldn't go deeper than that ... the little injustices of Kenya became shoddy and suburban beside it ... there are times of impatience, when one is less content to rest at the urban stage, when one is willing to suffer some discomfort for the chance of finding – there are a thousand names for it, King Solomon's Mines, the 'heart of darkness' if one is romantically inclined, or more simply ... one's place in time, based on a knowledge not only of one's present but of the past from which one has emerged.[17]

Such motives probably entered into the curiosity of travellers in most ages. What was special about these English people was that they no longer felt themselves to be taking off from or coming back to a solid base. Leonard Woolf, who epitomised – who in many ways organised – the culture of his class, had felt the appeal of the wilderness during his time as a District Officer in Ceylon. His memories of the first years of this century put him, with Conrad, near the source of this theme, this recurring motif – the savage menace that prowls around the edges of the civilised. At Jaffna his bungalow had been overshadowed by a huge banyan tree 'which had covered the whole area between the verandah and the edge of the bastion with the tangle of roots and branches which is the sinister method of the banyan's growth'. 'The tree was inhabited by a notorious and dangerous devil, so that the servants disliked the bungalow and would never go near the tree after dark.' Another devil lived in a hovel, chickens were sacrificed to it, and 'you saw the headless bodies fluttering about on the ground'. Pondering the differences between this Asiatic life and ours, Woolf puts it that we run on rails and live in boxes, and goes on:

It has normally nothing to do with the jungle where wild beasts like the leopard and the elephant roam or even the human jungle where the human beast roams. If we have a tree in our back garden, it has no devil, no Jakko in it. Of course, very deep down under the surface of the northern European the beliefs and desires and passions of primitive man still exist ready to burst out with catastrophic violence if, under prolonged pressure, social controls and inhibitions give way.

His feelings are significantly mixed. The jungle is dismaying. It also has more to it than our steel and tarmac and cement. It is 'cruel and dangerous', 'horribly ugly and cruel', yet 'fascinating.'[18] And he cannot feel it to be nearly as far from home as it looks on the map, because it is only another form of the barely controllable beasthood in us all.

This daunting insight was compounded by the view common among Woolf's class that their own civilisation was quaking.

In 1914 in the background of one's life and one's mind there were light and hope; by 1918 one had unconsciously accepted a perpetual public menace and darkness and had accepted into the privacy of one's mind or soul an iron fatalistic acquiescence in insecurity and barbarism.

The 'bases of European civilisation', he thought, were being destroyed. 'No period in the world's history has been more full of what are called great events, bringing disruption, disaster, cataclysms to the human race.' And finally 1933–9 are picked out as 'the six years in which civilisation was finally destroyed and which ended with war'.[19] To the extent that Woolf was feeling the agony on the Continent, this is a humane testimony. It is also clear that he believes his own civilised footholds to have given way. Yet throughout this period he and his wife Virginia wrote and published successfully, they lived exactly as they wished, printing and publishing their own books and their friends', with decorations by Virginia's sister Vanessa, they had a house in Bloomsbury and another in Sussex, and though they worked very hard it was never under the lash of money worries. Virginia had £400 a year from investments. The average wage for female workers was about 28s. a week and the minimum needed to maintain a single woman in full health was 31s.[20]

The feeling of being in jeopardy from some 'public menace' was therefore only partly rational. The Great War had been real all right and Germany was still a smouldering volcano. But from the viewpoint of the British upper-middle class the revolutionary upheaving and laying-low of their basis was a spectre, a panicky foreboding that probably betrayed guilt. This syndrome of un-nerved attitudes issued in the motif that runs through the literary record. The centres of right living, of civilisation, are felt to be of a kind of clearing uncertainly maintained against the savagery which may thrust in at any moment.

In one of Luis Buñuel's earliest films, *L'Age d'Or* (1930), couples in dinner-jackets and silk gowns are dancing in a big house. A bull bursts through the curtained windows, lowers its head, and charges the dancers, splintering the grand piano. (This is a memory of the film from many years ago but we believe it to be accurate in essence.) As the people scatter, a man looks at his hand appalled – it is crawling with ants. The Surrealists did not explain their insights, though Buñuel's sense of latent violence was confirmed: at the first showing, the audience turned so wild that police were called to clear the cinema. Novels are harder to create than films or poems without the kind of specifica-tion of social circumstances that makes plain where, in the writer's view, the heart of the darkness lies. *The Great Gatsby* (1926) at first seems to be unfolding smoothly when the surface bloom is roughened and then split. The Buchanans live in what has been the house of an 'oil man', amongst the 'white palaces' of a fashionable area on Long Island Sound. 'They had spent a year in France for no particular reason, and then drifted here and there unrestfully wherever people played polo and were rich together.' Tom Buchanan's assets are not specified but the sources of such wealth are pretty tangibly symbolised in the waste-land of industrial ash nearby – amidst which lives his mistress, the wife of an unsuccessful garage man. This all belongs to a familiar, though freshly expressed, view of exploitative society. But peculiar notes begin to be sounded. Tom is first seen 'standing with his legs apart on the front porch ... Two shining arrogant eyes had established dominance over his face and gave him the appear-ance of always leaning aggressively forward ... he seemed to fill those glistening boots until he strained the top lacing.' A few minutes later, when the word 'uncivilised' happens to be used, Tom 'breaks out violently': ' "Civilisation's going to pieces ... I've gotten to be a terrible pessimist about things. Have you read *The Rise of the Coloured Empires* by this man Goddard? ... The idea is that if we don't look out the white race will be – will be utterly submerged." '[21] The whole thing is an extraordinary anticipation (it was written early in 1924) of Fascist style and ideas, from the domineering posture, which is precisely Mussolini, to the Nazi racism of the man's opinions.

Lurking beasthood is then symbolically implied to be widespread through this class by the animal names given to one after another of Gatsby's guests (none of whom he actually knows) – there are leeches, civets, blackbuck, beaver, whitebait, hammerheads, beluga whales, roebuck, a ferret, a klipspringer, and a bull,[22] all touched in with details that deliberately allow us to half-glimpse a world of crime, accidents, and financed mania:

> Snell was there three days before he went to the penitentiary ... when Ferret wandered into the garden it meant he was cleaned out and Associated Traction would have to fluctuate profitably next day ... [there were] the young Quinns, divorced now, and Henry L. Palmetto, who killed himself by jumping in front of a subway train in Times Square ... and young Brewer, who had his nose shot off in the war.[23]

The novel ends in a welter of error – Tom Buchanan's mistress smashed to death on the road by Gatsby's car, Daisy Buchanan driving it, the dead woman's husband revenging himself on Gatsby supposing that it was he who had been his wife's lover, then shooting himself. Working-class mistresses kept by rich men must be as common in modern times as working-class wet-nurses to rich babies used to be. What must be rare, though Fitzgerald imagines it powerfully, is the poor man actually taking his revenge. He is seen as an 'ashy, fantastic figure gliding towards' Gatsby through the woods that surround his lavish house.[24] It is again the spectre of the underdog breaking as a destroyer into the handsomely-appointed demesne of the rich.

In L. H. Myers's *The 'Clio'* (1925) all the motifs in the vision, or syndrome, appear together. 'The most expensive steam-yacht in the world' is gliding southwards off the mouth of the Amazon estuary with a party of the rich and fashionable on board. The ship's doctor sees them as 'the fine flower of civilisation' who bring with them from Mayfair a 'sweetness' that is better than the 'convictions' of Hampstead, the 'ideas' of Bloomsbury, or the 'drawing-room topics' of Chelsea. A little later the narrative completes the spectrum of classes when it tells us, with uncertainly directed irony, that the crew are like 'prize pigs in a sty . . . lumps of brick-red flesh . . . worthy fellows, lying about like seals on a floe'.[25]

After calling at the city of Para (now Belém) on the Brazilian coast, the *Clio* begins to make its way inland, up the Amazon, towards the heart of the continent. It is making for Manaos, which was also Waugh's destination when he went to Brazil in 1932. (There are close parallels. *En route* Waugh was told that 'most people were sick in Boa Vist''. *En route* the owner of the *Clio*, Lady Oswestry, is told by a Brazilian that ' "most people die at Breves" '.) To those on board, the yacht, that sleek white piece of Europe, begins to look astonishingly small now that the jungle is closing round it, the 'dark glassy water' stretches away, the main channel is blocked by fallen trees, the maze of the wilderness surrounds them. Revolution has broken out. Amazonia is struggling to separate itself from metropolitan Brazil. Lady Oswestry's son Harry is a dilettante adventurer who speaks of the need for strong men in South America, ' 'a Mussolini, a Diaz, or a Lenin at the head of each State.'' He is obscurely in touch with the revolutionaries, and as the novel ends he is heading off into 'the darkness' of the mainland, where machine-guns are rattling. But the heart of the book's significance lies at the point where Harry suddenly wrenches the helm over to avoid some mines that the loyalist navy has sown in midstream and the *Clio* rams her bows too deeply into the jungle to be able to reverse out. Wasps and lizards start to shower down, a musky smell steals over the ship, there is a crocodile's lair under the bank, a huge branch has thrust through a porthole and made a cabin uninhabitable. The remaining chapters are an artfully balanced narrative which manages to disquiet us with suggestions of a disaster that we cannot quite believe in, which is scarcely likely (the ship and its crew and owners are very well equipped to preserve themselves), yet which rings true as an evocation of deteriorating morale.

Hugo, Lady Oswestry's younger son, wants to explore a little into the jungle. After two hours' walking he is stopped by 'a sheet of coal-black water' in which the towering boles of the trees appear inverted. As he stares at it, his spirits sink, his friends on board ship begin to seem unreal and insignificant. He moves on into a brighter space where a hurricane has made a clearing, as he watches snakes slipping out of the water into the undergrowth he is bitten on the foot, he is desperately afraid of dying, gives up hope ... but a girl from the boat finds him, the pain in his foot is due only to the handkerchief he had tied too tightly round the bite, and really they are not very far from the ship.[26] The objective danger has been nil. What has happened has been a collapse of morale in face of untamed, alien life. The whole feel of the sequence, physically and psychologically, is strikingly close to the Marabar Caves sequence in Forster's *A Passage to India*, in which Mrs Moore slumps into thinking that 'Everything exists, nothing has value' after being jostled, harmlessly, by Indians in the stifling darkness of the cave. Myers's art is thin in comparison to Forster's, but both men have felt how people in a colonising role – well-off, well equipped, venturing into the wilderness they have been accustomed to rule or exploit from a distance – can feel the props of their culture so easily knocked away by an incident which has been menacing only in fantasy. In the same way, in Camus' *The Outsider*, the white Algerian Meursault only thinks that one of the Arabs is looking menacingly at him. Yet he shoots him.

Actual disaster overtakes Sir James on the *Clio*, the older man with a 'distinguished' political, diplomatic, and literary career behind him (he comes over as a Harold Nicolson figure). He has been in India as a young man and at one point he feels oddly smitten by the tropical sunset: 'why was it that every evening at sundown he was seized with a distress so poignant that he positively feared for his sanity? Some sorrow within him reared its head ... Like a sea-monster ... What was it? And whence? And why? He looked into himself aghast.' Once the boat is grounded, he spends a sleepless night listening to howler monkeys in the jungle. Presently he is fevered, seriously ill. The monkeys almost obsess him, at dawn their noise is amazingly loud, it united 'the bellow of a bull with the howl of a wounded tigress. Sir James welcomed the uproar.' When he becomes delirious he mutters about the monkeys and in a lucid spell he asks for information about their habits. He is told that ' "The howling monkey stands about two feet high. He has long silky hair, of a reddish-brown colour on the back, golden on the flanks ... When he howls he sits at the top of some great tree which dominates the surrounding forest." ' The sick man takes this in and is pleased. 'He died not long afterwards, just before the monkeys began their concert.'[27] Although neither Sir James nor the animals have been developed with enough power or fullness to act out a symbolic drama on a level with *St Mawr*, it is still striking to find that Myers, writing in the same year as Lawrence, has arrived at so like a theme: effete and nerve-worn people with nothing much to do, who turn for a surrogate to the wilderness and the splendour of hot-blooded animal life that belongs there.

The elements of this vision are so potent that they even figure at the close of *The Great Gatsby*, although its material has nothing to do with any veritable jungle. In the wonderfully rich passage that ends it, we see the narrator, Nick Carraway, longing for the lost historical moment when America had appeared to those who landed there as an unbreached aboriginal forest. Briefly this terrain has been lit up by the rich men's windows but 'Most of the big shore places were closed now' and the old forest darkness is reappearing as 'that vast obscurity beyond the city, where the dark fields of the republic rolled on under the night'. We will meet this dauntedness at the overwhelming extent of America once again, in Studs Lonigan's glum feelings as he shuttles north through Indiana back to Chicago. But, naturally, the vision of civilisation as a small clearing in the darkness, and the nerving of oneself to explore the darkness, comes more commonly in the books of exploration beyond the industrialised areas of the world.

In Ceylon Leonard Woolf had had the daunting colonist's experience of being totally lost, isolated, marooned, in the midst of a huge virgin territory. In the southern jungle he had lost touch with his cart train and pony as he went from village to village and he found himself in a clearing a mile across. The forest was 'exactly the same all round the circle – and I could not tell which was south and which north'.[28] This is quite like the symbolic disorientation Mrs Moore feels in the Marabar Caves, and it is even more like what happens in a story from the days of the grab for empire, Kipling's 'The Strange Ride of Morrowbie Jukes' (1885). A white man in India, far from his base, ends up in a village of Hindu outcasts who live in a great dusty crater. The path out is unknown and dangerous and Jukes has to share the outcast life, living on the meat of crows and sleeping in a filthy hole in a sandbank.[29] In essence this is close to the sequence in Conrad's *Nostromo* where the super-civilised Decoud, the creole *boulevardier* who has tried to intervene as a journalist in the nationalist revolution in Costaguana, finds himself adrift in a small boat, with miles of empty tropical sea around him, and loses his grip on his own sense of self and on life.

We would expect accounts of tropical exploration to be full of passages where survival figures as a finding of the one cleared and narrow route through thickets of danger. As the traveller nears the verge of the safety zone composed of passports, telephones, piped water, and reliable maps, almost anything can strike him as a threat or a mystery. So Huxley in Barbados:

> Between the lamps, in the thickening night, every passing form was disquietingly without a face, and handless; blackness melted into blackness ... Every now and then we passed a chapel – always lighted up and always full of people singing hymns. For half a minute, perhaps, the noise of 'Abide With Me' would drown the noises of the tropical night; then, as one moved further away, the frogs and the cicadas would reassert themselves, and one was aware of both noises vibrating with an equal hopelessness under the first stars.[30]

So Waugh in Guiana: 'All the time we passed only one human being – a Portuguese-speaking Indian, padding along on foot, going down the river on some inscrutable errand. For two days we travelled over grass land and then entered the bush ... the green, submarine darkness of the jungle.[31] Inscrutability is of course in the head of the uneasy colonial visitor: no doubt the Indian was going to market or carrying a message. In a betraying passage from *Passenger to Teheran* Victoria Sackville-West shows how deeply conditioned by class this whole experience was. Describing the bazaars, she writes: '[One] is oppressed only by the sense of dark life; then one imagines these separate, hurrying people coagulated suddenly into a mob, pressing forward with

some ardent purpose uniting them, and the same intent burning
in all those dark eyes.' Dismissing this spectre (which is the long-
standing bourgeois dread of a *jacquerie*) with rational argument,
she goes on:

> This is simply an effect of one's own strangeness; there is
> nothing really sinister about these people ... How curious
> a fact it is, that in a strange country, and more especially
> in the east, one should be so much concerned with the common
> people; at home one does not (except for more serious purposes)
> speculate about the secrets of the slums.[32]

The writer's guileless confidence that her readers share her actually
very blinkered viewpoint stops her from saying distinctly what
she means; but it seems most likely that the 'serious purposes'
she hints at were political: she and her kind were for ever speculat-
ing uneasily about the likelihood of revolution, or at least rebel-
liousness, among the people of 'the slums'. A few years later,
her husband, Harold Nicolson, had become one of Oswald Mos-
ley's closest advisers in the New Party – the British Fascists
– and was discussing the need to 'create a trained and disciplined
force' to resist (as he put it in an election address) 'a proletarian
revolt' springing out of 'The widespread dissatisfaction prevalent
in these islands'.[33]

For such people, alien life (if safely exotic) was to be savoured
for oddity and thrill. When the irrupting beast occurs, in the
form of a bandit, 'a wild, coloured figure on horseback' who
'came at full gallop into the glare of our headlights', she congratu-
lates herself on having refused an escort because 'I would not
in the world have missed the brief encounter with that marauding
apparition. I had felt, in seeing him, as one might feel who
sees a wild animal suddenly revealed in the jungle.'[34] A deeper
writer was liable to be more disquieted by alien life (as Lou
was by St Mawr) and also more respectful of it as a culture
in its own right. Graham Greene in Liberia was impressed by
the secret network of 'bush schools' and 'bush societies' which
initiated boys and girls into maturity through various devil cults
and tattooing ceremonies and later graduated them to more serious
ploys. 'All the way through the great forest of the interior one
comes on signs of them; a row of curiously cropped trees before

a narrow path disappearing into the thickest bush: a stockade of plaited palms: indications that no stranger may penetrate there.'[35] He knows too that white civilisation can work in clandestine and 'sinister' ways, and here he confirms Conrad's vision in 'Heart of Darkness'. Kurtz had been part of the system which exploited the Congo by extracting ivory and forcing people to work at the rubber on pain on amputation. Kurtz had a special interest in the indigenous culture and this had turned into a kind of morbid or addictive fascination with the 'black' rites of the jungle people. The rites are never specified – in 1899 Conrad was still at the stage of milking the 'inscrutable' for its ominous effects. A Kurtz in real life would probably have been presiding over the kind of human sacrifice practised by the bush society in Liberia, which needed for its rituals the heart, the palms of the hands, and the skin of the forehead. Greene is at one with Conrad in realising the squalor of imperial exploitation, of the sort of 'outpost of civilisation' which consists of 'an abandoned gold-working: a deep hole the size of a coffin, a few decaying wooden struts above a well of stagnant water, the ivy already creeping up'.

> This was the ruling passion of most white men in this dead bush, a passion just as secret, needing as much evasion, kept with perhaps as much fear, as the secrets of the bush houses which stood away from the path behind a row of stunted charred trees like funeral cypresses or a fence of woven palm leaves.[36]

Greene is historically beyond Conrad in being able to stretch his idea of civilisation to the extent of realising that it is in Africa too:

> However tired I became of the seven-hour trek through the untidy and unbeautiful forest, I never wearied of the villages in which I spent the night: the sense of a small courageous community barely existing above the desert of trees, hemmed in by a sun too fierce to work under and a darkness filled with evil spirits . . .
> . . . a hill, a stream, a palaver-house and forge, the burning ember carried round at dark, the cows and goats standing

between the huts, the little grove of banana-trees like clusters of green feathers gathering dust – not one was quite the same.[37]

We suggest that this openness to the foreign 'primitive' culture is possible only when you have got rid of the sense that you are justified in exploiting it, since the justification hinges on your classing the other culture as inferior, sub-human. As it says in the most recent study of 'European attitudes to the outside world in the imperial age':

> Between its two great wars Europe passed through a crisis of doubt and self-distrust that owed much to a declining confidence in its position in the world, and deepening uncertainty about what the world thought of it. Fascism was in one aspect a convulsive effort to shake off this mood, to restore the legend of virility by hysterical and suicidal violence. Loss of empire has set Europe free to begin finding better confidence, inspired by a new consciousness of itself and a new relationship with its neighbours, and to recollect in tranquillity its adventures across the seven seas.[38]

In the middle thirties writers were still feeling that reversion through stages of social evolution, back to savagery and perhaps beyond it to beasthood, was a menacing possibility. In the spring of 1935 Leonard Woolf was driving through Germany – keeping his Jewishness secret – and at a customs office a farmer failed to take off his cap to the big picture of Hitler. The officer 'immediately worked himself up into a violent tirade against the insolence of the swine who kept his cap on in front of the Führer's image ... I felt with some disquiet that I had passed in a few yards from civilisation to savagery.'[39] In Guatemala Aldous Huxley looked into the records of floggings at whipping-posts in the middle of the villages. These had been reintroduced in the 1840s 'at the wish of the Indians themselves, and in pursuance of the general plan to restore old usages and customs'. Huxley was disturbed by the startling likeness to Germany since the Nazis took power. He argued that the fomenting of sadism by the Nazis, the 'learning once more to punish' advocated in *Mein Kampf*, was part of a policy of making Germany primitive again. 'Mentally and emotionally, Germany is to be made as remote from Europe as New Guinea ... An ethic of head-hunters is to be justified by a philosophy of paranoiacs.'[40]

Huxley's analysis was precisely true of the primitivism which was a marked feature of the Nazi style. As early as 1920, Hitler had chosen the *hakenkreuz* or swastika as the symbol of the National Socialist Party. Its appeal was very wide partly because it had been used by anti-Jewish groups in Austria and partly because it was a mysterious emblem which pre-dated Christianity (it had been found on ancient sites in Troy and India). The Party's religious programme decreed that the swastika must replace the Christian cross in all churches as 'the only unconquerable symbol'. On the altars there should be only a copy of *Mein Kampf* 'and to the left of the altar a sword'. The cult of Jesus was to be supplanted by the worship of Wotan and of the sun. The aim in all this was 'to redirect the psychic energies of a public disoriented by the rise of industry and a mass-society towards the racial past, tribal duty and primeval customs'.[41] So the writers who had envisaged reversion to savagery had been true in their intuition. Only the beast had irrupted, not from the core of Asia, the sands of the desert, or the heart of darkness, but from the centre of European civilisation.

5. The Nullity of the Slump

We have said already that the economic slump from 1929 onwards worked also as a depression in the personal or psychological sense (see above, p. 34). The thing was a huge wave of shortages, worry, and suffering that fell upon thousands and millions of people. Pundits have recently tried to analyse it away to nothing, as they have done with the immiseration caused by the industrial revolution, in particular the Hungry Forties. They insist that the Gross National Product went on rising (as it did, apart from a drop in 1926 and again from 1929–32). They point out that work and people were moving into the south-east of England with the start of the 'third Industrial Revolution' in plastics, light engineering, consumer goods – industries which were not ruined by the Slump as were the older ones based on coal and steel and on cotton. But when the folk, the people, give a name to a time – the Slump, the Hungry Forties, hard times – there is more likely than not good reason for it. Millions *felt* that things had slumped. The facts were that from 1920, when the demobilised men had come back home, to 1940, by which time rearmament was well under way, there were never less than 10 per cent unemployed, or one million people. From 1929 to 1936 the number never fell below one and a half million, or one eighth of the working class. Even this figure disguises the number who were underfed, which can be put at ten million, since it included all the dependants of those on the dole or starvation wages. In Lancashire 40,000 mill workers got less than thirty shillings a week, and in 1931 nearly half the registered workers were jobless – this was reduced to a third by cutting many thousands off the Labour Exchange registers by ruthless use of the Means Test and the Anomalies Act.[1]

This experience gave rise to another undying collective image – a townscape of high factory walls with closed gates and smokeless tall chimneys, thin-faced men in scarves and cloth caps with broken peaks, leaning against the stonework or queuing quietly for soup, boots, or the dole. The meaning of this spoiled and stagnant townscape lay in the humiliation of society having no use for you, of your being worried to death about it and feeling helpless to change the situation. The thirties came to mean, for ordinary people, 'them days, 'the bad old days', the sort of times that must never ever return. Just before writing this, one of us was in a corner shop in a north of England town and heard a woman in her sixties saying to the shopkeeper: 'Bad unemployment – we don't want that back. We've seen it once already in our lifetimes. We was brought up to it.' There were no *coal*. Near Barrow there, in the woods, you could hear them cutting all over. In the summer. And in the winter there were nothing but a few sticks in't grate and us 'uddled over it. And then we grew up to't Depression. We beggared off to service and were glad to get it.' This experience was universal: 'No nation except Soviet Russia escaped. Industrial centres and colonial areas alike felt the impact of the general decline.'[2] From Berlin through France to Britain and the United States the look of the Slump was the same. In Lancashire Orwell found 'a monstrous scenery of slag-heaps, chimneys, piled scrap-iron, foul canals, paths of cindery mud criss-crossed by the prints of clogs . . . everywhere there were mounds of blackened snow.' In his diary he noted: 'heavy-set young women standing at street corners with their babies wrapped in their shawls, immense piles of broken chocolate in cut-price confectioners' windows.'[3] In *The Big Money* (1932) John Dos Passos described Pittsburgh: 'the crazy stairways zigzagging up and down the hills black and bare as slagpiles where the steelworkers lived in jumbled shanties and big black rows of smoke-gnawed clapboarded houses . . . the stench of cranky backhouses and kitchens with cabbage cooking and the clothes boiling and unwashed children and drying diapers.'[4] The cabbage smell, the smell of dampness and unnourishing food, is what Orwell made the atmosphere of ordinary life in his nightmare of the future, *Nineteen Eighty-four*. His specific image of helplessness amongst squalor is the same in both his books: a woman old before her time, poking helplessly at a blocked drainpipe.[5]

This was a crisis of capitalism (proclaimed by some over-enthusiastic Marxists as 'final'). But if 'crisis' suggests suddenness, emergency, something acute in the medical sense, it is misleading. The troubles were felt to be creeping and lingering ones. A Conservative prime minister used the image of a 'deep-rooted disease' to define the thirties. A Labour historian says that 'men regarded unemployment as a wasting disease, not as a crisis, and were glad that the crust of habit had been re-formed' when Lloyd George's proposals for a British 'New Deal' were defeated in the general election of 1929. An historian of no noticeable commitment describes the government as 'sunk in lethargy' and says that 'recovery in Germany and the United States seemed to have been achieved more dramatically and more consciously . . . whereas in Britain . . . there was a gnawing sense of national economic decline.'[6] This was indeed the feeling in the air. Commenting in 1940 on Malcolm Muggeridge's history of the thirties, Orwell objected to its 'defeatism', yet he himself had already said that during the thirties every creed, party, and programme had flopped: 'The only "ism" that has justified itself is pessimism.' To hit off what he called the 'all-pervading lethargy' he quoted Eliot's 'Hollow Men' (published the year before the General Strike):

> Shape without form, shade without colour,
> Paralysed force, gesture without motion.[7]

The terrible thing is that the paralysis was not only a metaphor, it was also a fact. A medical expert on the psychology of unemployed people cites the case of a girl of nineteen who had been a comptometer operator for four years when the Slump put her out of work. She developed acute pains in her right arm, which then became paralysed. If her mother had not saved enough money to open a small shop for her, 'she would probably have become a chronic neurotic and dependant, incapable in any circumstances of working for her living, always ill. There are thousands of such cases.' He concludes: 'As a precipitating factor of ill-health, unemployment is unequalled.' The government report of 1932 *On the State of the Public Health* found a tendency to mental depression verging on neurasthenia among older men who had large families dependent on them.[8]

Early in 1936 Orwell was trying to trace the paralysis to its source by exploring the industrial heartland of Lancashire. On 19 February he went to a social, organised by the mine-workers' union in aid of the defence fund for Ernst Thaelmann, the German Communist leader who was arrested by the Nazis and later killed in Buchenwald during the war:

> About 200 people, preponderantly women, largely members of the Co-op, in one of whose rooms it was held, and I suppose for the most part living directly or indirectly on the dole ... Round the back a few aged miners sitting looking on benevolently, a lot of very young girls in front ... I suppose these people represented a fair cross-section of the more revolutionary element in Wigan. If so, God help us. Exactly the same sheeplike crowd – gaping girls and shapeless middle-aged women dozing over their knitting – that you see everywhere else. There is no *turbulence* left in England.[9]

This rings true enough, in its blunt, rather overbearing way, and the loss of 'turbulence' is a crucial notion to which we will come back. But it is not enough to size people up for their potential as combustible political materials. The lethargy noted by all those commentators must also be understood inwardly, as a blight on the lives of persons, and for this we need good novels (and memoirs and plays and films). A dilemma of the time is that it did not stimulate expression of the widespread tragedy. The editors of *Memoirs of the Unemployed* remark that 'Drab monotony makes impoverished spirits'. 'The authentic voice of the unemployed' has almost never 'been heard in the long discussion of unemployment that has dragged on for so many years.'[10]

That is just the voice we are trying to catch, and it is hard to find in the literary record. What books can count as the classics of that time, as *The Waste Land* and *St Mawr* are for the years after the Great War? There are possibles – Grassic Gibbon's *A Scots Quair* (1932–4), MacDiarmid's *Hymn to Lenin* books (1931, 1935), Auden's *Look, Stranger* (1936). These have remarkable qualities but the relevant parts of them do not amount to anything like the contemporary American work. *U.S.A.*, Farrell's *Studs Lonigan*, and *The Grapes of Wrath* make up a *family* of works comparable with the English novel of the 1840s and 1850s in the sense they give of a complete society living through the gamut of experiences possible in their time and place. In Britain, especially in England, writers were turning away from native experience.

Waugh was finding many of his more telling experiences in Africa
and South America, Isherwood in Germany, Orwell in Burma
and Spain. Joyce Cary, then little known, based most of his
first five novels in Africa and did not turn to the England of
the General Strike until his last trilogy, written in the 1950s.
Graham Greene particularly advised a young writer to start from
his own country yet he himself was becoming famous for doing
the opposite.[11] No unquestionably masterly writer found everyday
life in the Depression of such engrossing interest that he was
moved to absorb it into his own vision of what it was to be
in the world. The writers who dealt with it at all made it the
whole subject of quite small works, not part of a panorama.
The book from England that is still read is Walter Greenwood's
Love on the Dole (1933), but the authentic things in it mingle
with novelette and melodrama. We would like to take as our
touchstone Walter Brierley's much less 'striking' novel *Means
Test Man* (1934).[12]

The book is a scrupulous recreation of how an out-of-work
miner in Derbyshire, his wife, and their seven-year-old boy live
on the dole. It is as sensitive to emotions as we would be entitled
to expect from a 'psychological novel'. It never treats the family
as a case – they are wholly persons, in no way set up as luridly
or grimly typical for the benefit of spectators from London or
elsewhere. The poignancy of their denuded life is hard to bear,
and it arises from the noting of emotional and domestic particulars,
it is not larded on by atmospherics or authorial special-pleading.

The novel opens as Jack Cook wakes up on Saturday morning.
The dazzle of sunlight on the brass knob of the bedstead catches
his eyes. 'The only thought that came to him was that he had
polished the knob yesterday when he had helped his wife to
clean the bedroom.' The prevailing atmosphere of a man who
is doing 'women's work' because he is 'idle' begins to arise from
the insistent household details – the cold tap in the kitchen,
the black-leaded range, the brick lavatory at the end of the garden.
The home is loved, it is well-kempt, it is oppressive – their existence
is too much bounded by these walls and gates and windows.
As the 5.30 hooter sounds from the nearby ironworks on the
Saturday morning, Jack looks at his wife and sees her 'lying
on her back heavy in sleep, her mouth slightly open ... Lines
beneath her eyes and on the forehead cut into the soft, smooth

flesh; it must be upon these that folks based the assertion that the past three years had aged her.' On Friday night, at the end of the novel, he looks at her (gone to bed early, worn out with repressed sick rage at the monthly visit of the Public Assistance inspector) and sees her face by moonlight: 'She looked ghastly, but she was sleeping a heavy sleep of exhaustion. The sound she made was frightening; half-snore, half-whine.' The action of the novel is hemmed in between stretches of sleep from which the people have to wake to face more of the same. Nothing has changed, except their balance in the Co-op, which has dropped from £2 to one penny, and their dole, which has risen from 25s. 3d. to 28s.

Against this iron blank of sameness, the least worry (the breaking of a good cup with a handle, losing a threepenny bit through a hole in a worn pocket, the boy catching a cold) stands out with neurotic acuteness:

When he used to waken in the morning after he had been to the pit, his whole frame had a fine, almost joyful feeling. He used to smile to himself and stretch out his arms and legs, opening his chest and working his abdomen, conscious that he had shape and substance and power, that his body registered a certain resistance to things. His wife had been real to him then, her body necessary; he had felt big and strong, surging with life and action, and she had been there to tone him down to normal, to take from him the almost dangerous driving. But his waking now was infinitely different, merely a matter of opening the eyes, it seemed. In the old days his mind would go out at once and probe among the stuff of existence, arranging it, cutting a path through it; but now, the opening of his eyes seemed to be just the baring of his mind to matters which were waiting, and had been waiting all night long, to beat upon it, eager to busy it with the inevitable things.

As the eggs boil for breakfast,

He sat on the edge of the table, the spoon in his hand, waiting until four minutes should have passed. Two streams were feeding his emotion, which sickened him slightly, taking away all desire for food. His whole being was finely poised, the last three years' experience had been one persistent refinement until now the very essence of him was bared, feeling pain at the mildest breath of disturbing.

The week goes by, they quarrel about the broken cup, the lost coin, and because Jack has not gone out to play hell with a neighbour who has clouted his son:

'I'm a woman first and a wife next. I want the decencies of life and I could have got them if I'd stopped single and in service. I married you and *you've* an obligation to provide. And more besides – you've a son.' The clock began striking nine. 'We thought of him doing something, going to a secondary school. His next move looks like being to the workhouse or a home.'

'And you think I can stop it, eh? That's what you're hinting at. Ah, you make me sick ... But I suppose that money or no money will be your measures always. It's a pity in one sense, but a good thing in another. Before you can suffer you'll always need some one to compare yourself with and that sort of suffering doesn't do you a deal of harm, or good if you look at it another road.'

On Friday the Means Test man comes on his motor-bike and writes down on his form their names, address, rent, insurance payments, all the details:

'You don't let no rooms? No trade union pay? No pension or compensation? No charity or outdoor relief? No help from relatives or friends?'

'No,' Jack answered quietly, not showing his disgust. The man wrote more than a dozen 'nils' down a column, then sat up again faintly fatigued.

Jane winces at his insistence on seeing their Co-op share book: 'She didn't want anyone to see the book, the graph of their fortunes, rising steadily for five years after the 1926 strike, then falling, falling, falling all the time.' After he has gone she breaks down in tears, he braces himself to bear this 'drab, pinioned existence without hope' and makes himself comfort her: ' "Buck up, lassie . . . If all the women in England could feel for a minute what you've gone through this morning, there'd be no more of it, no more homes upset . . . it's like the war, only worse." ' Inside himself he is deeply daunted:

> She sat on the sofa again, and he stood watching. Of course she would die sooner than was necessary, she'd be worn out with worry long before old age approached her. There would be no lustiness for him unless work came again, and soon. All the nature was going from him, he felt sluggish most of the time, and the animal in him seemed to have died . . . they had thought they would like a daughter – well – he had, he'd have loved a daughter. But they hadn't to think of such things.

The gamut of experience in *Means Test Man* is not curtailed: the daily paper brings news of public happenings, Jack gossips about the job scene when he goes downtown to shop alongside other jobless men, he walks twenty miles to Derby and back to buy a suit with the last two pounds. These interludes do not relieve but only make more irksome the chafing conditions, since everything comes down to pennies and shillings. Brierley never swerves from the aim of showing lives that are (in Words-worth's phrase) 'intense and frugal' – too much so, under the duress of shortage and helplessness. Skilled and healthy people are made to bend all their powers to surviving by drawing cheap seed potatoes from the town hall or getting into the cricket match at the children's rate by showing their dole cards. This is from plumb in the centre of the Slump experience. In *Memoirs of the Unemployed* a colliery banksman sums up the psychological hardship:

> Family life is made more difficult, testiness creeps in and often condemnation of a system is transferred illogically to the irksome limitations of the married state.
> 'If only one were single, without restraint, limitations.'
> 'If it were not for the child.'
> These thoughts, sometimes expressed, give, when they do find an outlet in speech, occasion for a warm altercation, the

resulting bitterness of which is only erased by periods of unintelligent silence.

A Derbyshire miner's wife records that she has gone to hospital every week for two years to have an ulcerated leg dressed but now she has to do it herself because they cannot afford the bus fare. She writes about her husband:

> He gardens every day, and the vegetables keep us going half the year. He goes to the unemployed centre every evening and he spends a lot of his time reading. But he is a changed man these last two years. He never complains, but I wish he would. It makes me unhappy to find him becoming quieter and quieter when I know what he must be feeling. If I had someone to talk to about my troubles I should feel better. But having to keep them to myself, as my husband does, makes everything so much worse. We quarrel far more now than we have ever done in our lives before. We would both rather be dead than go on like this.[13]

This is the 'loss of *turbulence*' with a vengeance. It is the modern, Western style of poverty. It is measured and monitored by the State, it is provided for (minimally, in case idleness should become too attractive) out of public funds, it is put up with by the sufferers in a way that can be seen as either stoic or passive. The sunken or nullified quality of it shows in its powerlessness to fire memorable expression – passages that could become the permanent types of such a life, like the drama of innocence surrounded by heartless greed in the earlier parts of *Oliver Twist*, or the clerk's defiant verve in John Davidson's 'Thirty Bob a Week', or the monumental weight given to hunger and indebtedness in Anna Seghers's *The Price of a Head*. To remain reasonably true to such a life and the possibilities that could be imagined in it, the writer would have had to avoid any suggestion of a magical standing jump out of the paralysis. Earlier, the ardour of immature revolutionism had prompted even realists like Tressell and Upton Sinclair to soar into peroration as they closed:

> That atrocious system [capitalism] . . . was now fast crumbling into ruin, inevitably doomed to be overwhelmed because it

was all so wicked and abominable . . . But from these ruins was surely growing the glorious fabric of the Co-operative Commonwealth . . . The golden light that will be diffused throughout all the happy world from the rays of the risen sun of Socialism.

And then will begin the rush that will never be checked, the tide that will never turn till it has reached its flood – that will be irresistible, overwhelming – the rallying of the outraged working men of Chicago to our standard! And we shall organise them, we shall drill them, we shall marshal them for victory! We shall bear down the opposition, we shall sweep it before us – and Chicago will be ours! *Chicago will be ours!* CHICAGO WILL BE OURS![14]

The most nearly comparable work of the thirties – fiction that takes a broad view of society and is fired by militancy – was Gibbon's *A Scots Quair* and particularly the last book of the trilogy, *Grey Granite* 1934. At the end the young Communist, Ewan Tavendale, is readying himself to set off on a hunger march from the north-east of Scotland to London:

his thoughts had gone back to other things in Segget: that day that Robert [his step-father, a minister] had died in the kirk – did Chris [his mother] mind the creed he'd bade men seek out, a creed as clear and sharp as a knife? He'd never thought till this minute that that was what he himself had found – in a way, he supposed, Robert wouldn't have acknowledged, a sentimentalist and a softie, though a decent sort, Robert.[15]

But this is not the last word. That lies with his mother, who has major symbolic status, developed throughout the trilogy, as the embodiment of the whole nation, Scotland. She says to Ewan, ' "The world's sought faith for thousands of years and found only death or unease in them. Yours is just another dark cloud to me – or a great rock you're trying to push up a hill." ' And as the novel ends her life bends finally back towards the hill farm she came from, in a nearly religious or pantheist acceptance of nature and change.

The conclusion would seem to be that class struggle in Britain was not sufficiently outright to give good grounds – grounds that could pass the test of a full creative rendering – for a perspective of decisive social change. Struggle had regularly come to little, from the day in the spring of 1848 when hundreds of thousands of Chartists had marched to Kennington Common and then, bowing to a ban on meetings within a mile of Westminster, had quietly dispersed and left their petition to be taken to the Houses of Parliament in three cabs. Early this century the Great Unrest drew to a climax which nervous employers and officials called 'a revolution' – a year or two later, the bitterly militant workers were enlisting by the hundred thousand for the war.[16] This trend has been defined by a leading social historian as 'the fundamental political fact of modern Britain':

> this country could not and cannot be run in flat defiance of its working-class majority, and . . . it could always afford the modest cost of conciliating a crucial section of this majority . . . Between British employers and workers, British rulers and ruled, there is no chasm labelled 'Paris Commune', or 'Homestead Strike', or 'Free Corps' and 'SS'.[17]

A most revealing case of this in the years that went to form the thirties occurred in February 1919, when the Triple Alliance of railwaymen, transport workers, and miners bid fair to launch a general strike with revolutionary implications. The miners had voted heavily for strike action in support of a 30 per cent pay rise, a six-hour day, and nationalisation of the mines with elements of workers' control. The railwaymen and transport workers were concerting similar demands. London had three days' coal left. The government reacted by threatening to use the army to put down any strike and promising a full enquiry into the coal industry. The strike was suspended. The Royal Commission recommended nationalisation with an 'effective voice' for the workers: this was carried out, minus workers' control, a quarter of a century later. The army would probably have been helpless: during the rail strike six months later, so many soldiers fraternised with pickets that troops were withdrawn to barracks and the Higher Command warned the Cabinet not to use them but to send them instead to '*our* coming storm centres' such as Ireland and India. But the reaction of the miners' leaders was to persuade the workers to back down: 'A fatalistic anticipation of violence and bloodshed deluging the coalfields, weighed heavily with the Federation leaders, notably with President Smillie. From this anticipation the dour president recoiled, saying privately to his colleagues, "If there is a strike, they will use the soldiers. My people will be shot down. Anything rather than that!" [18]

To speculate on what 'might have happened' if a militant initiative had been tried in 1919, or 1926, is clearly absurd – a kind of retrospective prayer. What happened was what had to happen, the resultant of the forces then in motion. Forward impulses from the grass roots of society were dying away, and this is what people had in their systems as the blight of the Slump closed in. There was some resistance – much more than we hear about in the usual histories. The Battle of Cable Street in 1936, between Communists and Fascists in east London, is rightly famous. But who has heard of the battles between unemployed and State machine which were of more direct concern to the millions out of work? The standard police strategy was to charge with horses and batons at legal and orderly demonstrations, which were organised in dozens of cities. In Birkenhead in September 1932, hundreds of workers were injured and thirty-seven police. After four days of fighting, lorry-loads of police went into the back streets at night, smashed down doors, beat people up, and took many off to the police station. More than a hundred working people were treated in hospital for broken pelvises, ruptured kidneys, broken ribs, arms, and legs. In Belfast in October of that year, workers fought the mounted police and armoured cars from behind barricades, five men were seriously injured by rifle and revolver bullets, and one died in hospital. The following day another was killed and a curfew enforced at night for the first time since 1922. In November a million signed a petition to end the Means Test, 100,000 demonstrated in Hyde Park, and the leadership of the National Unemployed Workers' Movement were arrested and imprisoned. [19]

Barricades, the clubbing and gunning-down of demonstrators, night arrests, and political prisoners sounds more like the Britisher's idea of Russia or Germany than of his own country, yet those are the facts. They were known to the novelists. Grassic Gibbon has his hero, Ewan, undergo agony at the hands of police in the cells after they have harried the pickets at an engineering works. Walter Greenwood has two accounts (fairly detailed but with irksome discrepancies) of the clubbing down of a demo in Salford town hall square in 1931.[20] Yet what came of it was small in literary terms. World literature of Slump and Depression had two leading characteristics. Human nature was being tested to the quick by long-drawn-out erosion, and this showed in novels that pictured people in large and typical (rather than minutely individualised) strokes, usually against a stark or denuded landscape (Silone's *Fontamara*, Seghers's *Price of a Head* and *The Revolt of the Fishermen of Santa Barbara*, Brecht's *St Joan of the Stockyards* and *The Mother*). Secondly, whole societies became bitterly aware of the ills creeping through all their arteries and joints, and this showed in series of novels that took their characters through long spans of time and across wide tracts of social living (*A Scots Quair*, *USA*, *Studs Lonigan*, *The Grapes of Wrath*). From England not much comes – Auden's lyric laments for disused industry, the decent small-scale fiction of domestic hardship (*Love on the Dole*, *Means Test Man*, Orwell's *Keep the Aspidistra Flying*). It is Gissing and Elizabeth Gaskell rather than Dickens, George Eliot, and Hardy.

A contrast with the American historical and literary record will show up more palpably our cultural exhaustion. Unemployment in the United States took a severe toll. In 1932–3, the number out of work was estimated by trade unions and government agencies as at least thirteen million – an estimate, not a firm figure, because 'some Freudian resistance deterred the government from taking a census'. The total is six times the British, for a population about four times the British. Monopoly was further developed in the States; firms and also individual factories were much larger.[21] This meant that the masses of people made idle by a single strike or lay-off were enormous – enough to be qualitatively different from the British or French situation. The American police used the same strategy as those in Europe – harrying pickets and demonstrators, then gunning them down, but the scale was so large (and American habits still so raw and aggressive) that the clashes between the State and the jobless moved near the level of civil war. The demonstrators in Salford town hall square were beaten back with truncheons and fire hoses. In America, at Republic Steel and Bethlehem Steel, in Illinois and Pennsylvania, the weapons were grenades, tear gas, revolvers, and repeating rifles. In Chicago in the summer of 1937, legal pickets who

had their wives and children with them were massacred by the
police:

> The cops squealed with excitement. They ran after fleeing pickets,
> pressed revolvers to their backs, shot them down, and then
> continued to shoot as the victims lay on their faces, retching
> blood. When a woman tripped and fell, four cops gathered
> above her, smashing her flesh and bones and face.

Seven were killed and more than a hundred wounded. The massacre
was unusually fully covered by newsreel and still cameras, and
Senate investigations proved how thoroughly the bosses had prepared for war on the workers. Big firms such as the steel corporations and the Goodyear Tyre Company had bought loads of
small-arms and also army-type machine-guns, gas-guns, and gas-
grenades 'entirely unsuited for use except in carrying out offensive
action of a military character against large crowds of people'.
The tear-gas was 'in quantities many times greater than those
required by the police departments of some of our largest cities'.
Guards and deputies with criminal records were signed on by
the company armies, trade union offices were wrecked, labour
organisers were injured, murdered, run out of town. Some coal
companies owned not only the coalfields, mines, shops, and houses
but their own prisons.[22]
Against this system were ranged the organised workers, who
were struggling for life itself. The wage cuts in the Kentucky
coalfields were crushing them to death. In one mining camp of
125 families, seven children a week were dying of pellagra. The
civil war character of the resistance which the miners now began
to organise (the revival of the United Mine Workers) comes out
in an eye-witness account by a member of the National Committee
for the Defence of Political Prisoners:

> On the hillsides, in the woods, and in the homes of miners,
> groups of men – white and Negro – armed with rifles and
> pistols which are more common in the Harlan camps than
> toothbrushes, drifted together for whispered conferences and
> to listen to low voiced speeches. In at least one case a machine
> gun nest was discovered, covering the spot planned for a mine
> meeting. I have in my possession a photograph of one gathering

held in a barn that was blown to bits by dynamite, not half an hour after the miners had left it.[23]

The nakedness of such a struggle between the haves and the have-nots was bound to make it stand out in the eyes of artists as they strove to single out the most significant things in the life around them. In the Twenties, American writers had not been notable for a deep interest in the daily life of their own society, or a committed concern about it. In spite of the efforts of Dreiser and the Chicago novelists, the more skilful writers kept up much of the nineteenth-century fascination with Europe, especially France and Italy. In April 1929, six months before the Wall Street Crash, with real wages still at their highest point in American history, Edmund Wilson could write in the *New Republic*: 'Dos Passos is now almost alone among the writers of his generation in continuing to take the social organism seriously.'[24] In a year or two this was transformed and the writers, not only in their subjects but also in their styles and their ways of getting to know their country, were responding to the full extremity of the situation. Dreiser, Dos Passos, and Sherwood Anderson served on the committee which did the (dangerous) investigations and report on Harlan County. Farrell, when he began writing *Studs Lonigan* in 1929, was directly inspired by, among other things, the pioneering Chicago sociologists, who had been using interviews and newspaper evidence for their studies of rooming-houses, taxi dance halls, and boy gangs.[25] In 1938 when Steinbeck went with a photographer to the West Coast fruitpickers' camps to write a feature for *Life* on the migrant workers, he found a tragedy of such scope that it needed a major novel to do it justice. There were a few English counterparts, notably Orwell's stay in Lancashire to gather material for *The Road to Wigan Pier*. But the condition for major literature was not achieved: that is, when the channels of communication are so open, the pressure points in society so exposed, that writers can feel they have access to the whole of the human condition as it is in their time.

6. Social Tragedy

The experience of millions of lives in jeopardy because of economic collapse gave rise to a sort of writing we suggest should be known as social tragedy. A complex trap of disasters closes in on people, and while they (whether individuals, a family, or a bigger community) are not stereotyped into mere cases, the historical circumstances bearing down on them are unusually fully specified, the region or nation or class they belong to is clearly visible all around them, the conditions they *share* with thousands of others matter as much and bulk as large as their special characters. Such work is not born only of the Depression. Most of Arthur Miller's plays, for example, right through into the early Seventies, have many of those qualities. But he was decisively formed by the Slump. His mother's business failed in 1932, he grafted his way through college on odd jobs, he worked on the Federal Theatre Project, a typical piece of New Deal subsidising of the arts; and when he produced *A Memory of Two Mondays*, its image of the drab toil and insecurity of warehouse work struck people as so thirties that they assumed it was a twenty-year old play which Miller had 'exhumed'.[1]

Farrell's *Studs Lonigan* deserves to be the touchstone for social tragedy, and it is in our view a modern classic, both because it is steeped in its epoch and because it makes one very fully-created character the bearer of the whole suffering of his time. Farrell follows a typical life through from young manhood to (premature) death. In so doing he is able to show society as the articulated and cohering whole that it actually is, however deeply split by stress between classes, races, and generations. *Studs Lonigan* has enjoyed much lower prestige than its Modernist counterpart, Joyce's *Portrait of the Artist as a Young Man*, because Farrell is 'naturalistic', which these days means mundane, predictable, and nearer the sort of sociology which amasses data with a minimum of slanting or reshaping. Farrell's trilogy has something of this, and it works as a strength, not as a shortcoming. On the one hand he uses a great deal of sociological material. He takes excerpts from pop lyrics and newspaper small-ads and transcribes in full such items from the mass media as B-pictures, movie newsreels, and Roman Catholic sermons. Where most novelists would have transposed these into their own style, Farrell pastes them unaltered onto his otherwise novelistic texture. At the same time, like no other writer before him and few since, he is scrupulously true to the way most people speak. Not until page 772 of the one-volume edition is there a single phrase from the consciously peculiar or clever language which is the dialect of the intelligentsia. It is also the language of prestige fiction from Henry James to Iris Murdoch. In Farrell's trilogy it occurs when Studs, who works as a housepainter with his father's small firm, happens to hear an arty young couple talking in the street. Its rarity in the whole big work makes at a stroke the culturally important point that most people have little or no contact with the life-style, including the language, which academics tend to take for granted, or else esteem as the acme of the expressive, because it is their own.

Studs Lonigan grew out of a more deliberately sociological concern than any other important fiction known to us. Farrell majored in sociology at the University of Chicago in the years just after researchers based there had pioneered theoretical and field studies of city life. Burgess's *The City* appeared in 1915 and F. M. Thrasher's *The Gang* in 1927. Farrell later acknowledged that it was studying the social sciences which had weighed most in his decision to become a writer. The first edition of the first novel, *Young Lonigan*, came out in 1932 with an introduction by Thrasher. So as to prevent prosecution for obscenity or the like, it was limited for sale to 'physicians ... social workers, teachers and other persons having a professional interest in the psychology of adolescents'.[2] Farrell knew at first hand the Chicago youth culture of the 1920s which gives the bulk of his themes. He was helped to see how it meshed with the wider social fabric by the sociological researches of Thrasher, Burgess, Park, Wirth, and others. The specific setting of the novel was, in their terms, on the margin of an 'interstitial area' – a physically spoiled city section located between areas which had a more cohesive and therefore supportive culture. Their research showed that it was in such 'interstices' that the most dissatisfied and violent behaviour occurred. Studs, in his rather run-down Catholic neighbourhood, is so situated that his life and character partake both of the disturbed and brutal minority experiences in American life and of a sub-community which (like most others) is living at a reasonable level materially. So we have a major character who is rare in modern Western literature in being neither exceptionally privileged nor exceptionally deprived. At the same time Farrell is able, with no trace of wanton melodrama, to give due place to the gang bangs and pool-room punch-ups which characterise a way of life that is in trouble, that has symptoms of what Reich called 'emotional plague' or epidemics of irrational destructiveness.[3]

Studs leaves school at fifteen, repudiates his parents, fails to grow beyond them – he spends ten years working for his father's firm. He is short, tough, none too bright, and the high point in his life occurs when he is fifteen and fights a bloody draw with the local street bully. The acclaim and respect earned in that moment is sucked to a dry husk for the rest of his life. Equally, his sweetest experience occurs with his first girl-friend while he is still adolescent. Later, he courts a young woman but their engagement is unnaturally prolonged because Studs is now out of work as a result of the 1929 crash. Apathetically he tries for unskilled jobs, fails to get them, frequents burlesque houses and betting shops for want of anything better. When the money runs out he walks the streets, gets cold and soaked in the rain. His resistance is lowered by years of cheap food, bad booze, and the anxiety that comes with the realisation that he has reached some sort of dead-end. He catches pneumonia. He dies.

The double question we have to consider is: How does Farrell manage to make the mainly average flow of Stud's life interesting? How does he manage to see the exceptional – the unusually unfortunate – side of Studs as an aspect of that same normality?

In 1929 Farrell wrote a review of a co-operative study called *Personality and the Social Group*. He argues that the sociological case method 'merely approximates personality' and so fails as an analysis. 'Spiritual loneliness' is the worst contemporary problem but the sociologist 'splits it up into cause and effect, and while giving it a healthy objectification, loses the individual, unique emotional colouring.'[4] What Farrell does in his masterpiece is to fuse healthy objectification (the minimum intrusion of the author's ego) with emotional colouring which is not so individual as to lose touch with how most people speak and think but individual enough not to become featureless.

It is hard to illustrate this convincingly because such a book accumulates unobtrusive effects instead of working by flights of eloquence or stunning images. One nodal passage must stand for the whole. Near the start of the final book, *Judgement Day*, Studs and some of his friends are journeying home by train after going to a funeral. The train clatters through the Indiana countryside, through small stations, past farms, cars on the road, glimpses of others' lives. Studs is bored by his friends' small-talk and sinks into his own thoughts:

> The train crawled through a station and a moustached man, lazily pushing a station truck containing a few mail sacks, reminded him of many such characters from movies. He did not catch the town name lettered above the station window, and as the engine picked up speed, he saw scattered wooden houses standing at the other end of the town like so many lonely sentinels. And then again, the altering picture of flat farmlands, dreary and patched with dirty snow at the end of February, houses, barns, silos, telephone posts, steel towers connecting lines of strung wire, with a row of wintry trees in the distance, bare like death, and appearing to speed as swiftly as the train travelled . . .
>
> His mind drifting from their talk, he thought of how this trip to Terre Haute had broken up the monotony of living in one place all the time. The world was full of places and things he had never seen, and would probably never see. If only, when he'd been younger, he'd bummed around and seen something of the world, gone through many towns and cities, and even villages, like the one they had just passed, seeing the stores and movie shows, and houses, listening to the people talk, meeting the girls. He might have made girls all over the country, and like a sailor leaving a girl in every port, he could have left a sweet little lay behind him in every town of the good old U. S. A. And one of them might have been prettier and keener than Catherine, and he might have liked her more

than he did Catherine. She might have been an heiress for whom he would have cared more than he had once cared for Lucy. And if he had, the fellows would often say to each other, I see where Studs Lonigan copped off a bim whose old man is lousy with dough, and is he up in the world now!

The train shot up an embankment and rattled along parallel to a cement road. Below, he saw a large and shiny automobile, probably a Cadillac, racing even with the smoking car, shooting ahead, slowing down and falling back at a right turn to a road that cut through the dreary fields, regaining its lost speed, darting forward until he could see only the back bumper and rear end. They whisked past a deserted and probably unused station platform, and he looked vacantly out at fields that were being covered with the lengthening shadows. It was funny that he should be riding home now from the funeral of Shrimp Haggerty, and so many things should have been changed from what they used to be, and from what he had expected them to become. But since his kid days, there had been many years, all piled on top of one another, and now, each year, each month, each week, each day, every hour, every minute, and every second even, carried him farther and farther away from them, just as if he was on a moving express train which was shooting him forever away from some place where he very much wanted to be, and all the while carrying him nearer and nearer . . . to his own death. He was going on thirty now, almost a third of a century. If he was going to die when he reached sixty, it meant that half of his life was already gone. If he would be called before sixty, it meant more than half of it was already spent. . . .

The dim light of a solitary farm house whisked before him, and again he heard the long, piercing engine whistle. Winter had never seemed so dreary to him as it did now, not even on some of those sunless days, when, as a kid, he had walked alone through Washington Park with the ground hard and chunky, the snow dirty and crusty, the trees and bushes stark and bare. From the train, the land here looked harder, the patches of snow dirtier, an ugly sight. He wondered how the people in these parts, cut off from the rest of the world, could stand looking at the earth on such days as this one, hearing nothing but silence or the wind, except for the passing trains and automobiles. He thought of how his father and mother would so often sit home in the evening, and not have a word to say, and asked himself how the farmers and their wives ever had anything to say to each other. Living like they did out here, their minds must, he felt, always be on such things as death.

He chuckled to himself thinking how glad he was that he lived in a big city like Chicago.[5]

There are few phrases there that could not have come from the mouth of someone who is a little, but not much, above average in powers of self-expression. Yet the passage reverberates and gives off meaning more or less indefinitely. Every detail is both symbolic and plainly itself, unaltered. Studs is insulated by the pane of glass, lifted above ordinary living by the embankment, the speed of the train, the special feel of leaving your usual place and of going to a funeral. The landscape has the character of a map and of a picture. It is multifarious and infinite-seeming yet all too dauntingly well known. He is caught in it, a particle in a tight circuit, and the fact of being one small organism hauled quickly along a pair of steel rails heightens this. The passage of time, the four or five hours north through Indiana and back into Illinois, telescopes out to seem the span of his whole life. By the time Studs is consciously thinking things like these, the reader has intuited them, and more, from the sequence of the details.

The analysis could easily be continued without exhausting the meaning. But enough has been said to show how Farrell, without grafting insights implausibly onto a not exceptionally imaginative character, has given the chosen moment this wonderfully wide and deep reference.

That sequence is typical of the trilogy. Consider one other moment, one of the italicised sections which step for a page or two out of the continuum of Studs's life in order to enlarge its context. Near the end of the middle book, *Young Manhood*, there is a young man, Danny O'Neill, who is unlike all the others because he is studying at university. In the evenings he works at a gas station at the edge of a black people's slum. Late at night Danny, rather like Studs on the train, is looking out on the world surrounding him from the glassed-in box of the office. An old black man comes in and buys four cents' worth of kerosene. Danny is led to make the connection between the hardship of poor folk and the economics he has been studying at university. The passage ends on an up-beat: Danny feels he will settle accounts with this existence some day ('He wanted to be a writer') and he feels too that some day the world will be cleansed and renewed.

This is a moment of heightened consciousness, it is what critics (after Joyce) call an epiphany. But its power comes more from the placing or timing of it than from the character's extraordinary powers of feeling or perception. Danny is in a glass (or triplex) box, part insulated against the atmosphere outside, part all the more in touch with it because through the transparency his surroundings flow in on him. It is as though he were in a hide observing the wild life all around. He feels keenly different from his environment. An old man comes in – an old black man. The big dark box of the factory is over against his small light box. His friends stroll by while he is tethered to his job. Every detail, commonplace yet in sum intensified, drives him to realise himself *in life*, situated, and he is moved to take stock of his position with more than the usual looking before and after (which actually occurs in the Swinburne poem he has been reading as a break from his studies:

> We look before and after
> And pine for what is not . . .)[6]

Too many of such nodal passages would make the book veer away from the daily continuum which Farrel is intent on evoking. But when they do come, they knot together all the fibres already threading through the work and radiate them out again into what is still to come.

If, then, Farrell so keeps to the dull quotidian, how does it come about that, without implausibility, he can make Studs abnormal in his misfortunes? (He never marries, he has no home of his own, no happy love-making, and he dies miserably at thirty.) It is done by historicising Studs's life. He is situated in his epoch, and the history he is embroiled in is one of world war, growing fascism, workers organising for revolt, economic collapse. As America slumps, so does Studs. It is done by so many ordinary details that there is never any sense of a forced parallel. Dates are always specified, whether the moment is ordinarily domestic or in some way public. 'At the supper table early in 1927, Mrs Lonigan sighed that she was glad because soon it would be time for Father Shannon, the missionary, to be coming back to the parish to conduct the first mission in his new church.'[7] Early in *Judgement Day* Studs and Catherine, his fiancée, are walking through the lit-up city at night. She says, '"And wait until we have The Century of Progress in 1933. Won't that be grand! Mr Brenckenbridge says that by then Prosperity will be back and everyone will be making money hand over fist."' Studs replies, '"I hope so"', wondering 'how his health would be in two years. Would he even be alive? Two years ago, Shrimp, Tommy Doyle, Slug, lots of people now dead, had been alive, and in better health than he was now.'[8] Everything happening globally is noticed, in a natural way, by the characters. A Greek café owner in the first book, *Youth*, is anguished to read in the papers about what is happening over in Europe, in the Great War. Kids in the street parrot chauvinistic slogans and mime bits of military behaviour. If someone is reading the paper twenty or thirty head-lines and sub-headings are given in full and then the character comments.

Most of this historical material is a passing show to Studs, it does not affect him. Until the Slump. It kills him. At first it too is part of the show: he sees a newsreel, which Farrel represents literally by transcribing headlines:

. . . CALIFORNIA
BUSINESS ORGANISATIONS AND FRATERNAL
SOCIETIES DEVISE NOVEL WAY OF COMBINING CIVIC
SPIRIT AND FUN TO ATTACK DEPRESSION

followed by film of businessmen pelting each other with surplus eggs from huge piles 'guarded by shapely girls in bathing suits'.

PITCHED BATTLE BETWEEN STRIKERS AND POLICE

followed by film of policemen in a mid-Western town clubbing strikers who had been on picket duty when blacklegs were coming in to work. The Slump itself is then magicked into a show. In a city somewhere a procession moves along, a hearse appears with a banner on its side:

OLD MAN DEPRESSION DIED 1931. R. I. P.

A float laden with flowers carries ' a stately virginal girl in white seated on a bedecked throne'. She is the 'QUEEN OF OPTIMISM', and as the newsreel draws to a close a 'puffy' banker is trotted on to read a prepared statement assuring viewers that the worst of the Slump is over. Studs waits impatiently for the feature – *Doomed Victory*.[9]

Within two years Studs has been caught up and killed by the downward spiral of over-production – glut – workers laid off – decreased national spending power – still more unsold goods – more sackings – economic standstill. The final book is called *Judgement Day* because Studs has been terrified by death ever since the priests bullied him with hellfire sermons as a child. It is also a judgement on an economic system that has been found wanting.

Reading between the lines and drawing the inference from the sum of the details, we realise well before the end that Farrell is bearing witness as a radical against this America. On page 814, with twenty-six to go, this protest comes out from between the lines in the form of a socialist march. It lasts for eleven pages (*Doomed Victory* had taken eight and the Mass in *Young Manhood* ten and a half) and it puts before us a wealth of slogans and songs: the 'Red Flag', the 'Internationale', 'Hallelujah, I'm a Bum', Joe Hill songs like 'Long-haired Preachers'; 'Defend the Soviet Union', 'Remember Sacco and Vanzetti', 'Hands Off Haiti'. The only important English critic to take the trilogy seriously and give it due praise was Mrs Leavis: she calls it 'a work of art equally remarkable for its subject-matter and its distinction of style and tone'. Yet even she has to qualify this: 'Mr Farrell is an extreme left-wing novelist and the space given to direct propaganda at the end of the saga may be thought by many of us to be excessive.'[10] We have shown how modest the space is in proportion to the various other things in the culture. No named character takes part in the march. Studs's father glowers sourly at it from the sidewalk and offers a policeman a cigar. At home Studs is unconscious, dying. The march could not be more estranged, in Brecht's sense. Of course to give it that much space, close to the tragic climax of a panoramically large work, was, in that America, to stress that socialism had a strong claim to attention. Farrell's books may well have been burned by the Ku Klux Klan, as Steinbeck's were, and in Philadelphia in 1948 the police tried to stop the sale of the trilogy: Farrell and his publishers won the law-suit.[11] But the estranging of the march makes it wholly unlike the sort of Grand Finale quoted already from Tressell and Sinclair, where the writer is swept beyond the facts to an unlikely vision of a revolutionary future somewhere beyond the skyline. Farrell makes no vainglorious forecasts. His determination to tell it like it was is felt in the remorseless trend downwards to Studs's death.

If one were to infer a perspective from the trilogy – and so large a work will seem spineless, a scrapheap of random experiences, if it can envisage no tendency – it would be that American capitalism would continue to operate at the expense of the people as a whole and sweep aside any attempt at opposition. In late 1974 the *Guardian* published a piece from Harlow Unger in New York with the headline 'Depressing reminders of the 1930s'. Unemployment had reached 6.5 per cent or six million out of work, the highest for thirteen years, and the Secretary of State, Kissinger, was telling the NATO conference in Europe that 'he personally felt there was no solution' to America's economic problems.[12]

In the truth of its perspective Farrell's work is clear-sighted compared with the third of the great socially tragic works which came from that America, *The Grapes of Wrath*. So long as Steinbeck roots his style in the speech and day-by-day behaviour of the working people, he is incomparable at presenting their way of life, with an attention to people's manual skills and their self-expression which is signally missing from nearly all literature to date. But he craves more of a solution to the crisis than history has actually offered. This comes out in the recurrent forecasts (envisaged in the title itself) of a day of reckoning when *les damnés de la terre* will feel their powers and rise up:

> And the companies, the banks worked at their own doom
> and they did not know it. The fields were fruitful, and starving
> men moved on the roads. The granaries were full and the
> children of the poor grew up rachitic, and the pustules of

pellagra swelled on their sides. The great companies did not know that the line between hunger and anger is a thin line. And money that might have gone to wages went for gas, for guns, for agents and spies, for blacklists, for drilling. On the highways the people moved like ants and searched for work, for food. And the anger began to ferment.

The people come with nets to fish for potatoes in the river, and the guards hold them back; they come in rattling cars to get the dumped oranges, but the kerosene is sprayed. And they stand still and watch the potatoes float by, listen to the screaming pigs being killed in a ditch and covered with quick-lime, watch the mountains of oranges slop down to a putrefying ooze; and in the eyes of the people there is the failure; and in the eyes of the hungry there is a growing wrath. In the souls of the people the grapes of wrath are filling and growing heavy, for the vintage.

All such passages come from the alternate chapters, where there are no named characters, little dramatisation, and the prose swells out into a sterotyped imitation of the Hebrew prophets. The result is a rhetoric that booms hollowly, and from the point of view of now we can see that the novel was bound to falter in those places because it had nothing to go on. The migrant workers never organised. No political party of the exploited whites ever has got anywhere in America (and the blacks do not figure in *The Grapes of Wrath* at all). Until these past few years the tyranny of the big fruit and vegetable farmers was becoming ever stronger, buttressed by the corrupt contracts negotiated by the Teamsters' Union with the personal support of President Nixon. Since 1972 we have seen the first breach in this alliance. It has come not from the whites of California or the migrants from the Middle West – the sons or grandsons of the Joads – but from the landless peasants from Mexico, migrating for work, allowed to cross the border illegally, then treated as non-persons, but now organised in the United Farm Workers by Cesar Chavez; and their song has been, not the 'Battle Hymn of the Republic', but 'We shall Overcome', sung in Spanish.

That vein of wishfulness does not pervade *The Grapes of Wrath*. The bulk of it is unrivalled in Western literature for describing, dramatising, and *explaining* a large socio-historical process – a deathblow to the American yeoman farmer, the migration of 350,000 working people from the Dust Bowl to California between 1934 and 1939 – from the point of view and *in the language* of those who lived this huge movement, not those who supervised it or lived off it at a remove. No detail that we need is missing. The humour, family loyalty, and practical skills of the Oklahoma families are richly evoked with barely a trace of false heroics. The largest trends are epitomised in snatches of idiomatic speech, as when the men camping beside the road west talk in the evening about what has forced them out:

I don' know what it's coming to, they said. The country's spoilt.

It'll come back though, on'y we won't be there.

Maybe, they thought, maybe we sinned some way we didn't know about. Fella says to me, gov'ment fella, an' he says, she's gullied up on ya. Gov'ment fella. He says: if ya ploughed 'cross the contour, she won't gully. Never did have no chance to try her. An' the new super' ain't ploughin' 'cross the contour. Runnin' a furrow four miles long that ain't stoppin' or goin' aroun' Jesus Christ hisself.

And they spoke softly of their homes: They was a little coolhouse under the win'mill. Use' ta keep milk in there ta cream up, an' water-melons. Go in there midday when she was hotter'n a heifer, an she'd be jus' as cool, as cool as you'd want. Cut open a melon in there an' she'd hurt your mouth, she was so cool. Water drippin' down from the tank.

They spoke of their tragedies: Had a brother Charley, hair as yella as corn, an' him a growed man. Played the 'cordeen nice, too. He was harrowin' one day an' he went up to clear his lines. Well, a rattlesnake buzzed an' them horses bolted an' the harrow went over Charley, an' the points dug into his guts an' his stomach, an' they pulled his face off an' – God Almighty!

They spoke of the future: Wonder what it's like out there?

Well, the pitchers sure do look nice. I seen one where it's hot an' fine, an' walnut trees an' berries; an' right behind, close as a mule's ass to his withers, they's a tall up mountain covered with snow. That was a pretty thing to see.[14]

When the big caterpillar tractors come, 'laying the track and

rolling on it', to plough up hundreds of farms for one cash
crop before the soil-crumb is finally pulverised, the men argue
through the economic process that has seized on them:

'And that reminds me,' the driver said, 'you better get out
soon. I'm going through the door-yard after dinner.'

'You filled in the well this morning.'

'I know. Had to keep the line straight. But I'm going through
the door-yard after dinner. Got to keep the lines straight. And
– well, you know Joe Davis, my old man, so I'll tell you
this. I got orders wherever there's a family not moved out
– if I have an accident – you know, get too close and cave
the house in a little – well, I might get a couple of dollars.
And my youngest kid never had no shoes yet.'

'I built it with my hands. Straightened old nails to put the
sheathing on. Rafters are wired to the stringers with baling
wire. It's mine. I built it. You bump it down – I'll be in
the window with a rifle. You even come too close and I'll
pot you like a rabbit.'

It's not me. There's nothing I can do. I'll lose my job if
I don't do it. And look – suppose you kill me? They'll just
hang you, but long before you're hung there'll be another guy
on the tractor, and he'll bump the house down. You're not
killing the right guy.'

'That's so,' the tenant said. 'Who gave you orders? I'll go
after him. He's the one to kill.'

'You're wrong. He got his orders from the bank. The bank
told him: "Clear those people out or it's your job." '

'Well, there's a president of the bank. There's a board of
directors. I'll fill up the magazine of the rifle and go into
the bank.'

The driver said: 'Fellow was telling me the bank gets orders
from the east. The orders were: "Make the land show profit
or we'll close you up." '

'But where does it stop? Who can we shoot? I don't aim
to starve to death before I kill the man that's starving me.'

'I don't know. Maybe there's nobody to shoot at. Maybe
the thing isn't men at all. Maybe, like you said, the property's
doing it'.[15]

When the families reach California on the trek for work, they describe the Peach Bowl with the utter finality of those who have no privileges, no private means, no padding between themselves and necessity:

'They's a big son-of-a-bitch of a peach orchard I worked in. Takes nine men all the year round.' He paused impressively. 'Takes three thousan' men for two weeks when them peaches is ripe. Got to have 'em or them peaches'll rot. So what do they do? They send out han'bills all over hell. They need three thousan', an' they get six thousan'. They get them men for what they wanta pay. If ya don' wanta take what they pay, goddam it, they's a thousan' men waitin' for your job. So ya pick, an' pick, an' then she's done. Whole part a the country's peaches. All ripe together. When ya get 'em picked, ever' goddamn one is picked. There ain't another damn thing in that part a the country to do. An' then them owners don' want you there no more. Three thousan' of you. The work's done. You might steal, you might get drunk, you might jus' raise hell. An' besides, you don' look nice, livin' in ol' tents; an' it's a pretty country, but you stink it up. They don' want you aroun'. So they kick you out, they move you along. That's how it is.'[16]

It is hard to imagine the situation more trenchantly expressed. This is the strength of native idiom which led Dos Passos to say in the Harlan County report: 'It's a shame that all the speeches were not taken down as the miners who spoke put the situation far better than I can.'[17] The same realisation led the authors of the classic 'Record of Human Erosion', the sociologist Paul Schuster Taylor and his wife, the photographer Dorothea Lange, to use the working people's language wherever they could, for example in the captions to their pictures.[18] It is no accident that during this decade two large works on the despoliation of the land, Gibbon's *A Scots Quair* and Steinbeck's *The Grapes of Wrath*, should have used versions of the people's own language not only for dialogue but even for the narrative. The size of the crisis, the numbers of suffering people it had thrust into view, had opened literature to the language of the majority.

Precisely this had never before been done. In the words of Lu Hsun, greatest writer of the biggest peasant country in the world, the country-people 'grew up during four thousand years in silence, withering like grass under a huge and heavy stone'. Writers tend to 'amuse themselves by using erudite terms which only a small minority understands. We cannot be sure that even this minority understands; and since the great majority certainly does not, this too is tantamount to silence . . . Hence our people, unable to understand each other, are like a great dish of loose sand.'[19] By the start of the twentieth century the majority were beginning to speak up in their own voices. Zola's *Germinal*, about the French miners, and Upton Sinclair's *The Jungle*, about the Chicago meat-packers, are researched books. But Gorky's *Mother*, about the militant factory hands in north-west Russia, and Tressell's *The Ragged Trousered Philanthropists*, about the house-painters in south-east England, are written from the authors' own experience of working life, in styles often painfully pieced together from the shop-talk, demagogy, and pamphlet literature which bulked large in the language-culture of working men.

Many things were coming together to force the mass of the people into social awareness: the total mobilisation of the Great War; the Russian Revolution, with kindred eruptions in Ireland, the Clydeside, Germany, Hungary; the founding of the Chinese Communist Party in 1923, and Mao's classic report on 'The Peasant Movement in Hunan' – his recognition that a strong new tide was setting from the country nearly got him expelled from his Party. In Italy, Marxists in such working-class bases as Turin were calling attention to 'the Southern question'. In America, the Agrarian movement was pressing, in a futile way, for the regeneration of America from the old country heartlands. In Russia the government started in on the crushing of the richer peasants, and the rare, terrible photographs of this, along with such classic films as *The General Line*, *Earth*, and *Grass* made real again, an archetype which had always been current, usually as a social alibi for the townspeople's nostalgia: people with cloths round their heads, faces seamed like dried leather, clothes worn to their colourless warp, scraping the ground for their subsistence.

Such is the trend embroiling many countries which raises the head of water and sends pressure throughout the culture – the collective imagination – of the people involved, issuing now here, now there, in quintessential works. In Gibbon's *Sunset Song* we feel the traumas of a thinly populated community who had so few to spare that the Great War, and the boom/slump cycle it stimulated, were fatal to a way of life. In Silone's *Fontamara* a nearly destitute hill village, holding on like a dried-out twisted tree with its roots exposed, enacts in a legendary way, a stylised way, the whole series of changes that has given towns the upper hand: enclosure, land hunger, soil erosion, dispossession under laws made by townspeople for townspeople, and finally the enlistment of peasants as tame voters by town-based parties. Anna Seghers's *The Price of a Head* shows how the slide of the German poor and middle peasants into irredeemable debt poses crippling problems, such as marrying a frail girl to a brute of a young man because a farmer needs a bearer of future working sons and daughters, and how these normal human problems of neediness, hunger, and sexual vulnerability came to be mixed, in the Fascist times, with political terror until the peasant community had no security left. In *The Grapes of Wrath* the tenant farmers and share-croppers, people with a small tough root in the very ground whose first ever tilling is still a family memory, are foreclosed on and actually ploughed out and the families must go on to the labour market as commodities – people with nothing to sell but their own power to labour.

In Gibbon's trilogy, the girl Chris Guthrie, growing up on a hill farm in the north east of Scotland early this century, is made to enact the whole evolution of her people in modern times: working on her father's land, getting a grammar-school education but marrying a farm hand who rents a place of his own, being widowed by the Great War, marrying a minister and going to live in a small mill town that keeps many village ways, and moving to the city with her son who works in a foundry as rearmament gets under way in the middle Thirties. The scattered community, more parish than village, in which the trilogy starts loses two tenant farmers, a miller, and a farm hand become farmer, in the course of the Great War. The sermon preached in their honour epitomises the social process which makes *Sunset Song* a death-knell:

> The last of the peasants, those four that you knew, took that with them to the darkness and quietness of the places where they sleep. And the land changes, their parks and their steadings are a desolation where the sheep are pastured, we are told

that great machines come soon to till the land, and the great
herds come to feed on it, the crofter has gone, the man with
the house and the steading of his own and the land closer
to his heart than the flesh of his body. Nothing, it has been
said, is true but change, nothing abides, and here in Kinraddie
where we watch the building of those little prides and those
little fortunes on the ruins of the little farms we must give
heed that these also do not abide, that a new spirit shall come
to the land with the greater herd and the great machines.[20]

In 1821, half a million people had been on the land, or one
in four of the population. By 1911 it was 200,000 or one in
twenty. The population had more than doubled but the agricultural
counties were losing people. 'Hill pastures, rough grazings and
woodlands had everywhere encroached on the farm-land, and
while fields were larger, corn-fields were fewer.' The historian
comments: 'This was deplored, not only by the farmers, but
by those who felt that an unbalanced economy was a tragedy
for the whole nation.'[21] A tragedy because it left Scotland nothing
to fall back on when the Slump hit heavy industry after 1929.
The colouring of Gibbon's work had to be dark, its tendency
a downward curve, like Hardy's, with the difference that Gibbon,
closer to the land (as the son of a small farmer) than Hardy
and with a Nationalist and Marxist understanding of its problems,
was fully conscious of his themes and therefore less inclined than
Hardy to make the personal disasters of the country folk hinge
on melodramatic chance or Fate. From his knowledge of Kincar-
dineshire he was placed to write the final account in *British* literature of a people whose place of work and work-team were one
and the same as their own homes and families. Wordsworth had
put it like this in a letter of 1801 recording the squeezing out
of the self-employed farmers in Cumberland:

Their little tract of land serves as a kind of permanent rallying
point for their domestic feelings, as a tablet upon which they
are written which makes them objects of memory in a thousand
instances when they would otherwise be forgotten. It is a fountain fitted to the nature of social man from which supplies
of affection, as pure as his heart was intended for, are daily
drawn.[22]

The English Highlands were being ruined at the same time as
the Scottish Highlands. The thing took longer in the Lowlands
with their deeper soil. But in the years before Gibbon drew his
panorama, the price of wheat dropped from 70s. a quarter in
1918 to 50s. in 1921 and 20s. 6d. by 1933. A ploughman's weekly
wage (including payments in kind) dropped from the artificial
wartime high of 53s. 9d. in 1920 to 37s. in 1932, the year of
Gibbon's novel. 'The farmer now stood on the brink of despair.'[23]

Sunset Song has a wholeness of human nature which should be
common in our literature yet is rare. Its form is not contrived
– *données*, build-up, *dénouement*; instead it is based on the rhythms
of life, from pre-history through history to the present, from
ploughing through seed-time to harvest, from childhood through
adolescence to middle age and death. It is often tragic or dire
yet it breaks out at any moment into outrageous jokes. It has
a collective voice, that gossips and reminisces, yet the main voice
is the deep and vivid introspecting of the main character, Chris.
It is both local and national. The freedom across the whole gamut
is in the language, which is physical, colloquial, politically radical,
heart-searching, all in a breath:

> You could go never a road but farmer billies were leaning over
> the gates, glowering at the weather, and road-menders, poor
> stocks, chapping away at their hillocks with the sweat fair
> dripping off them, and the only folk that seemed to have a
> fine time were the shepherds up in the hills. But they swore
> themselves dry when folk cried that to them, the hill springs
> about a shepherd's herd would dry up or seep away all in
> an hour and the sheep go straying and baying and driving
> the man fair senseless till he'd led them weary miles to the
> nearest burn. So everbody was fair snappy, staring up at the
> sky, and the ministers all over the Howe were offering up
> prayers for rain in between the bit about the Army and the
> Prince of Wales' rheumatics. But feint the good it did for
> rain; and Long Rob of the Mill said he'd heard both Army
> and rheumatics were much the same as before.[24]

It was a tremendously hard thing to do, to take the whole social
character of a people for his subject, and Gibbon's touch becomes
less steady as the trilogy unfolds. More and more he too easily

turns on and hands over to a few images – the changing sky, the wind, the call of curlew and snipe – that palpably hold an overwhelming emotion for the writer but which he uses more for rhetorical heightening than as something to be understood, evoked concretely, and traced down to its source. In *Sunset Song* this emotion is grounded enough but by the middle book, *Cloud Howe*, it is turning into this:

> She minded then as she worked at that tree, an apple tree, and set smooth the earth, and reached her hands in the cling of the mould, that saying of Robert's, long, long ago, the day he unveiled the new-hallowed Stones up by the loch on Blawearie brae – that we'd seen the sunset come on the land and this was the end of the peasants' age. But she thought, as often, we saw more than that – the end forever of creeds and of faiths, hopes and beliefs men followed and loved: religion and God, socialism, nationalism – Clouds that sailed darkling into the night. Others might arise but these went by, folk saw them but clouds and knew them at last, and turned to the Howe from the splendid hills – folk were doing so all over the world, she thought, back to the sheltered places and ease, to sloth or toil or the lees of lust, from the shining splendour of the cloudy hills and those hopes they had followed and believed everlasting. She herself did neither, watching, unsure: was there nothing between the Clouds and the Howe?
>
> This life she lived now could never endure, she knew that well as she looked about her, however it ended it could not go on; she was halted here, in these Segget years, waiting the sound of unhastening feet, waiting a Something unnamed.[25]

This is a sort of soaring high note which the writer can let fly whenever he wants that sort of thrill. Psychologically it has the marks of what D. W. Harding has called nostalgia in the sense of 'the feeling of distress for no localised, isolated cause, together with a feeling that one's environment is strange, and vaguely wrong and unacceptable.[26] In *Sunset Song* the growing 'wrongness' of the environment has been solidly established, as the Great War saps the countryfolk. There is no equivalent cause from the historical mainstream for the much stronger emotional woundedness of *Cloud Howe*; and although there is such a cause in the final book, *Grey Granite*, in the poverty and police brutality of the industrial heartlands during the Slump, the heroine and all-inclusive consciousness of the trilogy, Chris, stands outside all that. Her son, as we saw in the last section, experiences it to the full, as a militant who joins the hunger marchers. But this is felt to be less from the core than the experience that closes the whole series – Chris's return to her father's old farm which she'd left at the time of her first memories, 'the coarse little place that hadn't had a tenant this many a year'. She is supposed to be about to bring this land back into cultivation:

> And she'd open her eyes and see only the land, enduring, encompassing, the summer hills gurling in summer heat, unceasing the wail of the peesies far off.
> And the folk around helped, were kind in their way, careless of her, she would meet them and see them by this road and gate, they knew little of her, she less of them, she had found the last road she wanted and taken it, concerning none and concerned with none. . . .
> . . . No twilight land anywhere for shade, sun or night the portion of all, her little shelter in Cairndhu a dream of no-life that could not endure. And that was the best deliverance of all, as she saw it now, sitting here quiet – that that Change who ruled the earth and the sky and the waters underneath the earth, Change whose face she'd once feared to see, whose right hand was Death and whose left hand Life, might be stayed by none of the dreams of men, love, hate, compassion, anger or pity, gods or devils or wild crying to the sky. He passed and repassed in the ways of the wind, Deliverer, Destroyer and Friend in one.[27]

If we were to take this seriously as a perspective, then the change of life immediately in view at this point would need to be plausible, distinctly done, and an inevitable development of the objective series that runs from the farm of Chris's formative years, Blawearie, through the small town of her second marriage, Segget, to the city of her middle age, Duncairn. What is that ending but a swoon, on the writer's part, of the emotion that Harding defines as most akin to nostalgia – homesickness? Critics should try to be constructive, and this can mean, where a basic

misdirection in a novel is concerned, suggesting an alternative
ending. We suggest that *A Scots Quair* should have ended with
Chris paying a last visit to the old farm, out of family piety
– finding it gone to bog and bracken – and getting back on
the bus that will return her for good to the smoky city. Anything
else, and especially the ending as it stands, is a heartsore evasion
of the fact that the land could no longer be a base for more
than a small percentage of the people.

Anna Seghers's novel *The Price of a Head* faces up to this
squeezing of the country people with a remorseless, but not heartless, clearsightedness. The book is set in the poor farmland of
the north German plain, just before and after the elections to
the *Reichstag* in November 1932. It was a low ebb for the farmers.
The annual value of the sale of their produce had dropped from
DM. 10 billion in 1928 to DM. 6.5 billion, and the repayment
of the interest on their debts now used up 15 per cent of the
total agrarian income.[28] Seghers gives us the feel of nearly helpless
poverty with an impersonality that is the opposite of Gibbon's
wholehearted identification, and this means that the country people's point of view and their own voice are not nearly so present.
What she does is specify, with unrivalled accuracy, the psycho-
social snares and bonds that beset a people who are struggling
to live off a shrinking productivity. Andreas Bastian, main representative of the poorest class in the village, on coming back
from the war has been given by his brother 'a rather sandy
piece [of land] near the river' with a steading and kitchen garden
inconveniently half an hour's walk from the fields. He does not
mean to marry but is drawn to a widow with two cows, furniture,
and linen. Disastrously, their union is fertile: they have five
children, no sons. To save his wife, sickly with childbearing, the
labour of carrying water, he installs a pump – after his neighbour
has refused to let him connect his pipes to the well that he
has drilled. He falls hopelessly behind on his payments to the
city dealer in machinery because of a glut that brings down the
price of fruit. If one egg cracks and leaks, it means 'a pinch
of salt less, a needle less or no thread', which recalls the funny
story from Donegal, which is not really funny, about the farmer
who had one potato stolen by a crow and chased the bird all
day till he got it back. Bastian's neighbour, Schuechlin, has married
the mentally sub-normal daughter of a middle peasant because

the father-in-law's property will go to any children of the marriage. This enables Schuechlin to make Bastian an offer which he cannot refuse – to shift a fence, take the pump into his farm, and so take over both the water supply and the payments on the pump. But Schuechlin's last action in the novel is to join with other villagers in beating to a pulp a socialist on the run from the police in Leipzig: his fury is due to missing the 500 marks' reward because his shame at having married such a wife for money has led him to lie low on his farm and so miss seeing the poster advertising the wanted man ... So these people turn and twist, driven at every point by toil, debt, and acquisition.

The totally oppressive and chafing force of their economic chains is done partly by the density of the plotting in which every link hinges on some move in the struggle to compete, acquire, hold on, not sink one notch lower in status or real security. This shapes every attitude. Andreas's father was killed by a kick from the first horse he ever owned, and the richest peasants in the village called this mismanagement – because they already owned two horses . . . The other main element is the style, which takes us close in to the experiences and the people, close enough for us to feel their anguish without its misting our vision with their tears. Here is their work and hunger:

Bastian was the last to come from the field; he closed the gate in the fence, scraped the dirt off the hoe, put it in its place in the shed, washed his face and hands under the pump. His head remained bent and his shoulders drawn forward, for his back was strained from too much bending. In front of the door of the house he stooped for a last time. He wanted to pick up two potatoes, which Dora had dropped from her basket. The effort made his head reel. For a moment he stood there, on all fours, his hands on the ground so as not to topple over. An unbearable weight seemed to pin his shoulders to the ground. Close behind him stood Death, hand uplifted, ready to unload another burden on him, and this time it would have meant his end.

He pushed himself up from the ground not a moment too soon, and stood up, groaning. The two potatoes in his left hand, he reached for the handle of the door with his right. The woman was sitting behind the laid table opposite the door. Next to her, on the bench, in order of height, the four children. On her lap she held the fifth child. The immobile faces were veiled by a soft cloud of steam which rose from the bowl on the table. The smell of the steam made his faintness come on again, although this attack was not as acute as the first. His insides contracted sharply with greed. He had only one desire – to throw himself on the full bowl, his head in the food. He stepped up to his chair, the only one at this broad side of the table. His heart beat as his head plunged deeper into the steam. But he pulled himself together, the way he had done a short while ago. He twirled his moustache between thumb and forefinger. The children watched him intently, their nostrils quivering. Their folded hands made little roofs which covered the plates. At last the silence was broken by the first words of the prayer, the bulwark around the steaming bowl.[29]

Each movement is so distinct and so exactly specified that the action is slowed, as though forcing its way through some resistant medium. Each action feels compelled – the one way to satisfy a need that cannot be avoided. There is no fling or lift of freely springing emotion. The people are locked into the most curbed form of themselves because to relate freely might mean a crunch between Andreas and his distant relative Johann, the man on the run. The trouble is whether Andreas should hand over his weakly daughter Dora to his better-off brother, the middle peasant Konrad, and so have one less mouth to feed (they are so short that the innards of their geese are already sold to a dealer in town, and they can only drink a little of their own milk – the bulk must stand in pails at the front door waiting for a buyer).

Dora's face was as grey as the air. There was nothing light in the room now, except her eyes. She was looking at Johann, only at him. Johann got up, bent forward slightly and caught hold of the table with both hands.

The farmer was unable to understand the meaning of this gesture. He looked up at Johann, from his jacket hem to his face. Exertion made Johann hunch his shoulders. His face changed. The man and the woman looked open-mouthed at this new face. They would never have taken in a face like that, never. Johann said in a new voice: 'You're giving her to them, really?' He tilted the table, pressing the edge against the farmer's chest, who now repeated, cramped in as he was between table and wall: 'Its got to be.' And added: 'If it needs must be, better with your flesh and blood.'

Johann did not dare to squeeze the farmer hard against the wall. He dug his nails into the palms of his hands. . . .

. . . Bastian said: 'What're you standing around for? Sit down, Johann. What can I do? Should I let 'em take the roof from over my head?'

Johann said: 'Yes, better than that, yes, yes!'

'That wouldn't help nobody, it wouldn't.'

'Yes, it would, it would.'

At last the farmer said: 'Sit down or get out. I don't know what you're all excited about. That's the way things are around here. And anyhow, what business is it of yours? It ain't your sister, and you ain't my son.'

He knew at once that he had said something terrible. He was startled. He had said Johann was not his son. But Johann had arrived one evening when he himself was on the point of breaking down from exhaustion. And during these past weeks he had often thought that the boy could have been his own son, born in time. He looked up at Johann, who was still standing, and Johann well knew that something terrible had been said:

For a moment it looked as though he was contemplating an appropriate answer. Then the expression on his face changed. He sat down. Bastian looked at his lowered head, his light hair. Only now did he realise the reason for the turmoil in his heart. A feeling of deep surprise overwhelmed him, a tenderness which tormented him, because he dared not lay his hand on this boy's head, dared not make the gesture which would have gone beyond the boundaries of his life.[30]

The novel is deliberately set at the time of the German people's last nominally free act of collective political choice – the election that gave the Nazi Party 43 per cent of the vote. The peasants typically inclined much more to Fascism than the city workers: farmers made up 10.6 per cent of the population but 14 per cent of the Nazi vote, workers 45.9 per cent of the population but only 28.1 per cent of the Nazi vote; and throughout that crucial year the electoral districts which were most pro-Nazi had a majority of the population working in agriculture.[31] Hitler was wooing the peasantry with promises of easier credit and reduced interest rates, in keeping with the policy announced in *Mein Kampf*: 'A solid stock of small and middle peasants has at all times been the best defence against social ills such as we possess today.' As soon as the Nazis seized power, in March 1933, they published a typically muddled edict whose propagandist aim was to stress the 'indissoluble unity of blood and soil' embodied in 'handing down the farmstead from generation to generation' and whose *realpolitik* was to exclude from the law of entail any farmer with a single Jew among the previous four generations in his family.[32]

Reich saw deeply into the link between the work-and-family nexus in peasant living and the coercive or domineering type of social control which Nazism brought to its peak. Hitler's *Mein Programm* for the presidential election in 1932 had proclaimed that in a healthy society men and women were companions in work. Reich points out that this 'does not apply to the body of industrial workers' (precisely this had been destroyed in the industrial revolution) and 'Even to the peasant it applies only formally, for in reality the peasant's wife is the peasant's servant'.[33] We already saw this in action in the Bastian family. Seghers traces the matter back to its personally most deforming results in the habit of the teenage sons having to ask their fathers to *provide* them with a wife. The rich peasant, old Merz, provides his son Paul with Sophie, the sexually terrified and wholly inexperienced daughter of the middle peasant Konrad Bastian. Then old Merz listens, chuckling, outside the door on the wedding night while his son carries out what is really a rape: 'the weak, broken voice of the girl:"Don't! Don't! Don't!" and the soft, happy cursing of his son.'[34] What the novelist evokes the social psychologist diagnoses: 'owing to the strictly patriarchal education ... the [rural] youth are sexually very disturbed or even brutal; sexuality is practised in secret, sexual frigidity is the rule among girls; sexual murder and brutal jealousy, as well as enslavement of the women, are typical occurrences among the peasantry. Hysteria is nowhere so rampant as it is in the country.'[35] This is plain enough in Gibbon too, especially in John Guthrie's savage hatred of his son's and daughter's sexual maturing. What Seghers does with the completeness of the great novelist is to see how her themes, starvation and bondage in that particular place and time, are simultaneously expressed in all the relationships, economic, personal, political.

Germany industrialised early and thoroughly enough for her peasantry to be fully penetrated by politics based on the city. The late and uneven industrialisation in Italy meant that in a region like Silone's Abruzzi, well down the eastern side of the Appenines, modern developments like the paying of rates and taxes and taking part in national politics are not understood – they make sudden inroads, like electric storms or floods, and are resisted, if at all, by spasmodic violence. There are striking overlaps with the social tragedies presented in *A Scots Quair* and *The Price of a Head* but the mode is again quite different. Gibbon imitated the voices of spontaneous gossip and reminiscence. Seghers set up her shots and sequences with the exactitude and lack of authorial intrusion that make great cinema. Silone adapts the anecdotes and legends of a traditional village storyteller. Whole areas of exploitation, racketeering, and shortage are imagined in a single page of stylised prose – as liable to be comic as painful. An agent is sent to the village by the Mussolini government to explain policy and get peasant support. In the stylisation this comes out as each villager being expected to sign a blank sheet, the blankness symbolising their total ignorance of what the government in Rome has in store for them. The peasants of course sign. Their one means of retaliation is to humiliate the agent by crowding in on him with flights of satire, unanswerable questions, seemingly irrelevant stories with a buried sting (like the one about how lice came to the region: Christ was going through the land with a bag on his shoulder and the Pope behind him took out of it whatever the peasants needed. He gave the Marsica a cloud of lice, saying, ' "Take them, my beloved children, and scratch yourselves. Thus in your moments of leisure you will have something to distract your thoughts from sin" '). The great clinching joke (if joke is the word) goes as follows:

'And the hierarchy? What about the hierarchy?' asked the townsman, who was probably a hierarch himself. You see, we didn't yet know what the word meant. The man had to

repeat it over and over again, and explain in different terms.
In the end Michele answered:

'At the head of everything is God, Lord of Heaven.

'After Him comes Prince Torlonia, lord of the earth.

'Then come Prince Torlonia's armed guards.

'Then come Prince Torlonia's armed guards' dogs.

'Then nothing at all. Then nothing at all. Then nothing at
all. Then come the peasants. And that's all.'

'And the authorities, where do they come in?' asked the
man from town, more angrily than ever.

Ponzio Pilato interrupted to explain that the authorities were
divided between the third and fourth categories, according to
the pay. The fourth category (that of the dogs) was a very
large one.

The Hon. Pelino rose to his feet. He was trembling with
rage. He said:

'I promise you you'll hear more of this.' And away he went.[36]

The gist of the novel is how the expropriation of a village
is completed, for the good of one titled landlord and one nameless
businessman called the Contractor, and to the ruin of the peasants,
who are already either poor peasants, who get up at three in
the morning to walk to their parched fields many miles below
their hill village, or else hired labourers, who have to sign on
with an employing farmer each morning at a peasant market.
This ruination is made to turn realistically on the water supply
but the mode is stylised comedy. At the big political rally in
chapter 4, with fast cars flashing through the small-town square
and platoons of youths in black shirts standing by, the job of
the peasant contingent from Fontamara is to stand up every
so often and shout ' "Long live ... so-and-so!" ' The meeting
is to announce the settling of the local land question:

'. . . The important thing is to know how to work the land.
The Fucino to the people who cultivate it. That's Don Circostanza's principle.'

'The minister accepted that principle,' the official replied.
'The Fucino to the people who cultivate it. The Fucino to
the people who have the means to cultivate it, and the means
to have it cultivated. In other words, the Fucino to the people

who have sufficient capital. The Fucino must be freed from
the wretched small tenant-farmers and handed over to the
wealthy farmers. Those without great capital resources have
no right to rent land at the Fucino.'

'What did our representative say?'

'The Hon. Pelino, representing the peasants, said that in
the interests of national production the peasants must be elim-
inated from the distribution of the rentable land of the Fucino.
To achieve this he proposed that the rents of the bigger lessees
be diminished and those of the smaller lessees increased by
twenty per cent. Payment of rent is to be in kind, especially
sugar beet, the price of which will be regulated by Prince Torlonia's administration. Small cultivators who do not grow
beet will pay seven hundred lire per hectare. I may add that
the proposals of your representative were accepted in their
entirety. The peasants who gathered at Avezzano from the
whole Fucino basin demonstrated their satisfaction by the magnificent reception they gave the minister, the prefect, and the
other authorities. Is there anything else you want to know?'

'It's perfectly clear,' we said.

It was perfectly clear.[37]

The means of the expropriation has already been shown in the
great water-supply trick. The blank petition, it turned out, had
then had written onto it a request from the Fontamaresi to
the government ' "in the interests of increased production to divert
the stream from the insufficiently cultivated land belonging to
the Fontamaresi towards the fields belonging to the town, whose
proprietors can devote more capital towards its exploitation"'.
But how is the water to be divided up?

The contractor didn't say anything. He let the other talk.
Don Circostanza found the real solution.

'These women say that half the stream is not sufficient to
irrigate their lands. That is, if I rightly interpret their wishes,
they want more than half. They are right, ten times right.
There's one solution and one solution only. The *podestà* must
be left three-quarters of the water of the stream, and three-
quarters of the water that's left must be preserved for the
people of Fontamara. In other words, they'll have three-quarters

each, that is, a little more than half each. That is the only possible way out. I realize that my proposal inflicts an enormous hardship on the *podestà*, but I appeal to him as a philanthropist and public benefactor, accustomed to give and not to receive. . . .'

Don Ciccone, Don Cuceavascio, Don Tarandella, Don Pomponio, and the captain, having by this time recovered from their fright, surrounded the Contractor and implored him to make this sacrifice on our behalf.

After a little reflection the Thinker joined them, too.

After a lot of persuasion the Contractor gave in.

Somebody brought a piece of paper.

The notary wrote down the terms of the compromise and made the Contractor sign it. The captain of the carabinieri signed it, and Don Circostanza signed it too, as the representative of the people of Fontamara.

After that we all started walking home.

(As a matter of fact not one of us understood what the agreement really amounted to.)

A dam is built with two sluices and the division of the stream begins, in the presence of a hundred *carabinieri* who keep the peasants away from the water-course itself:

It was arranged that we should appoint a committee of elders to witness the division of the water. . . . The other peasants were given permission to gather on the high-road, behind a cordon of carabinieri. . . .

. . . Six carabinieri came up to us and led us to where the other people of Fontamara were standing on the high road, while Don Circostanza shouted to us:

'Keep calm! keep calm! Put your trust in me!'

From behind the cordon of carabinieri we could hardly make out what was happening near the stream. Secretly that did not altogether displease us, because it rid us of all responsibility towards the other inhabitants of Fontamara. It was better that our interests should be protected by an educated man like Don Circostanza.

Raffaele was the first to see the water-level sink. Not one of us had believed that we should be left as much water as we had before, but when we actually saw it sinking we all began to shout and curse at the Contractor and his guests.

'Thieves, thieves, thieves!' we shouted.

Filomena Quaterna, Recchiuta, the daughter of Cannarozzo, Giuditta, Scarpone, Lisabetta Limona, and a number of other women went down on their knees and began the litany of curses:

'May they lose as much blood as they are stealing water from us!

'May they shed as many tears as they are stealing water from us!

'May toads be born in their bellies! May sea serpents be born in their bellies!

'May none of them ever see their wives and children again.

'Jesus, Joseph, St. Anne and Mary,

'Do me this grace for my soul!'

Meanwhile the water-level sank lower still, until we could see the stones, tufts and weeds that lined the bottom.

'*Consummatum est!*' we heard Don Abbacchio say. . . .

Don Circostanza came towards us along the bank of the road and started one of his usual speeches.

'Have you lost confidence in me? That's why things are going badly with you, because you've lost confidence in me. Do you think you will gain anything by shouting and violence?'

Then he turned to the Contractor and said:

'The dissatisfaction of these people is justified. A compromise must be found. I appeal to your sense of humanity, I appeal to you as a friend of the people. The good people of Fontamara deserve to be respected. The commune has borne the expense of digging the new bed for the stream. What is done is done. it is one of the sayings of Christ, *quod factum est factum est* _ '

'Quite right,' interrupted Don Abbacchio.

'I therefore propose that a term be established after which the stream must be returned in its entirety to the people of Fontamara. That should console the people of Fontamara. Their loss is legal, but not eternal! Let someone propose a term.'

But every new proposal was howled down by the whole mass of peasants.

Don Circostanza came forward again.

'Permit me to make another proposal in the name of the good and industrious people of Fontamara. I propose a term of ten lustres. I appeal to the *podestà* in his kindness of heart to accept this great sacrifice!'

Don Tarandella, Don Ciccone, Don Pomponio, Don Cuccavascio and the Thinker all gathered round the Contractor to implore him to make this sacrifice on our behalf.

After a lot of persuasion the Contractor gave in.

A sheet of paper was produced, and the notary wrote out the form of words suggested by Don Circostanza and had it signed by the Contractor and by the Hon. Pelino and the author of the proposal himself as representing the people of Fontamara.

(As a matter of fact, not one of us had any idea how long ten lustres were.)[38]

The thing is absurd, it may be said, Dickensian exaggeration, with the common implication that Dickens turned his social originals into 'caricature' for the sake of the comedy or was carried away by his own powers of invention. Of course Silone's mode is not realistic, but is his stylisation valid? In November 1973 at Lancaster we had a visit from the leader of the Pakistan Workers' and Peasants' Party, Mohammad Aszal Bangash, and listening to his detailed account of the peasants' struggle in the north-west province of Pakistan was like hearing *Fontamara* over again – with the difference that things had moved forward, into effective militant counter-attack against the alliance of feudal landlords, rural capitalists (the merchant–moneylenders who are a great bane of the poorer countries), and the government agencies backing them. The three-quarters trick? The Pakistani hill peasants grow tobacco and sugar, which they sell for milling and re-sale. The receipt they get from the miller or wholesaler is issued *in the name of their landlord*, so if he wants to change the proportion of the income allotted to the cultivators, he has only to wave the paper in front of them. They pay rent; and now that evictions are on the increase, for political as well as economic reasons, the only proof admitted that a man is entitled to the land he holds is a receipt for rent. But *no receipts are given*. Now the Party has organised the peasants to demand receipts, they are being refused, the landlords' bully boys are ambushing known militant peasants, and so far eighty have been killed. But here is the crucial difference from Italy in the Twenties: no peasant has been killed in defence of his *own* land, all have been elsewhere – taking part in drilled and armed struggle to protect the land or safe-conduct of others. Contrast the bad blood in Fontamara: 'Furious quarrels about sharing out the water break out [between the cultivators] every year. In years of drought these quarrels end in stabbing affrays.'[39] Compare the present quarrels over the ownership of an unmade road in the hill village of Mynydd Bach in Monmouthshire. It has lasted seven years. There have been incidents with pitchforks, guns have been fired in the night, three people have been assaulted, one man's cesspit went unemptied for eighteen months because his neighbours would not allow the Council lorry along the road, two dogs have been poisoned, one car damaged nine times, and by the end of 1973 nine of the villagers had applied for shotgun licences.[40]

So every year life confirms the most outrageous catches and extremes that Silone sees as typical of the old-style scrabble for livelihood in the country. The movement of population between town and country is the same in Italy then as in Pakistan now. 90 per cent of workers in Karachi come from peasant villages in the north-west province, people who have become landless and are now earning a wage in town and sending it back to buy land for the family. Compare the rebellious hero of *Fontamara*, Berardo Viola, who had always gloried in being landless because he had no ties but went off and scoured Rome for a job as soon as he wanted to marry. In June 1972 in Karachi skirmishes started in the streets, leading to the occupation of the textile mills in the autumn. Of forty-four workers killed in the summer, forty-three were from the north-western province. Compare the death of Berardo at the hands of Fascist policemen, with the crucial difference that he was on his own and was under torture to give away details of a ramshackle underground movement to mobilise the Fontamaresi, whereas in Karachi the workers of country origin are now organised from a country base, admittedly 1100 miles away, but militant and expanding. Compare Mao Tse-tung's insistence on the possibility of revolution originating in the village[41] or Lenin's slogan of 31 May 1913, 'Backward Europe, Advanced Asia'.

What Silone shows in *Fontamara* is a condition of the country folk that corresponds at every point to Gramsci's analysis in 'The Southern Question':

> The southern peasants are in perpetual ferment, but as a mass they are incapable of giving a unified expression to their aspirations and their needs ... the old type [of educated man] has remained prevalent, providing most of the State personnel and locally, in the small towns and rural centres, carrying out the function of intermediary between the peasant and the administration ... democratic in its peasant face, reactionary when its face is turned towards the big property owner ... [with] a most refined skill in deceiving and breaking the peasant masses.

Earlier Gramsci has quoted a manifesto of the northern city Communists, based in Turin, who in the years just before Mussolini took power were planning to 'give credit to the peasants, institute co-operatives, guarantee personal security and property against plunderers, and carry out public expenditure for development and irrigation'.[42] Of course this was not carried out: the Fascist dictatorship took over, the big estates were left untouched, thousands of peasants left the land in the twenties, and by the thirties they had not even the escape of emigration since it was now forbidden by law. *Fontamara* seems to be set in about 1926, towards the end of the time that Mussolini himself called 'the period of reprisals, devastation, and violence'[43], when the *squadristi*, counterpart of the German S.A. who are unforgettably embodied in Anna Seghers's character Zillich, had been encouraged and equipped to carry out the ferocious raids on rural trouble-spots such as Silone describes in chapter 5. The disunity of peasant resistance is something Silone must show. What he craves on their behalf is effective retaliation but the makings of this were not to be had in the real situation. The Communist underground is personified in the Mystery Man:

> 'For some time an unknown person, called the Mystery Man, has been endangering public safety,' the young man explained. 'The Mystery Man is mentioned in every case before the Special Tribunal. He prints pamphlets and distributes them secretly. Everyone caught carrying illegal papers and documents always

admits having received them from the Mystery Man. First the Mystery Man used to work at a few big factories, then in the city suburbs and the barracks. Then he put in an appearance at the university. One morning he was reported to have been at several places at once, and on the same day he was reported to be on the frontier.'[44]

The Mystery Man is a young man who appears suddenly here and there. By pure chance he runs into Berardo Viola who has come to Rome for a job; the two of them have talks in prison which suddenly open Berardo's eyes to the real nature of the system which holds him down and to the need for class unity. This part of the novel is so implausible, and passes so quickly, that it cannot begin to signify some possible alliance of city and peasant revolutionaries. Here is how literature tests the wisdom and likelihood of a writer's views. That which cannot be brought to the point of a fully dramatised or descriptive rendering is thereby suspect – is more likely than not to signify some deep-seated wishfulness on the part of the artist.

The ending of *Fontamara* moves back into reality and in so doing reaches one of the high-points of modern literature. With a scarcely credible mixing of humour and the most painful tragedy, the Fontamaresi are shown creating on a lithographic stone 'the first peasants' own paper', *Che faré?*, 'What are we to do?' – the great question first asked by Chernyshevsky at the dawn of Russian socialism in the 1860s and again by Lenin in his famous pamphlet of 1902. A germ of the Fontamara paper may lie in the hundreds of collective letters sent by villages to the socialist paper *Avanti!*, in which Silone's own writings first appeared.[45] But he knew that the political and economic enslavement of the countryfolk was more or less total, and the novel ends in massacre, flight, and exile: 'After so much strife and anguish and tears, and wounds and blood, and hatred and despair – what are we to do?'

7. *Thwarted Revolutionaries*

As 1917 receded, the literature of revolution darkened. The vista of society transformed – what Alan Sillitoe calls in 'The Good Women' 'a great space of freedom and change not too far beyond the feet and eyes' – seemed to become clouded and then blocked. Silone's Fontamaresi had undergone their agony of persecution. In his next two novels, *Bread and Wine* and *The Seed Beneath the Snow* (1943), which completed the core of his life's work, the rebel bearer of humanness, Pietro Spina, the Communist on the run, can find fewer and fewer beings to make common cause with. He relates to a gentle deaf-mute, then to a donkey, then to one seed prematurely putting out its root from a little neuk in a snowdrift which he sees as though in cross-section through the wall of the barn where he is hiding. In Anna Seghers's *Revolt of the Fishermen of Santa Barbara* (1930), Hull the roving agitator (a convincing version of Silone's flimsy Mystery Man in *Fontamara*) is at last picked up by the police after failing quite to detonate the fishermen's revolt against their terms of employment. As they take him away in a cart, he craves a last glimpse of the sea, 'but the low buckling waves of the dunes telescoped into each other so softly, quickly and endlessly that his wish was never realised'. The last young fisherman who has tried to prevent the fleet from sailing has to hide in the cliffs. He ventures again into the village, then as the soldiers chase him through the rocks he is shot down 'till he came to rest with his face smashed beyond recognition, yet something of him kept on running, running, running, until at last it flew apart to the four winds in a joy and lightness beyond all description'.[1] As *The Quiet Don* nears its close, Grigory makes his way back home, his beloved woman dead, his peace of mind burnt out. He throws his rifle and pistol into the thawing Don, pours his bullets after them, then crosses the ice to his son who is playing near his home and does not recognise him:

> And now that little thing of which Gregor had dreamed
> during so many sleepless nights had come to pass. He stood
> at the gate of his own home, holding his son by the hands.
> This was all life had left to him, all that for a little longer
> gave him kinship with the earth and with the spacious world
> which lay glittering under the chilly sun.[2]

Serge's *Birth of Our Power* ends with the narrator looking back
at the Barcelona rising of summer 1917 from where he now
is in the 'necropolis' of Leningrad in winter 1919:

> The silence of the houses, the emptiness of the straight avenues
> no longer distressed us. We knew that within all those glacial
> houses, in the depths of their souls, they were burning bushes
> of anger, of fury, of perfidy; that the ground was mined every-
> where under our feet; that people were waiting – unatonable
> vengeances slowly ripening in brains debilitated by famine and
> terror – for the uprising brought on by hunger or the onslaught
> of the Finns, implacable wolf hunters who would massacre
> us like wolves; that the workers' quarters were being slowly
> drained of their living strength by the Army, the supply services,
> the State; that the dregs were rising and overflowing around
> the men of energy and truth: a swarm of adventurers, profiteers,
> speculators; the slow conquest of the factories by those without
> faith or devotion; that there were only enough foodstuffs for
> three days, not enough munitions for more than twenty-four
> hours of combat if the Finnish invasion took place, only enough
> combustibles – some wood cut last week – for five days on
> the Moscow railway . . .
> We had stopped for a moment in the middle of these white
> splendours, in front of the granite-banked Neva, a river of
> ice on which human ants were moving back and forth on
> yellowing paths. Behind us rose the Marble Palace, as dead
> as the Theban tombs, all in stern, sharp outlines, all in flat,
> polished surfaces of a light, dusklike grey. 'Men,' said Gregor,
> 'move across that hard ice never thinking of the deep river
> rolling along beneath. The revolution lives on a layer of ice
> too, and we do not know what dark ocean lies beneath, ready
> to engulf us tomorrow.'[3]

Such sequences – among the most gravely poignant we know of in modern literature – both dramatise and symbolise the literally unbearable stresses which the effort to make revolutions had put upon the activists; the near-impossibility, if you were in the thick of things, of keeping ardour unquenched; and the desire of those harried, maimed, and thwarted revolutionaries to melt back into some natural continuum in which new growth might yet take place.

Near the end of *Comrade Tulayev*, the prosecutor Fleischman is reading through the papers of the executed Old Bolshevik and historian Rublev. He notices a jotting made in response to a despairing comment of Bukharin's at his trial in March 1938. Rublev (and palpably Serge) mixes pessimism and optimism as he writes:

> we bear witness to the fullness of a victory which encroached too far upon the future and asked too much of men. We have not lived on the brink of a dark abyss, as Nicolas Ivanovich said, for he was subject to attacks of nervous depression – we are on the eve of a new cycle of storms and that is what darkens our conscience . . . . We are terribly disquieting because we might soon become terribly powerful again.[4]

It was this asking too much of men that weighed most heavily with the writers from the storm centres at that time. Serge was writing *Comrade Tulayev* as he fled through Marseilles and the Dominican Republic to harbour in Mexico – arriving there in the year, 1940, in which Trotsky had his head smashed in by a Stalinist assassin. Early in 1941, Arthur Koestler, in flight from Hungary-Germany-Spain-France, reached harbour in England – where he spent his first six weeks in Pentonville Prison during the Blitz. He then wrote *Scum of the Earth*, describing his time in what he called the Purgatory of Le Vernet, where the French government were holding thousands of revolutionary refugees (including Anna Seghers's husband) in conditions of destroying hardship. Barrack 32, the Leper Barrack, housed 150 men, the remnants of the International Brigades from Spain, 'once the pride of the European revolutionary movement, the vanguard of the Left'.

Not one of them was allowed to enter the Fatherland of the Proletariat, the country which had acclaimed them in hysterical hero-worship, which had boasted of having abolished unemployment and of having work for all. The gates of Russia were closed, the ears of the Party were deaf and the till of the *Secours Rouge* was empty; but then it had always been said that the Party was not a philanthropic institution.

So that was the end of the Crusade – the Leper Barrack in Le Vernet. Half of the human ruins who lived in it came from Germany and Austria, like Willy Schulz, a fair, blue-eyed, frail, and fanatical little fellow, who was spitting out his lungs in instalments on the straw of No. 32 (men of the Leper Barrack were hardly ever taken to the hospital); and their *curriculum vitae* was more or less on the same lines as his:

1930–3: living on the dole;
1933–5: concentration camp in Germany;
1935–6: unemployment in Paris, but no dole;
1936–9: volunteer in Spain, twice wounded, the second time in the lung;
1939–?: concentration camp in France.

That makes ten years of outcast life, and Willy was twenty-nine. For some it was only five or six years, for others eleven or twelve. Some of the younger ones had never known what work was like; some of the older ones still remembered vaguely the golden times when they were allowed to slave in a factory, workshop, or mine. Some had a wife and children in Germany of whom they had not heard for years; others had left a girl in Paris when they went to Spain, but that too was almost four years ago now. In the beginning there had been letters; later they became rare; gradually all ties with the outside world became thin and frayed, and finally they tore. Communism? Democracy? Fascism? A cigarette end in the gutter was a reality, while political ideas had gradually lost all meaning; but few admitted this. The sectarian hatred between Stalinists, Trotskyists, and Reformists still existed; fractional conspiracies and denunciations still went on – and whispered memories of political controversies which had been settled by a bullet in the back on the battlefields of Spain. Some of these were legends, many of them were true; and the dark silhouette of the Tchekist, the 'Apparatchik,' or G.P.U. agent had replaced the once bright and lively symbols of the struggle for a happier world. . . .

Ten years of constant defeat had reduced them to what they were; and their fate merely exemplified what had happened to all of us, the European Left. They had done nothing but put into practice what we had preached and believed; they had been admired and worshipped, and thrown on the rubbish-heap like a sackful of rotten potatoes, to putrefy.[5]

This family of writers, then, had been through an extraordinary gamut of experience. Their concern with what was happening in the world could not have been more first-hand. They were totally *in history*. They deserve to count as the social conscience of humanity (on this continent) in the age immediately before the present. Thirty years ago Orwell, with his unrivalled sense of what mattered most, already saw that they formed a cluster: 'Silone, Malraux, Salvemini, Borkenau, Victor Serge and Koestler himself . . . are all alike in that they try to write contemporary history, but *unofficial* history, the kind that is ignored in the text-books and lied about in the newspapers.' But their achievement was greater than he credited them with 'that they wrote about totalitarianism from the inside' as no English writer did.[6] For one thing, our writers (with a few exceptions like Orwell himself) just were not there – in Madrid or Berlin or Leningrad. For another thing, Silone, Serge, Malraux and Koestler managed to do far more than be on the spot or see through Fascism or Stalinism. They knew human nature when it was laid bare and tried to the utmost. They felt incomparably fully what it was to be alive at that time, for the reason that the struggle of the hungry, the hounded, the enslaved to remain alive and to free themselves had become theirs by their own choice. Our touchstone for work on this plane is Malraux' novel about the Chinese revolution in 1927, *La Condition Humaine*, now called in English *Man's Estate* (1933).

It may seem odd to treat as a key source a book by an author alien to the society he was presenting, and it is true that most of the Chinese people in *Man's Estate* are nameless – labourers going home from work in the fog, units of armed workers in the thick of a battle – while the main characters are half or wholly foreign: Katow the Russian revolutionary; Kyo, son of a French father and Japanese mother; Hemmelrich, a German small shopkeeper with a Chinese partner and a Chinese wife. The alien presence in China is completed by Ferral, head of one of the main French trading cartels in the Far East, and Clappique, ageing playboy from the nightclubs, a Graham Greene-ish go-between in various undercover deals. The fact is that this national mixture typifies what China had become. Mao termed it a 'semi-colony'. The native peoples were nominally free – no white judges, officials, or army of occupation except in one or two international enclaves. In practice the Chinese had sunk into the role of spectators, at a show in which their fates were acted out and decided for them by foreigners and the few native-born individuals who had become tools in the hands of foreign businessmen and political agents (for example, the Comintern's representatives). The thing is analysed with sardonic clarity by China's master-writer, Lu Hsun, in an essay of May 1929:

However patriotic we are, we probably have to admit that our civilization is rather backward. Everything new has come to us from abroad, and most of us are quite bewildered by new powers. Peking has not yet been reduced to this, but in the International Settlement in Shanghai, for example, you have foreigners in the centre, surrounded by a cordon of inter-preters, detectives, police, 'boys' and so on, who understand their languages and know the rules of foreign concessions. Out-side this cordon are the common people.

When the common people come into contact with foreigners, they never know quite what is happening. If a foreigner says 'Yes,' his interpreter says: 'He told me to box your ears.' If the foreigner says 'No,' this is translated as 'Have the fellow shot.' To avoid such meaningless trouble you need more know-ledge, for then you can break through this cordon.[7]

It was natural, given such a history, that a key masterpiece should have sprung from the experience of a Western radical who knew at first hand the freedom movement in an under-developed country (in fact Vietnam, not China, which Malraux visited for only a few days in 1931). Sartre says in the fifth volume of his *Situations* that in imperial conditions the distinctive features and strains of modern life have been most fully bared, the conflict between haves and have-nots least disguised. The literary record bears this out. In the nineteenth century the master writers scarcely ever situated their work abroad. Foreign life came to notice at most as a kind of *chinoiserie* or its Persian, Indian, and other counterparts. But as 'the net of the world market' exported immiseration and class struggle to every country (the terms and ideas here are from chapter 32 of Marx's *Capital* I), the writers realised, and rapidly, that themes of extraordinary significance were now starting up everywhere and were not inaccessible. Conrad's travels as a seaman showed him the naked miseries of a colony, the Belgian Congo ('An Outpost of Progress', 'Heart of Darkness'), and the sinuous politics of intervention in the Latin-American semi-colonies (*Nostromo*). Since then we have had, in a kind of continuous series, Forster's *A Passage to India*, the Nigerian novels of Joyce Cary, L. H. Myers's Indian trilogy, *The Near and the Far*, novels by Graham Greene set in Mexico, West Africa, Congo, Vietnam, and Haiti, by Malraux in Indo-China and China, by Camus in Algeria. In nearly every case – even in that of Camus at his most philosophical and least lifelike – what stands out is the more or less poisoned, stormy, or otherwise 'impossible' relations between colonised and colonisers. It is not surprising that the most remarkable *ideas* so far on this subject have been those of a Caribbean black man who had helped an African people in their freedom struggle against European colonial masters, the psychiatrist and social psychologist Frantz Fanon. (See *The Wretched of the Earth*, 1965; *Black Skin, White Masks*, 1968; *A Dying Colonialism*, 1970.)

Man's worst inhumanities to man now began to occur in the empires (if Germany under Hitler may be said to have colonised Poland, Austria, Czechoslovakia, France . . .). So did the utmost heroism. This word nowadays sounds old-fashioned, sentimental. But the way Dr Rieux resists the plague in Camus' allegory of the Nazi occupation, *La Peste* (1947), or the inmates of Buchenwald keep alive the child who has been smuggled past the guards in a suitcase in Bruno Apitz's *Naked Among Wolves*, or the revolutionaries fight to their last grenade and bullet in *Man's Estate* – such works show us, in a perfectly unsentimental and graphically precise way, the quality without which we would all be slaves by now: the power of holding firm. We mean the bravery of the British, American, and other soldiers who landed in Normandy on D-Day, the nerve of the French partisans who faced torture, the stamina of the Soviet soldiers at Stalingrad, the self-sacrifice of the suicide cadres in the Vietnamese NLF, or the similar courage of the workers and students who fought the Soviet tanks in the streets of Budapest.

'Heroism' has to be defended because, rightly, we have for so long mistrusted the idea of the 'fearless and irreproachable cavalier'. What gave it its bad name was the attitudinising of a Sidney Carton: '"It is a far, far better thing that I do, than I have ever done"' – pauses, grits teeth, muscle tightens in jaw – '"it is a far, far better rest that I go to, than I have ever known"'. The real end of a modern revolutionary is more likely to be like Katow's in *Man's Estate* – maimed, in darkness, in a foreign country, one amongst a huge crowd of injured men whose collective emotions, voiced in the 'chorus' of their whispers and groans, matter as much as his pain and his selflessness. The difference is between writers who have taken part in the revolutionary effort of their time and writers in a historical impasse with little to go on but a wish for something lofty to look up to:

> This has been the fate of the realist writers after 1848. The lack of action, the mere description of *milieu*, the substitution of the average for the typical, although essential symptoms of the decline of realism, have their origins in real life and it is from there that they crept into literature. As writers grew more and more unable to participate in the life of capitalism as their own sort of life, they grew less and less capable of producing real plots and action. It is no accident that the great writers of this period, who reproduced important features of social evolution more or less correctly, almost without exception wrote novels without plots, while most of the novels of this time which had intricate and colourful plots were full enough of sound and fury, but signified nothing so far as social content was concerned. It is no accident that the few significant characters produced by this literature were almost still-life-like, static portraits of average people, while the figures pretending to above-the-average stature in the literature of this period could not be anything but caricature-like pseudo-heroes, empty phrase-mongers in a grandiloquent and hollow opposition to capitalism or an even hollower hypocritical vindication of it.[8]

To rise to a revolutionary occasion, a writer has to become expert in (among other things) violent actions, because at the

very point of an extreme or drastic situation the crux is not
so much an event in your inner life but *rather* an action where
you need to be able to do the effective thing on the spur of
the moment, not to flinch, to think on your feet, to have so
much primitive and vital momentum in yourself that you can
seize the moment, however hair-raising the odds against you.
That the inner life is not nullified shows in the way Malraux
starts his novel with the psychological dilemma of a man, Chen,
about to kill for the revolution (to steal a gun-runner's papers):

> He knew he was strong really, but for the moment it was
> only a blank realisation, powerless before that mass of white
> muslin which draped down from the ceiling over a body that
> was vaguer than a shadow; from which a foot protruded, the
> foot of a sleeper, angular but still convincingly human flesh
> ... the thought came to him, rose up till it sickened him,
> that he was not the fighter he expected, but one performing
> a sacrifice ... How much resistance did flesh offer? ... To
> kill him was nothing; it was touching him that was impossible.[9]

Chen as a person has been very much driven in on himself,
both by inborn nature and by upbringing, and he ends up as
an assassin who does not care if he destroys himself in the act
of killing an enemy. His estrangement from his fellows shows
acutely even at a time of the closest working together with his
comrades. By the middle of the day which takes up the first
third of the novel (21 March 1927, the day of the armed general
strike in Shanghai), the uprising has reached the point of attacking
the police stations, to be followed by the arsenal and the barracks.
Chen is an ex-student, the men in his section are all workers
from the spinning mills: 'Their course was clear enough; they
were fighting for bread to live on and for recognition as human
beings. As for him ... apart from their sufferings for the common
cause, he was quite unable even to talk to them. But he realised
that the coming hostilities would forge the strongest possible of
bonds between them.' This is palpably wishful: to feel like that
already implies an inability to carry it out. During the fight
for the station which takes up the next fifteen pages, Chen feels
his estrangement more and more, even when he is one of a
human chain on the roof and is trying to throw grenades down-

wards into the windows where the last of the police are holding out. When the other men catch sight of a leading worker – Ma, a typesetter who has spent twelve years founding printers' unions – they greet him happily with shouts and cheers. Chen 'looked at them. The world which they were preparing together involved not only the destruction of the social system of their enemies, but the end of his own life too. What would he do in the factory of the future? Stand and look at them all in their blue overalls?'[10] This passage is a telling forecast of the way in which People's China would have little room for self-conscious intellectuals; in its context it is part of Chen's individual tragedy:

> The man who was clinging on up at the top was beginning to weaken: he took his place. Even there, with his wounded arm encircling the cement and plaster decoration, and his right hand grasping the next man in the human chain, he still had that feeling of isolation. The weight of three men slipping was dragging at his arm, transfixing his chest like an iron bar.[11]

Although Chen is characterised as a complex person throughout this sequence, those inmost feelings of his take up no more than twenty-five lines. The sequence (like the whole novel) is created to show a collective action, resolved upon by 600,000 people and impossible without the pooling of all their drives, their natures, memories, skills, and purposes. 'Kuomintang and Communist workers were cautiously getting into position. They had stopped still when the fall occurred: now they were coming down again. Too many people had been tortured in the suppression of the February rising for there to be any lack of men who would stick at nothing.'[12] That is a group *motive* but what the novel must do (though not exclusively) is to show people in action, people showing the ability to face danger, bear pain, shoot accurately, arrive on time . . . the range of practical functions without which revolutionary politics is so much talk. The perfect art of the police-station sequence lies in the exact showing of things being done. The tactics of the attack are clear, so is the plan and situation of the building; there is no fudging or waving of wands:

Chen knew that the special police had been on the watch for three days, and the men were exhausted by the need for continual alertness. Here there were officers, some fifty policemen, well paid and armed with Mausers, and ten soldiers. . . . The arms would no doubt be in the racks on the ground floor; in the room on the right, the guard-room which led to an officer's room: Chen and two of his men had made their way into it several times during the week. He chose ten men without guns, made them hide revolvers in their blouses, and went forward with them. Once they passed the corner, the sentries had them in full view, but their suspicions had been aroused so often that they were now no longer suspicious. Delegations of workmen had kept coming to interview the officer in charge, usually to bring him offerings of money, a business which required the presence of numerous witnesses as a safeguard.

'Lieutenant Shuei Toun?' Chen said. As eight of his men went in, the last two slipped between the sentries and the wall, as if pushed aside by the rush of people coming in; and the moment the first lot were inside the passage, the sentries felt revolvers pressed against their ribs. They let themselves be disarmed – they were paid better than the other wretches, but not well enough to make them risk their lives. . . . He threw himself in front of the racks, levelling his revolver at the police. If they had shown any resolution, the attack would have failed. Well as he knew the disposition of the place, Chen had not had time to tell each of his men which particular policeman he was to hold up; and one or two of them had a chance to fire. But they all put their hands up. In an instant they were disarmed.[13]

The officers are on the first floor, they resist, the orders of the military committee have been to set fire to any strongpoints that hold out, but as the workers soak the building with petrol they get shot at from outside – by a new rebel detachment out in the town who have failed to reconnoitre, and assume that the station is still held by the police. Chen rushes to show the blue flag of the Kuomintang, is bowled over by blast as the officers start to throw grenades from the first floor, in the meantime the building is set alight, and he has to escape along its front – sheltering himself from grenades from inside, while signalling to the newly-arrived comrades outside not to do anything that might betray his presence. The beautifully sharp focus throughout the sequence can be typified by one detail. As he edges along the wall, 'He realised from the strong smell of burning, and the sudden absence of support behind him (he didn't turn round), that he was passing in front of the ground-floor window. "If I can catch the bomb I'll throw it into the guard-room before it bursts." '14

Because Western intellectuals tend to put ideas first and still often have the aesthete's superciliousness about physical activity – because, in short, of the division between manual and mental labour – they expect novels to work on the plane of the inward and excel at insight, nuance, and the rest. (The goddess of the cult is Virginia Woolf.) Faced with a novel which specialises in the stuff of history (social cause-and-effect, the working of institutions, the interlocking between the movements of groups and crowds), they wish onto it some deep Idea which it is 'really about'. With *Man's Estate* the favourite is *angoisse*, the human anguish at realising the lonely and futile state we live in. Malraux himself has abetted this. In a speech about his previous political novel, *Les Conquérants* (1928), he defined its theme as 'escape from this idea of the absurd by fleeing into the human'. In a letter to an early reader of *Man's Estate* he wrote: 'The framework is not fundamental, of course. The essence of the book is what you call the Pascalian element.'15 To this we say with D. H. Lawrence, 'Never trust the artist. Trust the tale.' *Man's Estate*, in its texture, detail, deep meaning, and upshot, is about an armed uprising by *les damnés de la terre* in order to seize power from their rulers – Chinese employers, generals, police, and politicians and foreign businessmen. It is about this, and this moulds its style, just as Conrad's *Nostromo* is about struggles to form a stable government in an underdeveloped country torn several ways by British mining and railroad interests, American financiers, and national politicians both liberal and reactionary. Because the novels share the theme of power struggle, they also share techniques: the precise time-tabling of the actions; the framing of the scenes to move forwards an historically decisive series of actions rather than personal relationships as such; and the siting of scenes amongst crowds or groups, much more than in the depths of an introspective individual.

Malraux had come to realise the need for collective action, and the meaning it could have for him personally, during his first effective political work. This was his founding and editing of the anti-imperialist newspaper *L'Indochine* which he and a few others (including the original of Chen) ran in Saigon in the middle twenties. At a meal given to say thank you to donors from among the Kuomintang supporters in the Chinese community in Cholon, he 'became aware for the first time', according to his wife Clara, 'that a body of men was not the sum of the individuals that composed it, but a new element that went beyond them'. In the Preface to *Le Temps de Mépris* (1934), his short novel about a prisoner in a Nazi jail, he wrote:

> It is difficult to be a man. But it is not more difficult to become one by enriching one's fellowship with other men than by cultivating one's peculiarities. The former nourishes with at least as much force as the latter that which makes man human, which enables him to surpass himself, to create, invent, or realise himself.[16]

Individualism has been in many ways the core value of Western literature in recent times. Eliot based himself on it when he scorned intimate personal relations – sexual love – because in them we become *most like each other*. Leavis is in a similar position when he writes: 'it is only in individuals that society lives'.[17] This is only a half-truth unless we add that it is only in society that individuals live. The frame of mind is well diagnosed by Christopher Caudwell where he says that the modernist writer 'dreads even the social bond of having instincts common with other men'.[18]

Man's Estate is charged with this realisation. Not one main character other than Chen is 'fleeing into the human'. Kyo's marriage is losing its way but this follows well after his commitment to the revolution, it has not caused it. The extremely powerful external or historical factors that have brought these two men into the revolution are defined concretely in a passage early on:

> Kyo had chosen action, gravely and deliberately, as others choose a military career or the sea; he had left his father [a French academic married to a Japanese], and gone to Canton and Tientsin, to live as the manual labourers and the rickshaw-

coolies lived, and to help organise the unions. Then Chen's uncle was held as a hostage after the fall of Swatow, and executed because he couldn't pay his ransom; and there he was, at the age of twenty-four, with no money and a string of unmarketable diplomas; face to face with China.[19]

In other words Chen is faced with a dilemma which is not metaphysical but typical of the semi-colonies. The unplanned, lopsided, westernised growth of their economies first produces and then finds little use for great numbers of graduates, who therefore become part of the militant vanguard. Kyo's has been an ideological decision, made with a perfectly clear mind. Out of this clarity, even after the atrocious ordeal with the sadistic jailer in the cell, he can utter his motive to Konig, the police officer, when he interrogates him:

'I think that Communism will make dignity possible for those who are fighting with me. In any case, the forces that are opposed to Communism oblige them to have none, unless they happen to possess a wisdom which is as rare in them as in the others – more rare, maybe, by very reason of the fact that they are poor and that their work separates them from their true lives. Why ask me this question, if you're not listening to my answer?'[20]

Of the others, Katow, the Russian, has been utterly strong and devoted in his militancy for a good twenty years, and no quirk or qualm in his character suggests he is using politics as a surrogate for something wanting in himself. (He had been in the Social-Revolutionary Party before going over to the Bolsheviks; and a decisive experience for him had been facing a White-Guard firing squad on the Lithuanian front in the Civil War, when all Communists were being picked out for execution, being left for dead, and then picked up still alive when the Red Army recaptured the village.) The other main character, Hemmelrich, a German immigrant who runs a small, failing shop, has entered mass struggle after undergoing Chinese poverty at first hand. He has bought his Chinese wife, a prostitute, for twelve dollars, to save her from the streets; and he now takes up arms to fight against *the unbearable thing*:

There was more pain in the world than there were stars in the sky, but nothing to equal the pain which he could make that woman endure if he were to abandon her by dying. Like the starving Russian, living almost next door to him, who one day found life as a factory-hand a little more intolerable than he could bear, and committed suicide; and whose wife, mad with anger, had slapped the corpse which was leaving her to her fate; with four children crouching in the corners of the room, and one of them saying: 'Why are you fighting?'[21]

When Hemmelrich strangles and bayonets the Kuomintang soldier at the end of Part 5, the supreme and terrible physical force of the scene flows from its being the revenge of the underdog. In the likes of Hemmelrich, in Silone's Fontamaresi, in Anna Seghers's Johann and Georg, in Steinbeck's Tom Joad, we see not people 'escaping from the absurd' but *les damnés de la terre* retaliating against their oppressors.

Malraux is equally backing away from his own best insights when he slights the historical backbone of his novel as a 'framework' and not 'fundamental'. The extraordinary value of *Man's Estate* comes in large part from its analysis, in thoroughly dramatised and novelistic terms, of a struggle for power between classes. Highly aware people with convinced political ideas are shown relating, often in conflict, as they thrash out together those views of theirs which are going into the making of history. It has long been thought that politics can enter fiction only in undigested chunks, and this has too often been the case: the articulate and committed are unbelievably glib, they make speeches at each other, they are given no detailed behaviour, only large poses, and someone or other is set up by the author as the uncriticised and irreproachable embodiment of the Revolution. There is no trace of these faults in *Man's Estate*. Political people are shown being political with as scrupulous a weighing of each move they must make as in any of the classic dramatisations of personal decision-making (for example, Gwendolen Harleth in the 'Maidens Choosing' section of George Eliot's *Daniel Deronda*).

Two classic sequences show this – sequences in which the writer dares to make his gist explicit and manages it with no loss of dramatic energy. In Part 3 (27 March) Kyo goes up-river for an interview with Vologuin, the Soviet representative of the Comintern in China. Their discussion puts into words the issues on which the lives of many thousands, and China's next twenty years, were then pivotting. Kyo's mission is to put the case against the organised workers giving up their rifles to the Kuomintang and for the constituting of a fully independent Chinese Communist Party, outside the KMT and based on the trade unions. Vologuin meets this with the canny case: to play for time by leaving political leadership with Chiang Kai-shek, leave him with his well equipped army to defeat the right-wing generals, and so move through, 'ultimately', to socialism. The issue of who was right can never now be settled: it is a might-have-been. At the time the Oppositionists in the Soviet Union believed that the Cantonese workers' blockade of Hong Kong, the formation of a socialist republic in south China, and the solidarity of the armed workers in Shanghai could have won through. Serge wrote on 1927:

By this time the bureaucracy has, in actual fact, driven the workers from power in the USSR. Of the dictatorship of the proletariat, only the name remains. In the key positions, revolutionists have been replaced by functionaries. Policies are no longer inspired by the general interests of the Russian and international proletariat, but by the functionaries' wish not to be bothered. Stalin becomes their idol. They fear the victory of the Chinese Revolution even more than they pretend to desire it. They never dare when the hour for daring has struck. Their entire tactics consist in maneuvers to avoid complications. This leads to worse complications, but then it is too late.

We *know* that Chiang Kai-shek is preparing the open betrayal of the unions and his communist allies. We know that he is preparing a coup against the proletariat of Shanghai, which has accomplished one of the finest insurrections in modern history. We are not permitted to speak. And Stalin takes the floor in Moscow before thousands of workers and solemnly assures them that we have nothing to fear from Chiang Kai-shek. 'We shall break him after having made use of him.' This speech had not yet been published when, on the following day, the wires informed us of the event we had predicted: the massacre of the workers of Shanghai (1927). Stalin has the text and the proofs of his unfortunate speech removed from the office of *Pravda*; they will never be seen again.[22]

This was also the view of a Communist on the spot, Mao Tse-tung. According to a Comintern liaison officer who was in touch with him between 1942–5, Mao said: 'Stalin does not and cannot know China. And yet he presumes to judge everything. All his so-called theories on our revolution are the blabberings of a fool. And in the Comintern, too, they blabber in the same way.'[23] In a conversation with Edgar Snow early in the thirties, Mao showed how considered and qualified his judgement was of the policy imposed by the Comintern in 1927. For the débâcle he blamed foremost the CP leader, Ch'en Tu-hsiu: 'Ch'en was really frightened of the workers and especially of the armed peasants. Confronted at last with the reality of armed insurrection he completely lost his senses.' The next most responsible, in Mao's view, was Borodin, the chief Soviet political adviser and a member of the Cabinet of the Communist republic in Kwangtung-Kwangsi. 'Mao explained that Borodin had completely reversed his position, favouring a radical land redistribution in 1926, but strongly opposing it in 1927, without any logical support for his vacillations. "Borodin stood just a little to the right of Ch'en Tu'hsiu," Mao said, "and was ready to do everything to please the bourgeoisie, even to the disarming of the workers, which he finally ordered." ' Mao's was no ultra-revolutionary position, he did not believe that a rising was right in any and every situation. For example, he did 'not think that the counter-revolution would have been defeated in 1927 ... even if the Communist Party had carried out a more aggressive policy, and created Communist armies from the workers and peasants before the split with the Kuomintang.' Yet he himself favoured that policy, because 'the Soviets could have got an immense start in the South, and a base in which, afterwards, they would never have been destroyed'.[24]

Kyo and Vologuin debate this crux with a thoroughness, and a parity between their opposing viewpoints, which brings home to us the momentousness of history in the making. Nothing is perfectly certain for the protagonists. Neither can be right yet both are cogent. No possible path is free of dire risks.

> 'At the moment a genuinely Communist programme would immediately bring all the generals into line against us: two hundred thousand men against twenty thousand. That is why you must come to an agreement with Chiang Kai Shek in Shanghai. If it is quite impossible, then give up the rifles.'

'On that basis, it was a mistake ever to attempt the October revolution: what were the numbers of the Bolsheviks?'

'By making "peace" our watchword, we got the support of the masses.'

'There are other watchwords.'

'They are premature. What are they, pray?'

'Immediate and total suppression of farm rents and interest-bearing loans. The agrarian revolution without any syndicates, and without any qualifications.'

The six days which he had spent making his way up the river had confirmed Kyo's opinion: in those mud towns which had existed at the river junctions from time immemorial, the poor were as likely to throw in their lot with the peasants as with the city workers.

'The peasant always waits for a lead,' said Vologuin. 'Whether it is the worker or the bourgeoisie, he waits for a lead.'

'No. A peasant movement only *lasts* when it attaches itself to the town; unaided, a peasant rising becomes a mere *jacquerie* – that is clear. But there's no question of separating the peasants from the proletariat: the abolition of loans is a battle-cry, and the only one which might make them fight.'

'In fact, peasant ownership of the land,' said Vologuin.

'More definite than that; there are many very poor peasants who own their land, but who are sweated by money-lenders. It is well known. But at Shanghai we must start the Trades Union guards training as quickly as possible. And not let them disarm under any pretext. Show them off as an argument when it comes to dealing with Chiang Kai Shek.'

'Directly that plan becomes known, we shall be annihilated'.

'So we will anyway, in that case. . . .'[25]

From this point the action trends remorselessly into débâcle. What saves it from anything in the way of overdone heroics is the sinew of clear explanation which runs through to the end. Although the characters are very interesting morally and psycho-logically, the historical forces involved are more important. You could say that social factors – monopoly, foreign investment, nationalism – virtually become protagonists. This comes out in the one scene set in the metropolitan country, France, where the main action ends. In Paris, three months after the débâcle, there is a conference between VIPs of the French political and banking world and Ferral, whom we have got to know intimately as a personification of French colonialism: intensely vain about his own style and mastery, scornful of the acquisitive Chinese with whom he deals, sexually unscrupulous. Now the Consortium he manages has to plead for credit to tide it over the slackening of trade and failure of business confidence that have resulted from the upheavals in Shanghai. Again it is a thing many novelists have tried, to show us how important people carry on their business, but in which few have succeeded (Disraeli is a rare case in English). The bankers and the Minister are not named by the novelist, all speak the same heavy professional style, all have the same wish to do the statesmanlike thing and help preserve a major French company from going bankrupt – without risking their own investors' money:

'. . . Which of us could claim that the depositors he represents would welcome the idea of a loan for the purpose of keeping a tottering concern on its feet? We know very well, sir, what they think – and are not alone in thinking. They are of the opinion that the stock market ought to be put on a sounder basis and all unpracticable enterprises abandoned; that to bolster them up artificially is to do a good turn to no one. What is the use of free competition, the keystone of all French trade, if unsound businesses are sustained automatically?'

('My good sir,' Ferral thought, 'only last month your firm asked the State for a thirty-two-per-cent increase on tariffs – presumably for the benefit of free competition.')

'. . . Am I not right? Our business is the lending of money against security, as our friend here has so rightly pointed out. The security offered to us by M. Ferral . . . why, you have heard M. Ferral himself on that subject. Does the State intend to take the place of M. Ferral in this matter and provide us with such securities as would justify us in advancing the Consortium the sum it needs? In a word, is the State offering no compensation and does it appeal to our devotion to its interests or are we being asked – by the State, not by M. Ferral – to facilitate a Treasury transaction, as a long-term investment? If the first of these alternatives is correct, let me say that we are ready to do our duty by the State, though,

of course, our share-holders, would have to be considered:
if the second, what guarantees are we offered?'

('There's symbolism for you,' thought Ferral. 'If we weren't
so busy play-acting, the Minister would reply: "I am charmed
by your so humorous use of the word 'devotion': By far the
greater part of your profits derives from your dealings with
the State. You live off commissions, which are the stock-in-trade
of your house, not by hard work or any trade-efficiency. The
State has this year paid you, in one way and another, a hundred
millions; it is taking back twenty; be duly grateful and clear
out." But there's no danger of that happening.')

The Minister drew a box of marshmallows from a drawer
in his desk and handed it round. They all took one, except
Ferral. He knew by now what the Banks wanted: they were
ready to lend the money, since it was going to be impossible
to leave this room without, to some extent, letting the Minister
have his way, but they would part with as little as possible.[26]

One of Ferral's main arguments has been that '"the present
revolutionary state of affairs in China cannot last forever"' –
presumably the novelist is ironically implying the opposite view
between the lines. By the end of the debate, however, the loans
offered by each capitalist have been so small that the Consortium
(a concern as big as Standard Oil or Mitsubishi) has been nominally
saved but actually crippled. The Minister calls on the only representative of a lending bank present for in effect a summing up.
His moustache makes 'a straight line, parallel to his pince-nez;
a bald dome, a look of utter weariness.' His first and last words
are cautious, grudging, negative; if the Consortium goes under,
'"some other company will be formed"' and anyway a share
in building railways is guaranteed to France by treaty. But Ferral
has already claimed that '"France *is* the Consortium"' and Malraux has him spell this out in his bitter peroration, in which
he characteristically prides himself on his lucidity even as he
words his own business obituary:

'And this new company,' Ferral observed, 'instead of indus-
trializing Indo-China, will pay dividends. But as it won't have
done anything for Chang Kai Shek it will find itself in exactly
the position you would find yourselves in here, if you had

never been of service to our Government: and the contracts will fall into the hands of any American or British firm sheltering behind a French name – that's quite obvious. Then of course you'll be lending them the money you won't lend me. We formed the Consortium because the French banks in Asia were so set on a policy of guarantees that they ended up by lending money to the British so as not to lend it to the Chinese.[27]

This lengthy sequence (5000 words of economic debate) holds our interest in its own right, partly because its dramatic edge is given extra sharpness by its place at the end of a series of actions, each one of which has had momentous results for thousands, partly because (as we said before) there is an invisible protagonist at least as interesting as the characters: in this case, monopoly capitalism. It is a fine case of what Brecht had in mind when he wrote that *knowledge* is necessary if writers are to show the 'great passions or great events' which 'influence the fate of nations'.

And yet there are writers who find business and politics nothing like so passionately interesting as the individual's lust for power ... They are scarcely likely to learn enough by going round and keeping their eyes open, though even then it is more than they would get by just rolling their eyes in an exalted frenzy. The foundation of a paper like the *Völkische Beobachter* or a business like Standard Oil is a pretty complicated affair, and such things cannot be conveyed just like that.[28]

From the reader's point of view, *Man's Estate* is useful, as well as moving, if he wants an explanation, and a particularly memorable and clear one, of how finance capital underpins international politics. It was in this spirit that Malraux planned a novel 'about oil' and wanted to visit the Soviet oilfield at Baku – the plan was only dropped because of the new and urgent need, in 1934, to write a book (*Days of Contempt*) that would open the eyes of the world to the régime of torture and unfreedom newly set up by the Nazis.[29]

In the works of Serge and Malraux, and in those that Brecht was about to write, such as *The Life of Galileo* (1937–9), socialist literature comes of age. It can now analyse major forces in society, for example science, business, and policing, with the kind of depth and eye for public behaviour that Shakespeare had brought to bear on feudal institutions such as kingship and warrior prowess. The socialist writers understood their world to the core and they were chastened, though not defeated, by what they saw. In a kind of epilogue to *Man's Estate*, Kyo's wife May gets news of Hemmelrich. He has taken refuge in Japan and found work as a fitter at a power station: 'his words to me were: "Before, I began to live when I left the works; now I start to live when I go there in the morning. It's the first time in my life that I work with knowledge of why I am working – not merely while waiting patiently for death . . ."'[30] But the very end of the novel is near to heartbreak. May's father-in-law Gisors takes her face between his hands and kisses her. 'Kyo had kissed her like that on their last day together, just like that. And never since then had a hand caressed her face. "I hardly ever weep now, any more," she said, with bitter pride.'[31] It is the same controlled pain at epochal suffering that we feel again and again in these writers – in the part of Serge's *Memoirs* that we quoted at the start or in Brecht's classic summation of the Thirties, 'To the Successors':

You, who will rise up out of the flood
In which we have gone under,
Think
When you talk about our weaknesses
Of the dark age, too,
Which you have escaped.

Still, we went, changing our country more often
   than our shoes
Through the war of the classes, despairing
When there was only injustice and no revolt.

Nevertheless we know:
Hatred even of degradation
Distorts the features.
Anger even against injustice
Makes the voice harsh. Oh, we
Who wanted to make the ground ready for friendliness
Could not be friendly ourselves.

But you, when things have got so far
That man is a help to man,
Think of us
With understanding.[32]

8. The Literature of Unfreedom

Among the most dynamic passages in Upton Sinclair's *The Jungle* is the portrayal of a prison in Chicago. The writer's barely controlled rage against injustice and his unwavering political analysis fuse in a concentrated piece of denunciation:

> There were hardened criminals and innocent men too poor to give bail; old men, and boys literally not yet in their teens. They were the drainage of the great festering ulcer of society; they were hideous to look upon, sickening to talk to. All life had turned to rottenness and stench in them – love was a beastliness, joy was a snare, and God was an imprecation. They strolled here and there about the courtyard, and Jurgis listened to them. He was ignorant and they were wise; they had been everywhere and tried everything. They could tell the whole hateful story of it, set forth the inner soul of a city in which justice and honour, women's bodies and men's souls, were for sale in the market place, and human beings writhed and fought and fell upon each other like wolves in a pit; in which lusts were raging fires, and men were fuel, and humanity was festering and stewing and wallowing in its own corruption. Into this wild-beast tangle these men had been born without their consent, they had taken part in it because they could not help it; that they were in gaol was no disgrace to them, for the game had never been fair, the dice were loaded. They were swindlers and thieves of pennies and dimes, and they had been trapped and put out of the way by the swindlers and thieves of millions of dollars.[1]

At the turn of the century, before Hitler, Mussolini, Stalin, Franco, Batista, Amin, Thieu . . . had made imprisonment in hellish conditions one of the dominating images of our times, such a sequence may have seemed excessive (and we would still want the eyes Sinclair turned on such conditions to have been more focussed and less bloodshot). Two generations ago, prisons could still be seen as a regrettable but necessary step that society took in its own defence. Since 1929, however, the year in which it was no longer possible to ignore the seismic faults and subsidings in the structure of capitalism, the best writing has focussed more and more on the facts of human unfreedom. One great piece of literature after another has had to deal in some degree with that characteristic political phenomenon of industrial society in trouble: the oppression of the individual by the State.

Imprisonment is among the most extreme of the situations in which the best modern writers have found themselves: for example, Sartre, Serge, Solzhenitsyn, Babel, Mandelstam, Koestler, Malraux, Elio Vittorini, and Brendan Behan; and Brecht, Silone, Anna Seghers, and Thomas Mann escaped it only by flight. The same is true of thinkers: for example, Reich, Gramsci, and Bruno Bettelheim; and Freud escaped it only by flight. There is now a very large body of writing concerned either directly or indirectly with the experience and its meaning, most of it written since the thirties. It is in all the forms – fiction, plays, poems, songs, and memoir – and it comes from very different lives in many countries; but there is enough overlap in the nature of the experience and in the perspectives taken of it to justify treating it as a new school of writing.

The literature of unfreedom ranges across the gamut from the most lifelike – unvarnished memoir (for example, Anatoly Marchenko's *My Testimony* (1969), a marvellously shrewd and precise account of life in Soviet prisons and prison camps from 1958–66) – to the most 'metaphorical'. Kafka's 'In the Penal Settlement' (1919) was one of the first fictions to generalise from the social facts of bondage and torture to modern human life at large. Throughout his work he came back to this theme and to the related institutions of the modern State – the courts, the political police, the dehumanising corporations and bureaucracies. In 'In the Penal Settlement', the self-destruction of the state-machine yields a grim, joyless liberation:

The condemned man especially seemed struck with the notion that a great change of fortune was impending. What had hap-

pened to him was now going to happen to the officer. Perhaps
even to the very end. Apparently the foreign explorer had given
the order for it. So this was revenge. Although he himself
had not suffered to the end, he was to be revenged to the
end. A broad, silent grin now appeared on his face and stayed
there all the rest of the time.[2]

When this story first came out in English in the *Partisan Review*,
people at once sensed that its power lay in the tense ambiguity
of what it signified. The content was akin to the raw slices of
fact which had begun to come from Germany, Russia, and elsewhere, but the uncanny detachment of Kafka's manner, which
cleansed the horrors in the tale of any trace of sado-masochism,
also detached the piece from any particular history, and left it
to stand as an ominous possibility which might become real anywhere at any time. The same is true of much pre-totalitarian
literature of unfreedom, from Aeschylus's *Prometheus Bound* to
Dostoevsky's Siberian writings. Prometheus on his rock or the
man in the iron mask came to symbolise any society felt to
be in chains. As freedom movements became more consciously
revolutionary, writers about unfreedom pointed ever more directly
at the agents of tyranny, as Shelley does in *Prometheus Unbound*
(1820) and *The Triumph of Life* (1822), where he names kings,
priests, judges, lawyers, jailers. In most recent times, the writer
has usually started from a socially specific subject and any wider
applications are for the reader to make.

Among the first imaginative uses of modern imprisonment was
Men in Prison (1930) by Serge. He drew directly on his own
time in jail on a charge of complicity in Anarchist violence in
France before and during the Great War. Part of his modernity
is his perception that prison organisation parallels or flows from
the intensive controlling of people in factories: he remarks ironically that the new prisons built on a radial plan are the one
architectural form originated by capitalism.[3] There are also nodal
prison sequences in his novel of the Purges, *Comrade Tulayev*,
and in his *Memoirs of a Revolutionary*, which are one of the
indispensable modern testimonies. *Men in Prison* was soon followed by Malraux' *Man's Estate*. The long prison sequence near
the end so brings to the mind's ear the muttered remarks and
groans of hundreds of the maimed and confined that it broadens

out into a kind of archetype of all human bondage. James Agee's notes for a film treatment of the sequence, especially its sounds, wonderfully capture this symbolic power. Malraux remarked that Agee had brought out more in the scene than he himself had realised was in it.[4]

In 1938 Koestler published *Spanish Testament*, one of the first accounts of life in a Fascist prison (Malraux had drawn on the memories of refugees to write *Days of Contempt*), and in 1940 he fused this with his experience of how Stalinism was deforming Communism to make *Darkness at Noon*, a bleak, analytic novel of the Purges. From its opening sentence, 'The cell door slammed behind Rubashov,' the sense of claustrophobia is crushing and the details of confinement palpably first hand. The book is misleading only in two respects. First, as recent evidence from Marchenko, Evgenya Ginzburg, and others has shown, Soviet prisons were even more brutal and dehumanising than Koestler imagined; and secondly, the Old Bolsheviks yielded less to philosophical suasion (which Koestler concentrates on) and more to sheer torture and threats to their families.

In England literary treatment of unfreedom has been, on the whole, limited to occasional documentary novels or memoirs, but during the New Wave of the late Fifties and early Sixties a new-found power of telling a hard life as it was issued in a cluster of works that included Behan's *Borstal Boy* and his play *The Quare Fellow*, Sillitoe's story 'The Loneliness of the Long-distance Runner', and Tony Parker's many transcripts of talks with prisoners, for example, Robert Allerton's 'autobiography' *The Courage of his Convictions*. For obvious reasons the continental material dwarfs the British. Most of the revelations about the Soviet Union have come out in the years following Khrushchev's speech to the Twentieth Congress of the CPSU, although there were important forerunners such as Alex Weissberg's massive and detailed *Conspiracy of Silence* (1952). The flow of material from Hitler's Germany began in the 1940s, although again there were forerunners: Gollancz published *The Yellow Spot: The Extermination of the Jews*, as early as 1936.

The earliest important imaginative treatment of the Nazi concentration camps was Anna Seghers's *The Seventh Cross*. It reaches out of the camps to follow the fugitives as trace elements in German society – each chance turning-up of a fugitive, for example in a doctor's surgery, forces on the law-abiding citizens a cruel dilemma to which most are not equal. The moral analysis of terrorism and the succinct but frightening images of its brutishness have lost none of the power they must have had when the terror system was still rampant, although the 'death camps' have by now been treated in countless sensational novels, films, pornographic books, and even an American TV comedy series. Camp after camp has been dealt with in agonising detail – Mauthausen, Treblinka, Belsen, Buchenwald – and there are also the exceptional works which deal in a whole or cohering way with the survival of personality, and even group solidarity, against the worst odds: Primo Levi's *Survival in Auschwitz* (1958) and *The Truce* (1963), Bruno Bettelheim's *The Informed Heart*, Apitz's *Naked Among Wolves*.

In France, partly because of the Occupation, unfreedom has given rise to especially potent work. We discuss Camus' deep fable of oppression, *La Peste*, in the final chapter. Sartre has returned to the theme and the facts almost compulsively. Even before the war he had understood, in his story 'The Wall', how the enforced stillness and introversion of a prisoner bears cruelly on his conscience and on his faith in his own nature. The war moulded the form as well as the experience of unfreedom: Simone de Beauvoir points out that to write for a legal newspaper, journal, or theatre was an act of collaboration, abhorrent to someone of good faith, and Sartre found himself writing a play that would have as few characters as possible and just one set: 'He at once thought of a situation *in camera* as it were: a group of people shut up in a cellar during a lengthy bombardment. Then he had the inspired notion of placing his characters in Hell, for all eternity.' Hence *Huis Clos* – *No Exit*, or *In Camera* as it is usually called in English.[5] The second part of his *Iron in the Soul* is the most memorable work we know about prisoners of war. The play *Men Without Shadows* shows among other things how people weaken, begin to dislike themselves and others, under threat of torture (Arthur Miller has dealt with this very recently in *Incident at Vichy*). And *The Condemned of Altona* (1960) explores the way unfree Nazism imprisoned the imprisoners: again Arthur Miller has dealt with this, in the passage in *After the Fall* about how workmen – wage-slaves – *do not refuse* to lay the concrete for the slave-camps.

The single largest body of work in this genre is Russian, since the USSR has had the greatest number of unfree people over the longest period of time. Estimates of the labour-camp population vary greatly and can never be accurate, since it is an obvious part of unfreedom to rewrite or wipe out its own history. Immediately after Stalin's death and during the Khrushchev liberalisation, there was a flow of information and a trickle of very fine literary works but the information was turned off again from the middle sixties onwards. A few fairly certain figures must stand for the whole. The 'archipelago' of forced-labour camps grew very fast: 30,000 in 1928, 600,000 by 1930, two million by 1932, six million by 1937. This compares with 32,000 people in forced-labour camps during Tsarist times and 183,949 in Tsarist prisons of all kinds – according to figures from Vyshinsky, the chief legal agent of Stalin's Purges.[6] Just after the collectivisation of the farms in the early thirties, seven-tenths of the five million in the camps were peasants. By the end of the thirties, one-eighth of the eight million were Communists. By then the mortality rate in the camps was 20 per cent. Nearly all the people imprisoned in 1936 were dead by 1940.[7]

There is no way of making real to oneself the colossal swarm of agony that such figures represent, but the best works available do at least give us many unforgettable sights of one of the most sustained and extreme of situations in the human record. Nadezhda Mandelstam's *Hope Against Hope* is especially valuable because her strong, clear reasoning powers and unforgiving memory enabled her to analyse the unfreedom system into its parts – the seizing and destroying of papers, the use (or uselessness) of personal influence, and so on – rather than simply to narrate what happened to her and her husband. But narrative can be as valuable, if a novelist's powers of observation flow into it, and Evgenya S. Ginzburg's *Into the Whirlwind* (1967) is at least as successful novelistically as *The First Circle*. Serge's fiction, memoirs, and histories (including *Destiny of a Revolution*, 1937) are all cut from the same cloth: his history is passionate, his fiction is socially exact. The three books of Solzhenitsyn's *Gulag Archipelago* (published in 1974–1978, written well before that) will stand permanently among the ordeals of realisation that we have to go through if we are to take the measure of what people have done to people in our time, although his invaluable facts are blurred from time to time by the nearly hysterical sarcasm of his obsessional polemics against Marxism. In our view it is necessary to complement those three books by getting similar and other data through minds with the deeply humane rationality of Zhores or Roy Medvedev.

Finally, there are a few lyrics that reach us like messages wrapped round stones thrown from the other side. Anna Akhmatova, by reputation the best Russian poet from the twenties onwards, was expelled from the Writers' Union in 1946 and then became its president at the height of the Khrushchev period in 1964. Her son was arrested in 1934 on vague charges and spent the next twenty-two years imprisoned except for the war years when they put him into the army. For seventeen months Akhmatova spent most of her days in the prison queues in Leningrad, waiting to find what had happened to her son, to send him letters and parcels – all to no avail:

Then a woman with lips blue with cold who was standing
behind me, and of course had never heard of my name,
came out of the numbness which affected us all and whispered
in my ear – (we all spoke in whispers there):
'Can you describe this?'
I said, 'I can.'
Then something resembling a smile slipped over what once
had been her face.

Akhmatova's 'description' was 'Requiem' (1935–40), a sequence of lyrics written out of so helpless a suffering that it feels to have nearly paralysed utterance:

No, this is not me – someone else suffers.
I couldn't stand this: let black drapes
cover what happened,
and let them take away the street lights . . .
    Night.

For seventeen months I have been screaming,
calling you home.
I flung myself at the executioner's feet.
You are my son and my terror.

Everything is confused for ever,
and I can no longer tell
beast from man,
and how long I must wait for execution.
Only the dusty flowers,
the clank of censers, and tracks
leading from somewhere to nowhere.
An enormous star
looks me straight in the eye
and threatens swift destruction.

Today I have much work to do:
I must finally kill my memory,
I must, so my soul can turn to stone,
I must learn to live again . . .

[madness] will not allow me to take
anything away with me
(however I beseech it,
however I pester it with prayer):

not the terrible eyes of my son,
the rock-like suffering,
not the day when the storm came,
not the prison visiting hour . . .

. . . even in blessed death I am terrified
that I will forget the thundering of the Black Marias,

forget how the hateful door slammed,
how an old woman howled like a wounded beast.

And let the melting snow stream
like tears from my motionless, bronze eyelids,

let the prison dove call in the distance
and the boats go quietly on the Neva.[8]

'Requiem' was never published in Akhmatova's own country,
but at Khrushchev's zenith Tvardovsky's great prestige as editor
of *Novy Mir* and author of the country's most popular long
poems (often read in public and broadcast on the radio) enabled
him to publish in an official paper some work which has that

same freezing quality of making a few sparse lines embody a
world of duress:

> There – row on row, according to years,
> Kolyma, Magadan,
> Vorkuta and Narym
> Marched in invisible columns.
>
> The region of eternal frost
> Wrote men off into eternity,
> Moved them from the category of 'living'
> To that of 'dead' (little difference between them) –
>
> Behind that barbed wire,
> White and grizzled –
> With that Special Article of the law code
> Clipped to their case files.
>
> Who and what for and by whose will –
> Figure it out, History.[9]

Unfreedom and its literature are not only the product of totali-
tarian societies. In countries like Britain, America, and France,
imprisonment is a fact of life for hundreds of thousands of people,
an increasing proportion of the population, housed in jails meant
for much smaller numbers. Moreover, although the category of
'political prisoner' does not exist in the West, this is a semantic
quibble. Are the Irish internment camps political prisons or not?
Was Frank Stagg of the IRA, who starved himself to death
in a British prison, a political prisoner or not? In West Germany,
where left-wing parties are often banned, and teachers who are
Communists have to hide the fact or else ruin their careers, were
the Bader-Meinhof 'gang' tried for political activities or not?
Angela Davis, the American philsophy teacher who was legally
persecuted for her Communism, argues these and kindred points
in *If They Come in the Morning* (1971). She shows through repeated
examples – the judicial murder of the IWW organiser Joe Hill,
the Sacco and Vanzetti case, Martin Luther King's arrests, the
legal harassment of the Black Panthers – that in the West 'the
political prisoner inevitably stands trial for a specific criminal
offence, not for a political act. Often the so-called crime does
not even have a nominal existence.'

The offence of the political prisoner is his political boldness, his persistent challenging – legally or extra-legally – of fundamental social wrongs fostered and reinforced by the State. He has opposed unjust laws and exploitative, racialist social conditions in general, with the ultimate aim of transforming these laws and this society into an order harmonious with the material and spiritual needs and interests of the vast majority of its members.[10]

There is a further, more complex point. Crimes against property, such as theft, if they are analysed in depth have a political dimension, though it may well not be uppermost in the mind of the offender. This dimension comes from the fact that private property is an historically determined system of ownership resting ultimately on the controlling and enforcing institutions of the State. Most prisoners in the West are working class, and in the United States mostly black. The remarks of Judge Webster Thayer, when he sentenced Bartolomeo Vanzetti to fifteen years in prison for attempted robbery, apply to most offenders against private property: 'This man, although he may not have actually committed the crime attributed to him, is nevertheless morally culpable, because he is the enemy [as an Anarchist] of our existing institutions.' The most sacred of 'our existing institutions' is private property – by which we mean, not a woman's purse or a man's car, but the blocks of houses or offices, the tracts of land or seabed, the seams of copper and stands of timber owned by capitalist companies.

It is in large part to deter people from rising against such a system of ownership that conditions of appalling cruelty exist in Western prisons. Consider the following report from an American newspaper, and note that the victim belongs to one of the most politically oppressed groups in the United States:

Eugene Austin is a 51-year-old Paiute Indian who spent the last 33 years in the Nevada State Prison. He was recently released on parole and his story was told in the NBC Nightly News.

In 1941 Austin was given a life sentence – he was 18 at the time – for murder. He had allegedly gone on a shooting spree one night when he'd been drinking and one of the shots killed a white woman.

The prison records say that his first seven years in the penitentiary were uneventful, but in 1948 he escaped for two days before being recaptured. A few weeks later he tried to escape again, but failed. He was then branded a troublemaker and was transferred from the prison's 'maximum security' wing to solitary confinement. For the next 14 years he was kept in a 7-foot by 7-foot cell called 'the ice-box'. According to the NBC news account:

'When Gene Austin was stored here, it was a dungeon. He was stripped naked and forced to sleep on a steel cot. Once a week, guards would hose him and the cell down together ... He was taken out of the "ice-box" only once – in 1953.'

Why were they letting him out? For exercise? Had the warden gotten a twinge of conscience? Not quite:

'They took him to a hospital in Reno where doctors performed a lobotomy. They destroyed about one-fifth of his brain . . . After the operation he was returned to the "ice-box", where he spent the next 11 years – most of it in total darkness. In 1964, they let him out – and discovered that sometime during his years of darkness in the "ice-box" Eugene Austin had gone blind.'

His blindness, prison officials claim, was caused by his beating his head on the walls and floor of the 'ice-box', something he began doing after the lobotomy. He still has a neurological tic that makes his head jerk to the side periodically.

So now, 51 years old, blind, lobotomised, Eugene Austin is no longer considered a threat to the established order and has been released. What's left of him now resides in a convalescent hospital in Sacramento, California.[11]

To this we need only add that Eugene Austin's offence, if he committed it, was caused socially by the trigger-happy tendency in American life and that this is caused by property-owning white America's fear of the working-class and coloured have-nots.

In that case the naked cruelty of the 'ice-box' was supplemented by the disguised cruelty of using psychiatric surgery like lobotomy on a 'deviant'. Although lobotomy and leucotomy became discredited and were dropped, they have now been replaced by an exactly equivalent operation on violent people: their skulls are cut open, the cerebral cortex retracted, and then this part of the brain – which could be called the centre of our humanness – is irradiated by various means. In 1975 in the United States a scandal got up when it became known that poorly-off prisoners had been tempted with cash and privileges to undergo, as guinea-pigs, these and other operations that change personality. This is an ultimately political type of bondage or unfreedom. A directly political kind is typified by the use of committal to mental hospitals, in America and Russia, of people who speak out against The System. Military critics of the Vietnam War were sent home to the States for psychotherapy, on pain of losing their careers, and in the Soviet Union intelligent and candid dissenting Communists such as Zhores Medvedev have been put into mental hospitals, which thereby become, not places for healing people, but prisons.[12] This type of extreme situation, which fuses physical bondage with deliberate subversion of a person's own self, so typifies modern unfreedom that it has given rise to a classic, Ken Kesey's *One Flew Over the Cuckoo's Nest* (1961), as well as to the recent intensive debates led by R. D. Laing, David Cooper, Thomas Szasz and others about psychiatry as a means of keeping people obedient and unfree.

At this point in the discussion sharper definitions are necessary. 'Unfreedom' as we have been using it includes the notions of restraint and confinement. So it is a negative category, defined in contrast to its positive, freedom or liberty. This raises some difficult issues. Our position, following recent discussions of freedom as a concept,[13] is that freedom is, first, an historically and socially relative idea, and secondly, that it can only be conceived of when qualified or modified by the words 'to' or 'from'. That is, it is not a political or human absolute, which is in some sense 'there', given, eternal, regardless of the conditions of life in which people find themselves. We are either free *to do* something or we are free *from* something else. We are at liberty, for instance, to organise in trade unions, assemble publicly, write and publish what we think, teach according to our consciences, etc.; or we are free from, for instance, hunger, thirst, endemic diseases, arbitrary arrest, etc. It is literally meaningless to speak of freedom without framing it in terms of sensuous human activity.

Unfreedom, then, is the condition where the freedoms to or from are lacking. The plural form, freedoms, is important since it is the accumulation of constraints which matters. Taking away a single freedom – for example, the freedom to rape, the freedom to make money from other people's labour – does not bring about a state of unfreedom, unless you are so far gone in idealism that you consider absolute freedom to be possible.

The social reality of the matter is that freedoms, to or from, flow into or depend upon each other. If a political party is denied freedom to speak to people (by being allocated no newsprint for its paper), then the freedom to associate in opposition to the ruling party is in danger and may presently disappear altogether. If groups cannot publish literary work (for the same practical reason), then censorship has begun, and may presently become all-powerful even if it is not in the constitution (it is not in the Soviet Constitution which Stalin launched with such publicity in 1936). This interlocking of freedoms was well described by Marx and Engels in the *Communist Manifesto*, when they wrote that in a socialist society 'the free development of each is the condition for the free development of all.' Unfreedom is that network of restraints which makes it difficult or impossible for people to express or develop their capacities. Under capitalism it is often disguised as its opposite, for example, the freedom to invest money and set up businesses, which has made most people unfree to find secure employment or have a say in the organisation of their life's work. It is true that more people are more free under capitalism than under slavery or feudalism. This does not mean that capitalist society is free ('the free world'), but rather that the experienced and conscious working class engendered by the factory system has been able to wring liberties from the bourgeois state which are important preliminary concessions on the way to the creation of socialism. Yet in this section we are arguing that some forms of unfreedom have been particularly baneful in modern times. The reasons are, first, that the practical agencies of unfreedom have become, like everything else in the industrial epoch, more efficient (you can bomb, burn, gas, or imprison people at a rate which tyrants of the past would envy); and, secondly, that our social arrangements (the sum of our behaviour as persons) for ever lag behind the potential latent in the techniques at our disposal:

The basic traits of the character structures corresponding to a definite historical situation are formed in early childhood, and are far more conservative than the forces of technical production. It results from this that, as time goes on, *the psychic structures lag behind the rapid changes of the social conditions from which they derived, and later come into conflict with new forms of life.* This is the basic trait of the nature of so-called tradition, i.e. of the contradiction between the old and the new social situation.[14]

The particular political restraints that concern us now have been imposed by present-day industrialised societies as the international economic system has run into ever more severe difficulties. A society is significantly unfree when many of its citizens fear arbitrary arrest; or when there is a highly developed prison system; or when there is a large and powerful secret police; or when there are a great many part-time police informers; or when there are many categories of social default and punishment; or when the State resorts to murdering its citizens, whether by execution or by enforced starvation or other shortages, as a means of control; or when personal habits (where you sit, where you live, where you excrete, whom you can make love with) are controlled by penal laws.

These conditions apply so widely, whether or not the society in question has the seeming apparatus of freedom such as trial with the right of defence or representative government, that the system of unfreedom expresses, at a high valency or in extreme form, conditions typical of modern social life. The psychiatrist Bruno Bettelheim had been a prisoner in Dachau soon after it was set up. In *The Informed Heart* (1961) he shows how closely labour in the Nazi camps resembles work under ordinary, 'free' conditions. One of his most piercing points is that it was alienated, that is, meaningless, work that the slaves in Dachau and Buchenwald found the most *destructive* of all activities:

> By contrast, it was the senseless tasks, the lack of almost any time to oneself, the inability to plan ahead because of sudden changes in camp policies, that was so deeply destructive. By destroying man's ability to act on his own or to predict the outcome of his actions, they destroyed the feeling that his actions had any purpose, so many prisoners stopped acting.[15]

This is close to the depression experienced by alienated workers under capitalism, as Studs Terkel crushingly shows in *Working* (1974), which collects hundreds of interviews with factory workers about their attitudes to production, and as Huw Beynon shows in his study of the Ford factory near Liverpool:

> You don't achieve anything here. A robot could do it. The line here is made for morons. It doesn't need any thought. They tell you that. 'We don't pay you for thinking' they say. Everyone comes to realize that they're not doing a worthwhile job. They're just on the line. For the money. Nobody likes to think that they're a failure. Its bad when you *know* that you're just a little cog. You just look at your pay packet – you look at what it does for your wife and kids. That's the only answer.

Beynon comments: 'Most of the Ford workers that I talked to expressed sentiments broadly similar to those quoted above.'

> It's a relief when you get off the moving line. It's such a tremendous relief. I can't put it into words. When you're on the line it's on top of you all the time. You may feel ill, not one hundred per cent but that line will be one hundred per cent. Being on sub-assembly is like getting off the round-about. Y'know ... day in day out ... never stopping. I still have nightmares about it. I couldn't go back on that line. Not for anything.
>
> And another on the Trim: It's the most boring job in the world. It's the same thing over and over again. There's no change in it, it wears you out. It makes you awful tired. It slows your thinking right down. There's no need to think. It's just a formality. You just carry on. You just endure it for the money. That's what we're paid for – to endure the boredom of it.
>
> It's strange this place. It's got no really good points. It's just convenient. It's got no interest. You couldn't take the job home. There's nothing to take. You just forget it. I don't want promotion at all, I've not got that approach to the job. I'm like a lot of people here. They're all working here but they're just really hanging around, waiting for something to

turn up . . . It's different for them in the office. They're *part* of Ford's. We're not, we're just working here, we're numbers.[16]

Bettelheim also discusses the fact that, again like the 'free' worker, the camp internees hated most of all 'any command where the tempo of work depended on the speed of machines', as it does in assembly-line production. It was under these conditions that the person felt he was ceasing to exist.

The parallel with factory production was felt also by the camp administrators, who became increasingly to resemble factory managers. Hoess, commandant of Auschwitz, 'wished to . . . run a clean and efficient factory; its function merely happened to be the destruction of human beings. To Hoess the perfect running of the factory mattered very much; that it "processed" human beings and not steel or aluminium had ceased to be his concern.' Bettelheim goes on to cite examples of the business correspondence carried on by the Auschwitz management. Although the subject is human corpses, the tone and vocabulary is exactly that of any business enterprise, with arguments over the 'price' of bodies provided and quibbles over the 'supply'.[17] Likening this to industrial organisation is no caricature, as Beynon found at Halewood:

They wouldn't stop that fucking line. You could be dying and they wouldn't stop it. If someone was hurt the first thing the supervisor thought about was filling the job. He'd start doing the work before he made sure the bloke was alright. I tell you you could have been dying and they wouldn't have bothered.

Occasionally men did die. One, a man of about forty, lay by the side of the line as his mates worked.

We were in the locker room before the shift had started and he collapsed with a pain in his chest. He went an awful colour but then he reckoned he was alright. We went down the stairs on to the shop floor, walked across to the line and he collapsed again. Y'know – flat on the floor. His face was an awful grey colour. We all rushed round him like and the buzzer went. The line started. The foreman came across shouting 'get to work . . . get on the line'. And there we were sticking things on the cars and he was lying there. He must have been lying there ten minutes . . . dead. In front of us.[18]

Primo Levi's unsparingly vivid memoir, *Survival in Auschwitz*, bears out Bettelheim's analysis in the closest way. Here is a typical moment in which he discovers in his own experiences what Bettelheim had worked out:

> Kraus misses his stroke, a lump of mud flies up and splatters over my knees. It is not the first time it has happened, I warn him to be careful, but without much hope: he is Hungarian, he understands German badly and does not know a word of French. He is tall and thin, wears glasses and has a curious, small, twisted face; when he laughs he looks like a child, and he often laughs. He works too much and too vigorously: he has not yet learnt our underground art of economising on everything, on breaths, movements, even thoughts. He does not know that it is better to be beaten, because one does not normally die of blows, but one does of exhaustion, and badly, and when one grows aware of it, it is already too late. He still thinks ... oh no, poor Kraus, he is not reasoning, it is only the stupid honesty of the small employee, he brought it along with him, and he seems to think that his present situation is like outside, where it is honest and logical to work, as well as being of advantage, because according to what everyone says, the more one works the more one earns and eats.[19]

Levi is also striking in the way he draws, probably unconsciously, on the perspectives and images of nineteenth-century European Naturalism. His memoir, like many others about the camps, compares in significant and chilling ways with the social-Darwinist savagery in the work of writers such as Zola, Jack London, Dreiser, and (as we have already seen) Upton Sinclair. This likeness is not accidental. On the one hand, the camp world was seen by inmates as a brutish struggle for survival because that is what it often was. Furthermore, it became that because of its close economic and ideological meshing with the system it was designed to protect – German monopoly capitalism, with its need for cheap labour and for what Hitler called *lebensraum*, and analysts of imperialism such as Hobson, Lenin, and Varga have called 'spheres of influence'. Since Fascism is capitalism evolved to its extreme, it is not surprising that writers such as Levi and Sinclair, in other ways so different, should use the same phrases about the life they had in view. For Levi the concentration camps brought everyone down to the level of animals in a ceaseless battle to live. In a typical passage he comments: 'Here the struggle to survive is without respite, because everyone is desperately and ferociously alone.' To take an almost random example from *The Jungle*, Sinclair has his main character, Jurgis, think at one point: 'Ah, God, the horror of it, the monstrous, hideous, demoniacal wickedness of it! He and his family, helpless women and children, struggling to live, ignorant and defenceless and forlorn as they were – and the enemies that had been lurking for them, crouching upon their trail and thirsting for their blood!'[20]

Sinclair can be too rhetorical, but it is not the self-centred, purely ejaculatory rhetoric of, say, the young Shelley or the abysmal Drury Lane tragedians of the eighteenth century. Sinclair flails around because he is feeling the desperation of the cornered immigrant workers almost too strongly for his style to cope with. He is aghast. He badly wants us to know how unbearable life is in the lower depths, and his voice rises as he thinks of the distance between a slaughterhouse in Chicago and the comfortable homes in which books get read. But elsewhere he realises that the most unanswerable form of the indictment is to give his evidence with the fullness of a good newspaperman, as in the description of making sausages at the end of chapter 13, and here he is at one with the European Naturalist movement.

Realism had been a process of class self-definition. It was the justifying aesthetic which allowed middle-class writers, for example George Eliot and Henry James, to engage artistically with their society. Since Realism* was deeply related to the growing social and political dominance of the ruling middle class, its metaphors were drawn from the most spectacular achievements of thought and technical innovation that had grown up along with the mercantile and industrial revolutions: empirical science, the experimental method, medical progress. So the 'Realist' typically insisted on the right, even the obligation, to operate on the social body with the detachment of a surgeon, observing impartially what

---

* In the next few pages we will use a triple distinction of Realism: firstly, the movement as its conscious practitioners understood it; secondly, Realism in the sense we give it today ('the Realists'; to be compared with 'the Romantics'); and thirdly, realism as the common, not necessarily literary word for any unidealising approach which does not flinch from unlovely detail.

was there and cutting away the cancerous flesh with pitiless precision. What this meant in literary practice was rejecting the Romantic, which was the dominant sensibility just before industrialisation
and the heyday of the bourgeoisie. The exotic, the exalted, the
inspirational came to be disparaged. In Flaubert's phrase Yvetot
(typical French provisional town) was worth as much as Constan-
tinople. The Victorian Realist, no less than the Victorian scientist,
experimented with techniques which would make his or her work
as indisputable a piece of analysis as possible.

Naturalism, in its early form, seemed at first to be little more
than the logical continuation of such an approach. If a writer
was free to select any subject and treat it without idealisation,
it followed that the least privileged groups – the worst-off workers,
the prostitutes and their pimps, the thieves and drunkards and
sexual misfits – were equally entitled, as Henry James said of
Milly Theale, to be 'wrapped in the Beauty and Dignity of Art'.
Stephen Crane's Maggie, 'a girl of the streets' in his own
euphemism, was as worthwhile a subject for fiction as James's
Maggie, the bourgeois princess of The Golden Bowl. And yet
Victorian society in general, and its literary-critical arbiters in
particular, firmly rejected Naturalism in practice. Why? James
himself repeatedly attacked Zola and others for exercising the
artistic freedom he was among the first to champion. He was
not alone in this. Zola repeatedly had to restate the case for
artistic freedom and it is notable that when he did, for example,
after the storm over Thérèse Raquin, he invoked the classic frames
of reference of 'Realist' aesthetics: 'I have simply done on living
bodies the work which surgeons perform on corpses . . . I have
written from pure scientific curiosity.' And again, in his Preface
to the same book:

I do not know if my novel is moral or immoral; I admit
that I never concerned myself about making it more or less
chaste. What I know is that I never for a moment thought
of putting in it the dirtiness that moral people find there;
this is because I wrote every scene, even the most heightened
ones, with pure scientific curiosity.[21]

The 'Realists' were undeceived by this, although they could
not formulate their objections clearly. They sensed with all their

class fibres that 'Naturalism',* despite its camouflage of objectivity, was deeply hostile to their genteel world-view. Reactions to 'Zolaism' or 'Naturalism' were almost uniformly antagonistic, stretching along the whole gamut of possibilities from Tolstoy's anxious confusion (Gorky should not write about drunk women) through James's moral censoriousness disguised as good taste to the persecution by imprisonment of people such as Vizitelly who had the courage to publish Zola.

A typical denunciation of 'Naturalism' was Tennyson's. It was the sort of attack that made the imprisonments and bannings respectable, and it is notable that in it the writer makes no attempt to distinguish between 'Naturalism' as a set of aesthetic ideas and as outright political subversion. His fusion of the aesthetics and the politics is clearly deliberate, and raises again the main issue of our discussion, the link between Naturalism and the literature of unfreedom. In 'Locksley Hall Sixty Years After' he wrote:

Tumble Nature o'er the head, and yelling with the yelling street,
Set the feet above the brain and swear the brain is in the feet.
Bring the old dark ages back without the faith, without the hope,
Break the State, the Church, the Throne, and roll the ruins
  down the slope.

Author – essayist, atheist, novelist, realist, rhymester, play
  your part,
Paint the mortal shame of nature with the living hues of Art.
Rip your brothers' vices open, strip your own foul passions bare;
Down with Reticence, down with Reverence – forward – naked
  let them stare.

Feed the budding rose of boyhood with the drainage of your
  sewer;
Send the drain into the fountain, lest the stream should issue
  pure.
Set the maiden fancies wallowing in the troughs of Zolaism -
Forward, forward, aye and backward, down too into the abysm.[22]

---

* We use the same triple distinction with Naturalism as with 'Realism', inverted commas for the conscious movement; a capital letter for the more loose or general literary use of it today; and a small letter for the word when it is interchangeable with realism, meaning an unidealising approach.

Tennyson is trying to thunder but the result is apoplexy. One word tumbles over another in uncontrollable spasms and the violence of it far outruns any solid evocation of what it is he loathes.

The general trend of Tennyson's argument and what we gather to be his bugbears are worth looking into.. He pretends to be appalled, and perhaps he was, by the Naturalist movement's frankness in sexual matters, yet he does seem to accept the *truth* of what they wrote. What he hates is that the truth should be told. 'Foul passions' and 'brothers' vices' exist but should not be mentioned. His reasons are eminently Victorian. First, young people may learn about sex, and he wants to chaperone them past all that. Secondly, the antagonism between rulers and ruled will be greatly intensified. When the city crowd 'yells', Church and State will collapse and power will pass to the mob. Of course, the poet hardly dares openly to advocate deception or censorship, though that is what his position comes to. What he commends is an awkward blend of silence and respect, of Reticence and Reverence (capitalised to suggest a force the abstractions alone do not have). The hidden teeth of such admonitions, however, are the courts and the prisons.

Naturalism, then, was felt as a challenge to the ruling class and its ideas, partly because it was honest about sex, and partly because it consistently treated the European working class with the sort of concern and sense of tragedy which the powers that be and their theorists have always thought should be reserved for themselves (for example, the long-standing theory, still taught a generation ago, that tragedy has to be about important people). To perceive the life of a maid-servant or a mill girl or a stonemason as tragic – to perceive the tragedy that there was in it – one must attend to their conditions of life with a fullness, a precision, which was sensed by the pundits to be subversive because it was bound to show, for example, that millions of people toiled inhuman hours for a pittance too small literally to survive on. So E. M. Forster, direct descendant of the nineteenth-century Realists, declares in *Howards End* (1910): 'We are not concerned with the very poor. They are unthinkable, and only to be approached by the statistician or the poet.'[23] Social science, he must be saying, can give us the facts of poverty, poetry can make us weep for it, but 'we' (the editorial we? the middle class?

the educated élite?) can dismiss the life experience of 30 percent of the British people from the attention of the prime medium of that time, the novel. He is being ironical, of course – he is not saying 'unthinkable' with the unadulterated arrogance of an aristocratic Conservative; but what his irony does is to help him fudge his way past the crying problems of his time.

Naturalism, then, concerned itself mainly with the life of the nineteenth-century working class, and this is a social and political category. Its best practitioners, however, were consciously concerned less with politics than with humanity as part of the natural world (hence 'Naturalism'). People were represented as animals or part of a continuum including animals. A good example is *The Jungle*, whose title suggests the close likeness between modern city life and popular images of the state of nature ('red in tooth and claw', as Tennyson put it, anticipating the vulgarisations of Darwin). Thomas Hardy's sense of people, Tess for example, as being amongst the stuff of life, the dairy cattle and root vegetables and fossil remnants of earlier epochs, is part of the same outlook. It was not possible to see Victorian working people as animals (but sympathetically and even heroically considered) without reaching the sort of socio-political judgement that runs like a red thread through much of the best Naturalist work. Its writers were nearly all Left-wing, for example Zola, London, Gorky, Wells, Sinclair, Dreiser. They *could* not have looked closely into how poor people lived without concluding that such things must not be, and must be changed.

This brings us back to the later relevance of the Naturalist movement: its capacity to present and analyse the experience of entrapment and unfreedom in society. It arose out of the Great Unrest during the fourth quarter of the nineteenth century, when volcanic revolutionary energies were stirring, and it helped supply the ingredient of raw, painful reportage to the literature of unfreedom once revolution and counter-revolution had made way for the age of dictatorships. Naturalism rested, as on a bedrock, on the spectacle of the trapped individual, unfree biologically, socially, and historically. Dreiser's characters struggle with their libido, their ambitions, the encircling city. Zola's are hounded by sexual urges and lack of money and the social consequences of trying to sell their sexuality for money; Jack London's by the need for food and shelter; Stephen Crane's by the natural elements and their own moral limitations; Hardy's by the same. Wells's work has striking images of the human and social trap. In *Kipps* (1906) Minton compares life to a drainpipe, '"and we've got to crawl along it till we die."' In *The History of Mr Polly* (1910) the morale of the failing small shopkeeper is compared to 'a badly managed industrial city during a period of depression' and the man himself puts the trap in his own words: '"Hole!" said Mr Polly, and then for a change, and with greatly increased emphasis: "'Ole!.. He paused, and then broke out with one of his private and peculiar idioms. "Oh! *Beastly* Silly Wheeze of a hole!"' [24]

The claustrophobic individual was trapped in an airless pit, either personal or social or historical or biological, and this vision or image of the unfree human being has been in the culture ever since. It has been said that Naturalism was 'that type of realism . . . in which the environment displaces its inhabitants in the role of hero.' The characters in Naturalist fiction, as in the later literature of unfreedom, are subjected to overwhelming pressures from outside themselves, as well as from their own conditioned natures. As such they contradict the wishful optimism of the many thousand middle-class readers who heard their own sentiments in Tennyson's *In Memoriam* ('one far-off divine event,/ To which the whole Creation moves').

The main reason for Naturalism's lasting reputation for gloom lies not in its preoccupation with entrapment but from the solutions or escapes the writers offered. Perhaps the most frequent is suicide, in *Sister Carrie, Death of a Salesman, Jude the Obscure*. Some characters give themselves up to death, as in *Tess of the D'Urbervilles* and Crane's story 'The Open Boat'. Sometimes the author opens up possibilities of flight, in *Mr Polly*, for example, and the middle sections of *The Jungle*. But Jurgis is driven back to the city and *Mr Polly* becomes frivolous. In only two cases we know of does the author recommend what might seem the obvious response: destroy the prison walls; and when he does, as we have seen already in *The Jungle* and *The Ragged Trousered Philanthropists* (see above, p. 147), all we have is a wishful rhetoric of a red dawn. As early as January 1919, Brecht had a foreboding that this might well be false. In 'Song of the Soldier of the Red Army' he wrote:

Often at night the sky turned red
They thought red dawn had come again.
That was a fire, but the dawn came also.
Freedom, my children, never came.

Later Brecht withdrew the poem,[25] but his foreboding had been right, and that it was so is the essence of the tragedy we discussed at the close of the section on Stalinism. Part of the same tragedy is the fact that most of the best literature from the first revolutionary country, the Soviet Union, has concerned unfreedom. Evgenya Ginzburg's *Into the Whirlwind* has all the unflinching accuracy in presenting squalor that is typical of both Naturalist literature and the literature of unfreedom, and one of her finest scenes sums up the gist of this section incomparably well:

The next to go was Maria Zacher. Before her death she suddenly forgot her small stock of Russian words. She couldn't even remember the word for water. As no one else in the ward understood German and as I was by now able to get up, it happened that I was with her at the last. Her end was so perfectly a literary death-bed scene that if a writer had described it the critics would certainly have accused him of using his imagination; but I was there and it really was like that. Lying on her bed, all skin and bone, her body scarcely raised the level of the bedclothes, her 'Aryan' face was now sharply pointed, her nose and chin and the blue line of her lips standing out like gothic lettering. Yet in this ghostly face her large brown eyes still glowed with intelligence and pain. To her last breath her mind was active, she remained a soldier of Thälmann's army, anxious about the fate of the communist movement.

'Shall I be able to read Russian again? Why have I suddenly forgotten all the words I knew?'

'Probably because not enough blood is reaching your brain. They'll come back to you.'

A few minutes before she died she started reciting some anti-fascist verses (I think they were by Erich Weinert); the refrain was 'Marxism isn't dead'. She took my hand into her ice-cold, bony one and with her last breath said: 'Marxism isn't dead, but we are dead.'[26]

9. Artists and the Ominous

A drastic sense that *the bad thing* was imminent, that it could no longer be stopped, is more and more the note of remarkable fiction, poetry, and painting in the middle and later thirties. Artists increasingly spoke up as beleaguered bearers of humanness in the teeth of massed forces of enslavement and destruction. It was not a question of looking towards only one 'wellspring of evil' (Germany). The thing reared up on all sides. In 1936, in *The Big Money*, Dos Passos looked back to the eve of Sacco and Vanzetti's execution on 23 August 1927 and symbolised it as a turning-point downward:

> they have clubbed us off the streets   they are stronger   they are rich they hire and fire the politicians the newspapereditors the old judges the small men with reputations the collegepresidents the wardheelers (listen businessmen collegepresidents judges   America will not forget her betrayers) they hire the men with guns the uniforms the policecars the patrolwagons
> all right you have won   you will kill the brave men our friends tonight . . .
> America our nation has been beaten by strangers who have turned our language inside out who have taken the clean words our fathers spoke and made them slimy and foul
> their hired men sit on the judge's bench they sit back with their feet on the tables under the dome of the State House they are ignorant of our beliefs they have the dollars the guns the armed forces the powerplants
> they have built the electricchair and hired the executioner to throw the switch
> all right we are two nations
> America our nation has been beaten by strangers who have bought the laws and fenced off the meadows and cut down

the woods for pulp and turned our pleasant cities into slums
and sweated the wealth out of our people and when they want
to they hire the executioner to throw the switch . . .

    they have won why are they scared to be seen on the streets?
on the streets you see only the downcast faces of the beaten
    the streets belong to the beaten nation   all the way to
the cemetery where the bodies of the immigrants are to be
burned   we line the curbs in the drizzling rain we crowd
the wet sidewalks elbow to elbow silent pale looking with scared
eyes at the coffins

    we stand defeated America[1]

That was a single defeat – two Anarchists framed on a murder
charge. In Germany the hired executioners were starting on a
programme of killing which would run to millions, and there
were writers who knew this. In 1933, in January, Hitler became
Chancellor of Germany; in March he was given powers, by a
Parliament meeting in a building surrounded by SS and SA men,
to govern by decree without consulting Parliament (the *Reichstag*);
and in July all parties were disbanded except the Nazis, whose
party was declared the vehicle of the State. Trade unions had
been disbanded in May. Brecht wrote one of his most despairing
political poems, 'Burial of the Trouble-maker in a Zinc Coffin'.
The humane value at the centre of it is the same as Dos Passos's:

    (Tell us, doctors of philosophy, what are the needs of a
man. At least a man needs to be notjailed notafraid nothungry
notcold not without love, not a worker for a power he has
never seen
    that cares nothing for the uses and needs of a man or a
woman or a child.)

Even Brecht's phrasing is similar:

    What lies in the zinc coffin
    Has agitated in favour of many things:
    For eating-your-fill
    For a-roof-over-your-head
    For feeding-your-children
    For holding-out-for-the-last-penny

And for solidarity with all
The oppressed who are like you
And in favour of thinking.

Brecht's perspective in this poem, as he faces uncountable years as an exile, is, like Dos Passos's, one of unrelieved impasse and defeat:

Here, in this zinc coffin,
Lies a dead man,
Or else his leg and his head,
Or still less of him,
Or nothing at all since he was
An agitator . . .

And whichever of you thinks and proclaims his solidarity
With all who are oppressed,
He shall from now until eternity
End in the zinc coffin like this man here
As an agitator and be shoved under the earth.[2]

A few years later Anna Seghers (like Trotsky and Serge) reached Mexico to live as a refugee. While she waited in Paris for her husband's release from the Purgatory of Le Vernet, she began her classic novel of *l'homme traqué*, the hounded man – *The Seventh Cross*. Its perspective differs a little from Dos Passos's and Brecht's because she sees defeat as probable but not quite certain:

Now that Wallau himself had been caught and brought back, we bawled as if we had been little children. We were all of us lost now, we thought. Wallau would be murdered, as all the others before him had been murdered. In the very first month of the Hitler régime hundreds of our leaders had been murdered in every part of the country, and every month more were murdered. Some were executed publicly, others were tortured to death in the concentration camps. A whole generation had to be annihilated. These were our thoughts on that terrible morning; then for the first time we voiced our conviction that if we were to be destroyed on that scale, all would perish

because there would be none to come after us. The almost
unprecedented in history, the most terrible thing that could
happen to a people, was now to be our fate: a no-man's-land
was to be established between the generations, which old experiences would not be able to traverse. If we fight and fall,
and another takes up the flag and fights and falls too, and
the next one grasps it and he too falls - that is natural, for
nothing can be gained without sacrifice. But what if there is
no longer anyone to take up the flag, simply because he does
not know its meaning? It was then that we felt sorry for the
fellows who were lined up for Wallau's reception, to stare
at him and spit on him. The best that grew in the land was
being torn out by the roots because the children had been
taught to regard it as weeds. All those lads and girls out there
once they had gone through the Hitler Youth, the Work Service,
and the Army, would be like the fabled children nurtured by
animals who finally tore their own mothers to pieces.[3]

This is from one of the passages where the collective voice
of the camp inmates is made to stand for all people who will
still say what they think. Seven prisoners have escaped, six have
been recaptured, the last torture-tree (the seventh cross) waits
for Georg Heisler who is still on the run. Wallau is the strong
man, staunch under any torture. At the very last he is still himself,
unbroken:

All of Wallau's sensations were now merged into one – thirst.
What a terrible thirst! Never would he be able to quench
it. Every bit of perspiration had been drained out of him.
He was drying up. What a fire! Smoke seemed to be pouring
from all his joints. Everything had turned to steam as if the
whole world were coming to an end, not just he – Wallau.
'You didn't care to say anything to Overkamp. All right.
But we two will get along better. Heisler was your intimate
friend. He told you everything. Quick – what is the name
of his girl?'
'Ah, so they still haven't got him,' thought Wallau, once
more drawn out of himself, out of the exclusiveness of his
own extinction. At the flash in Wallau's eyes, Bunsen's fist
shot out, and Wallau reeled against the wall. . . .

... From the door, Zillich looked over at him calmly. A faint light over his shoulder, a tiny blue corner of autumn, told Wallau for the last time that the structure of the world held firm and would continue to hold firm regardless of what struggles might come. For a moment Zillich stood rigid. Never before had anybody awaited him with so much calm, with so much dignity. 'This is death,' thought Wallau. Slowly Zillich pulled the door shut behind him.[4]

The same keeping open a breathing hole to a human future is expressed classically in one of Lu Hsun's many essays from the 1930s which he wrote like bulletins from the front line but composed into a form with a weight and edge that make them permanent. He is commemorating five young writers who had worked to radicalise and modernise Chinese literature, translating Petöfi from Hungary, and Gorky from the Soviet Union. In 1931 they were arrested, chained, shot full of bullets at police headquarters. 'In Memory of the Forgotten' ends like this:

Two years ago today, I was lying low in a hotel while they went to the execution ground. A year ago today I was escaping through gunfire to the International Settlement while they lay buried none knows where. Only this year I am sitting at home again on this day, while the whole world is asleep, including my wife and son. Once again I am profoundly conscious that I have lost very good friends and China very good young men. I grow calmer after my distress, but force of habit asserts itself in my calm, and has made me write.

If I go on, I shall still be unable to publish what I write in China today. When a lad I read Hsiang Tzu-chi's *Reminiscences* and blamed him for writing a few lines only, then finishing when he had barely begun. But now I understand.

It is not the young who are writing obituaries for the old, but during the last thirty years with my own eyes I have seen the blood of so many young people mounting up that now I am submerged and cannot breathe. All I can do is take up my pen and write a few articles, as if to make a hole in the clotted blood through which I can draw a few more wretched breaths. What sort of world is this? The night is so long, the way is so long, that I had better forget or else

remain silent. But I know, if I do not do so, a time will
come when others will remember and speak of them .[5]

Inside Britain people were not in serious danger, but the most
perceptive writers were already in their imaginations living on
the Continent, wincing and worrying as though the terrorism
and the re-arming were happening in the next street or next
town. Graham Greene gives his best thrillers (*Stamboul Train*
and *The Confidential Agent*) a social complexity and a reality
far beyond mere suspense and thrill by having his key characters,
Dr Czinner and the agent, bring with them from the east the
hounded, worn, and urgent behaviour of societies already in the
throes. From the spring of 1933 and the Nazis' launching in
earnest of the Terror against the Jews and the Left, W. H. Auden
is showing himself able to see the imminent catastrophes as though
they were already under his eyes – although he later did his
best to go back on this testimony, and therefore to withdraw
from history, first by muddling the sequence of his poems and
then by suppressing some of the best.[6] In 'A Bride in the 30's'
the choice and the change of living which go with marriage lead
him at once to see the woman as being situated amongst

>   . . . the tall tenements and the trees in the wood,
> Though sombre the sixteen skies of Europe
>   And the Danube flood.

The bridegroom is one rare piece of good fortune in 'the policed
unlucky city', and the 'music from our time' conjures up as attend-
ant ghosts

> Ten million of the desperate marching by,
> Five feet, six feet, seven feet high,
> Hitler and Mussolini in their wooing poses,
> Churchill acknowledging the voters' greeting,
> Roosevelt at the microphone, Van der Lubbe laughing,
>   And our first meeting . . .[7]

A little later, in the winter of 1939, Yeats's death over in France
makes Auden think of how a poet's work, resonating in the
heads of thousands, outlives the artist. This network of readers,

merging with the miles and miles of gripping cold, turns into a whole continent politically darkened:

> The brooks were frozen, the airports almost deserted,
> And snow disfigured the public statues;
> The mercury sank in the mouth of the dying day . . .

> But for him it was his last afternoon as himself,
> An afternoon of nurses and rumours;
> The provinces of his body revolted,
> The squares of his mind were empty,
> Silence invaded the suburbs,
> The current of his feeling failed: he became his admirers.[8]

The master-poem in which this vein of topical foreboding coheres into one vision is 'A Summer Night 1933'. It is a seamless train of thought that leads from privileged England at its ease, to threatened middle Europe, to the great holocaust, to the return of good things (peace, youth, growth). To take excerpts from it makes ugly gaps in a whole that is beautiful in its supple moves from image to image, but enough can be quoted to show how the Marxist sense of being implicated in a determined history that stretches ahead has been dissolved into lyrical rhythms and remains present in solution in them, enabling the poet to make firm (and accurate) forecasts. A run of five verses may suggest how the poetic flow is one with a flow of history that leads on at least fifteen years from the date of writing:

> To gravity attentive, she [the moon]
> Can notice nothing here, though we
>   Whom hunger does not move
> From gardens where we feel secure
> Look up and with a sigh endure
>   The tyrannies of love:

> And, gentle, do not care to know
> Where Poland draws her eastern bow,
>   What violence is done,
> Nor ask what doubtful act allows
> Our freedom in this English house,
>   Our picnics in the sun.

Soon, soon, through dykes of our content
The crumpling flood will force a rent
   And, taller than a tree,
Hold sudden death before our eyes
Whose river dreams long hid the size
   And vigours of the sea.

But when the waters make retreat
And through the black mud first the wheat
   In shy green stalks appears,
When stranded monsters gasping lie,
And sounds of riveting terrify
   Their whorled unsubtle ears,

May these delights we dread to lose,
This privacy, need no excuse
   But to that strength belong,
As through a child's rash happy cries
The drowned parental voices rise
   In unlamenting song.

   The poem would not *need* to have been an accurate forecast to give a rich sense of historical process, but it is surely a sign of an extraordinary imagination in complete touch with the life of its time to have been able to gauge in advance: the role of Poland in causing the war; appeasement; the German invasion of the Low Countries; the defeat of the Fascist Axis; the emergence of a particularly liberated youth after the war. The poem, both its view of history and its sensuous feel, finds an exact gloss in Sartre's passage on what it is to be *situated*: 'Each day we had lived revealed its true face; we had abandoned ourselves to it trustingly and it was leading us to a new war with secret rapidity, with a rigour hidden beneath its nonchalant airs.'[9] But Sartre was looking back from after the war, Auden was understanding what was to come.

   You may be thinking: 'But that's absurd – can they really be saying that a writer, or anybody, can take standing jumps into the future?' Of course not. Our point is that a forecast consists of detecting in the present those seeds or starting-points which, unlike the other millions of potential starting-points, will turn out to have had in them the makings of the future. This

is something that socialist artists constantly managed to do. It
is particularly striking in the medium of painting. Here we must
distinguish between distinct or unambiguous previsions, on the
one hand, and on the other hand symbols which do go on corresponding remarkably with the experiences of later times but which
are not so finite that they can count as real prefigurings. In
1824 Delacroix painted his 'Horse Frightened by a Storm'. Seventy
years before Rousseau had used the same image, in his *Origin
of Inequality*, to stand for pre-civilised man reacting violently
to threatened enslavement.[10] Early this century Picasso began
to use a more extreme form of the same image, a gored horse
collapsing in the bull-ring, to suggest animal nature under the
most extreme stress (and we have already seen what Lawrence
makes of this image in *St Mawr*). In 1937 the Spanish Civil War
enabled Picasso to see that the image meant also the brutalities
of modern warfare. He painted 'Guernica', in which the horse
is both archaic and modern, its body impaled by a spear and
turned into newsprint, while its legs begin to split at the knees
under the destroying impact from above.[11] So this image came
into its own. It had always meant the deformity to which mankind
subjected organic life. Now it could mean the most denaturing
single force yet unleashed in the human world – the saturation-
bombing of close-built towns with high explosives.

   This family of symbols, then, has been so long-lived and potent
that it should be recognised as coming from the heart of the
age that began with the French and Industrial Revolutions. However, its *literal* likeness to this or that event has not been close
enough for us to speak of forecast or prophecy; and art's responsibility of truth to history matters too much for words like 'prophetic'
to be bandied about. For example, in *The Condition of Man*
(1944) Lewis Mumford made some characteristically far-reaching
and deep suggestions about the impulses that have been driving
mankind in modern times. But can we accept his suggestion,
in his caption to the plate called 'Dream and Nightmare', that
'the emptiness of di Chirico's ominous urban perspectives' is the
'precursor of the fascist revolution'? or that Surrealists like Dali
were 'prophetically representing in symbol those utmost horrors
which the Nazis and the Japanese have consummated in fact'?[12]

   To bring the matter down to its roots in actual behaviour,
we would prefer to say this: Di Chirico was having a vision

of the modern city. It has become so large, and hence the relationships of people inside it so over-extended, that it is blighted by large tracts (dead-ends, waste ground, 'lost' tenements) which are, in the terms of the American architect Oscar Newman, undefended space – areas for which nobody is responsible, where anything can happen, where (in di Chirico's image) the little girl bowling her hoop can be raped by the psychotic man waiting round the corner. In these cities blighted by what Mumford elsewhere calls 'insensate' growth[13] Fascism flourished. But it was the large blight, not its specific political symptom, that di Chirico saw with uncanny clarity in 1913. Regarding Dali, what has to be explained is the matching between the extreme distortion of human bodies in his paintings and the extreme atrocities done in the death camps, the destruction of hair and bones and feelings by planned malnutrition, the surgical operations on healthy people such as the experimental removing of ovaries from women. It is true that such parallels are never coincidental, and it would beg the question to psychoanalyse Dali's sadism as though it was a purely individual condition. But why did he paint like that? Why those Modernist 'distortions' with academically sleek surfaces? We suggest that this was a painterly reaction to the new dominance of the camera. It was futile to go on painting the exact likeness of reality. Photography could do that better. The painter could drastically rearrange reality, and if he was vain, like Dali, he could do so while still preening himself on the power of his brush to render the exact consistency of flesh or clouds. This does not cut off the development of the medium, painting, from developments in history. In the first place, Dali could not have felt so utterly free to flout our normal expectations of the human image unless traditional respect for norms, for the basic sanity and coherence of things, had been drastically sapped. Secondly, both the power of the camera as a machine and the rootless and irresponsible skill of a painter like Dali are part of the same trend: technique has come to such a pitch that people can now do anything to life. They can split and fuse the nuclei of atoms. They can kill 2000 people in fifteen minutes, in chambers surrounded by neat lawns and flowerbeds, to the sound of *The Merry Widow* and *Tales of Hoffmann*.[14]

What those cases show is that the links between art and history are often at a remove rather than direct: what looks prophetic is really a cast ahead from what is already in being, not a jump forwards out of time. This does not lessen its value. There is a family of paintings from the heart of the European troubles in Germany which made such clear forecasts that they could have helped to forestall terrible things if it had been possible for them to win attention as warnings. These are the works of the Dresden painters Hans and Lea Grundig and Otto Dix.

The sight of men mutilated in the Great War fired Dix to make etchings in which traditional Gothic fantasies such as writhen thorn-trees, grimacing gap-toothed trolls, and branches that grab like hooked fingers became real because they are actually like barbed-wire entanglements, children with burnt faces, and the collapsing joists of houses split by bombs with bloodstained corpses falling out through holes torn in the walls.[15] Dix used ink partly to catch the liquefying mess of war. During the same years Georg Grosz was whetting his pen to draw generals, profiteers, murderers, and the skeletons of the war dead with a consuming interest in the details of uniforms, fashions, utensils, household furniture, as though precision of this kind were the last means left with which to fix the image of chaos.[16] The Grundigs found their style a little later, during the phase that lasted from the stabilisation of the mark and Hitler's failed Munich rising (1923) to the setting up of the Third Reich in 1933. In their portraits and street scenes of the twenties, hollow-eyed people stare out of an Expressionist gloom. This darkness wells from the canals, grimed brick chimneys, and tenement doorways of a world still spoiled by the Bleak Age of industrialisation. As many writers and painters have shown, it is easy to be so repelled by the Bleak Age city that you want only to disown it, to fix your eyes on the past or heaven or the countryside and leave the industrial heartlands to fester away by themselves.[17] As Lenin said in his obituary on Engels, people regarded 'the proletariat only as an *ulcer*, and observed with horror how this ulcer grew with the growth of industry'.[18] The Grundigs, like other humane artists, stayed with the bleak city and allowed it to decide their media, e.g. charcoal, ink wash. They were at one with the people of the cities, instead of seeing them as sub-human or spectres, and their pictures of Left-wing demonstrations have advantages over kindred work (for example 'The Strike, Evening' by the Belgian Eugene Laermans) in that the people in the militant crowds are seen close up, they are not like soldier-ants, and the lettering giving details of slogans and banners epitomises the people's thoughts: there would be no excuse for belittling them as a mob.

Presently, at a time when many artists were doodling or just giving up (including Picasso[19]), the Grundigs were able to bear witness to the extreme throes of the Slump and its political outcome. In 1933 Hans paints 'Lightning-weather in the City'. The images, for all their grubby ordinariness, turn menacing as we look. A roadmaker's trestle begins to suggest a gallows, the shadows are like jagged sheet-iron. Not one thing in this environment encourages life. Di Chirico's vision is 'coming true'. By 1934 the underlying menace has erupted. The buildings in 'Street in the "Third Reich"' are gay – with swastika flags. people have begun to throng into the empty vistas – the pandemonium of the Nazi rallies is just round the corner.[20] In that year Hans also paints 'Vision of the Burning City'. The title is from a painting by Bosch (the right-hand panel of his 'Garden of Earthly Delights'). The symbolic monsters of late-medieval times have been replaced by real horrors. Searchlights beam up over breached house-rows and bristling rafters. This painting and 'Vision of War' (1935)[21] are very like 'Devastation 1941' which Graham Sutherland painted as an official war artist. But Sutherland had seen blitzed London. And it took the bombing and machine-gunning of Guernica to move Picasso out of the very personal paintings of women which had preoccupied him through the thirties. Three years before the bombs began to drop, Hans Grundig could see the exact shape of the menace hanging above the cities.

In 1935 he painted 'Carnival', immediately after Dix's 'Seven Deadly Sins' and 'Triumph of Death'. Now the streets are jam-full, something is being celebrated. A close look at these crowds shows not one face. The people are all masked, with obscene stabbing noses or pointed hats that shield the face like Ku Klux Klan hoods or the headgear in Manzu's frightening sculptures and reliefs of cardinals or inquisitors. The façades are now well lit – with a harsh glare like acetylene. The banners on the poles have no badge or stripe, they express themselves in their shapes, which suggest not cloth but industrial scrap, steel whips, or scorpion stings. The same image occurs in chapter 4 of Fedin's *Conflagration*. Pastukhov is driving home to Moscow on the eve of the German invasion, wondering what horrors from the West the next news will bring. 'The griffin-like cloud retained its outline and hung quite still in the sky. Only the orange tail wrapped round the tucked-in paws fell slowly down as if the monster was preparing to crack it like a whip.' Without any overt emblem of Nazism, a deadly image of degeneracy is created.

In 1938 Hans Grundig paints 'Chaos'. The streets still swarm, the façades shine, balloons bob from windows. But there are no people at all. The erect forms in the streets are wolves stretching up their necks to bay and horses wracked by death-throes. The one human witness is the artist's wife Lea, painted in the bottom right-hand corner in enriched, softened tones deliberately out of keeping with the rest. The scorpion banners bristle still more thickly. Like those in 'Carnival' they are copied from the flag in the top right-hand corner of Brueghel's war allegory, 'The Triumph of Death' (a favourite of Brecht's), which in its turn takes the shape from the right-hand panel of Bosch's 'Garden of Earthly Delights'. It is as though only motifs from the grotesque hell of the medieval imagination can render the barbarisms with which the Nazis deliberately corrupted Germany.[22] This is the atmosphere Brecht caught in the refrain of his poem on the baiting of the Jews, especially the Nuremberg laws of 1935 against marriage and sex-relations between Jews and non-Jews:

> In the outlying slums meat prices rise,
> They're beating the drums with all their might.
> God, if they're hatching another surprise
> It will be tonight.[23]

The Grundigs' use of masks and beasts is akin to Picasso's drawings of beastly organisms in his black comic-strip 'Dream and Lie of Franco' of 1937.[24] The horse crashing on to its knees savaged by wolves occurs a year before Picasso similarly symbolised a tormented people in 'Guernica'. When such a cluster of kindred images crops up on all sides, from artists of quite different individual natures, experiences, and national cultures, you know you have found the heart of an epoch. The way in which banners, shadows, metal objects, gritty edges of buildings threaten vulnerable bodies in the paintings of the Grundigs and the others belongs with the Slump art in which the materials of the environment are shown to clash harshly with the tender human organism. We see this in Brecht's imagery of asphalt cities and zinc coffins and knee-deep concrete, in Dos Passos's imagery of pavements and harsh street-lights and pit heaps, the same things in Orwell, and Ben Shahn's paintings of American cities in the thirties: solitary people are shown against rearing structures, a boy plays amongst rubble under a huge windowless wall, a cripple climbs a red-leaded iron stairway beside a half-ruined building. Here is the art of an epoch in which barbed wire came to mean not field fencing but concentration camps, in which concrete suggests the raw floor of a cell, and rubber suggests a club.

In Hans Grundig's paintings from 1934 on, birds appeared with wings like dark blades. By 1936 they fly in formation, half bird of prey, half bomber, above the burning city, anticipating by a year or two the photos of Heinkels or Junkers flying in squadrons to destroy Warsaw or London which were to become familiar in the papers and newsreels. Grundig spent the years from 1938–45 in a concentration camp. In his first important work after his release, the 'Victims of Fascism' of 1946, the black birds fly in on heaped victims (with their striped pyjama-like camp clothes and stencilled numbers), their flight-feathers opened out and jointed like monstrous fingers. (In the 'Autumn' of 1947 we see the birds for the last time and his work takes on luxuriantly bright colours in the thankfulness of his liberation from unfreedom. One bird is now white and is sheering away like a bad dream beaten off by waking.) At about the same time Malcolm Lowry was struggling to finish *Under the Volcano* (1947). People have seen it as the tragedy of a self-destroying individual, and so it is, but it is also shot through with the awareness of the ominous, the imminent bad thing, which we have seen in so many artists who came into their own in the thirties.

The novel is set in Mexico, country of refugees, country of revolutions which had left too much unchanged:

Juarez had lived and died. Yet was it a country with free speech, and the guarantee of life, liberty, and the pursuit of happiness? A country of brilliantly muralled schools, and where even each little cold mountain village had its stone open-air stage, and the land was owned by its people free to express their native genius? A country of model farms: of hope? –

It was a country of slavery, where human beings were sold like cattle, and its native peoples, the Yaquis, the Papagos, the Tomasachics, exterminated through deportation, or reduced to worse than peonage their lands in thrall or the hands of foreigners . . . Juan knew this, having suffered it; and more. For later in the revolution, his mother was murdered. And later still Juan himself killed his father, who had fought with Huerta, but turned traitor.[25]

The main characters are foreigners: an ex-British Consul in the last stage of alcoholism, his wife who is in the throes of leaving him, his younger brother, a journalist with Left-wing views that he can never quite back up or feel sure of, sentimentally befriending Jews because their race is martyred, feeling guilty because he should still be in Spain where he has been covering the Civil War:

And they are losing the battle of the Ebro. Because of you, said the wind. A traitor even to your journalist friends you like to run down and who are really courageous men, admit it – *Ahh!* Hugh, as if to rid himself of these thoughts, turned the radio dial back and forth, trying to get San Antonio . . . How well he knew the jargon. Darkness, disaster! How the world fed on it. In the war to come correspondents would assume unheard of importance, plunging through flame to feed the public its little gobbets of dehydrated excrement.[26]

It is again the cosmopolitan milieu of rootlessness and crack-up, with the difference that chaos has now burst right in, killing people, demoralising them, deranging their perception of where reality ends and fantasy begins. The book works by long, confusing flashbacks to the Day of Death, the old Mexican festival, on which most of the action happens:

There were no children, however, in the garden; just a man sitting alone on a stone bench. This man was apparently the devil himself, with a huge dark red face and horns, fangs, and his tongue hanging out over his chin, and an expression of mingled evil, lechery, and terror. The devil lifted his mask to spit, rose, and shambled through the garden with a dancing,

loping step towards a church almost hidden by the trees. There
was a sound of clashing machetes. A native dance was going
on beyond some awnings by the church, on the steps of which
two Americans ... were watching on tiptoe, craning their
necks.[27]

It is again the 'medieval' inferno and it has its modern counterpart
which Lowry uses throughout as a leitmotiv, a poster of a nasty
thriller imported from the States: '6 y 8.30. Las Manos de Orlac,
con Peter Lorre' with a picture of 'a murderer's hands laced
with blood'.

As the novel ends, all the elements we have been seeing as
typical of the ominous collide with shattering effects. The Consul,
wandering around dazed with the virulent Mexican booze, finds
himself being hustled into a bar by a gang of policemen with
hifalutin titles and heavy revolvers at their hips – the Chief of
Gardens, the Chief of Rostrums, the Chief of Municipality ...
a diseased comedy of persecution has begun to work itself out.
The Consul has Hugh's papers on him and they incriminate him:

> Daily ... Londres Presse. Collect antisemitic campaign mex-
> press propetition ... textile manufacture's unquote ... German
> behind ... interiorwards. What was this? ... news ... jews
> ... country belief ... power ends conscience ... unquote stop
> Firmin. ...
>
> 'Where your papers? What for you have no papers?' the
> Chief of Rostrums asked, pocketing Hugh's cable. 'Where your
> pasaporte? What need for you to make disguise?'
>
> The Consul removed his dark glasses. Mutely to him, between
> sardonic thumb and forefinger, the Chief of Gardens held out
> the card: Federación Anarquista Iberica, it said. Sr Hugo Fir-
> min.[28]

In fact the Consul actively scorns political commitment, and here
Lowry is compounding the objective or social chaos by seeing
these final experiences through the mind of a man who now
finds himself by a mere accident typifying the millions of contemporary victims. The Consul has already (in a rather facile piece
of dramatisation) been made to rout Hugh in an argument about
fighting for causes:

'. . . All this, for instance, about going to fight for Spain
. . . and poor little defenceless China! Can't you see there's
a sort of determinism about the fate of nations? They all seem
to get what they deserve in the long run.'
  'Well . . .'
  'Not long ago it was poor little defenceless Ethiopia. Before
that, poor little defenceless Flanders. To say nothing of course
of the poor little defenceless Belgian Congo. And tomorrow
it will be poor little defenceless Latvia. Or Finland. Or Piddlede-
dee. Or even Russia. Read history. Go back a thousand years.
What is the use of interfering with its worthless stupid course?'[29]

Now the Consul becomes a scapegoat himself as the ruffian-police-
men identify him with every minority they have *carte blanche*
to crucify: '"You make a map of the Spain?"' They paw at
him with their questions. '"You Bolsheviki prick? You member
of the Brigade Internationale and stir up trouble?"' Someone
calls him Trotsky, someone else 'Juden', and Russian, and finally
(clearly the basic Mexican insult) '*antichrista* prik'.

  'You are no a de wrider, you are de espider, and we shoota
de espiders in Mejico . . . You Al Capón. You a Jew *chingao*
. . . *Norteamericano*, eh,' said the Chief. 'Ingles. You Jew . . .
I blow you wide open from your knees up, you Jew *chingao*
. . .' The Chief of Rostrums stepped aside, hand on his holster.
He drew his pistol. With his free hand he waved away some
tentative onlookers. 'I blow you wide open from your knees
up, you *cabrón*,' he said, 'you *pelado*.'

As mortal danger irrupts at last out of the tangle of ignorance,
bad English, bullying, and the drunken Consul's unsteady focus,
a horse rears, panicking at the revolver shots, and plunges neighing
into the forest. The final delirious image of a volcano erupting
turns into a nightmare of war: 'the world itself was bursting,
bursting into black spouts of villages catapulted into space, with
himself falling through it all, through the inconceivable pandemonium of a million tanks, through the blazing of ten million
burning bodies, falling into a forest, falling . . .'[30]

Our point is not that Lowry's novel is *about* the Spanish Civil

War or *about* Mexico after its revolutions but that a society so racked by war, corruption, and ill-controlled change could offer unlimited correlatives for the mentality of a deranged character. In the thirties and forties the tragedy of a man ruining himself with drink was likely to alert both writer and reader to the historical fact that every kind of chaos and destructiveness was now about to break loose.

10. Spain: Life Against Death

In the middle of 1975, some British papers carried stories about the treatment of captured fighters for the ETA, the Basque freedom movement. Torture has become the rule for hundreds of prisoners in the provinces of Vizcaya and Guipuzcoa since they came under emergency government in April of that year. Terror attacks are carried on against Basques by the extreme Right-wing *Christorei* or 'Fighters for Christ the King'. A priest has had his kidneys crushed by policemen jumping up and down on his back in a cell – he happened to be in custody on a night when Basque guerrillas killed an inspector of the Bilbao 'torture brigade'. A seventy-year-old farmer from near Guernica and his wife are in prison injured after sheltering a wounded young man who was being chased by the police. The sister of an ETA leader had her identity card snatched from her in the street by the police. She was then arrested for having no card and the police spat in her face in relays for two days. A conscript soldier, arrested as a suspect on the first day of the emergency, was beaten on the head and legs for twelve days and repeatedly put into a car and told he was about to be taken away and shot – 'a deliberate reminder of the Spanish Civil War when many people were executed in such a manner'.[1]

The fact that the battle continues like this in Spain is one ground for the abiding relevance of the Civil War of 1936–9, in addition to its well-known meaning as the 'dress rehearsal' for the total war of 1939–45. For example, German air-force officers fighting for Franco wanted to find out how city dwellers reacted to a planned attempt to set fire to their city, quarter by quarter. From 16–19 November 1936 Madrid was therefore bombed almost continuously, with special attention to hospitals and other buildings (such as the telephone exchange) which might arouse the worst panic. At least 1000 people were killed. The thing was unprecedented, although Republican journalists in Madrid at once forecast that it would be repeated many times in the next few years. And it was.[2] 'The terrible flames caused the capital to appear like some elemental place of torture. Over the crackle of fire, there could be heard the monotonous refrain, repeated syllabically, like a beat on a distant drum, "¡No pas-ar-án! ¡No pas-ar-án! ¡No pas-ar-án!"'[3] This audible evidence that people would *not* be cowed by such brutality of course had no effect on the thinking of the megadeath experts, whether Spanish, British, American, or German. On 26 April 1937, Heinkels and Junkers flown by German airmen bombed Guernica, ancient capital of the Basque land, in waves that arrived every twenty minutes for four hours. 70 per cent of the town was destroyed and one person in every four.[4] A year later Italian Fiats poured down bombs on the slums of Barcelona – the heartland of militancy described by Serge in *Birth of our Power*:

> Five hundred dead at ten a second
> is the world record so far reckoned;
> a hundred children in one street,
> their little hands and guts and feet,
> like offal round a butcher's stall,
> scattered where they'd been playing ball.[5]

The record was soon broken, in the carpet-bombing of working-class housing which now became standard. Our point is that the late thirties saw the intensifying of that class-struggle raised to the scale of war which has gone on ever since. In his poem Rickword specifies the international economic basis of Fascism and also makes many accurate detailed forecasts:

> Euzkadi's mines supply the ore
> to feed the Nazi dogs of war:
> Guernika's thermite rain transpires
> in doom on Oxford's dreaming spires:
> in Hitler's frantic mental haze
> already Hull and Cardiff blaze,
> and Paul's grey dome rocks to the blast
> of air-torpedoes screaming past.

'Euzkadi' was the Basque name for the province of Vizcaya (mentioned above), which during the Civil War proclaimed itself a free state. And now, again, in the north of Spain you can see 'Euzkadi' on the aerosol slogans and students' wall newspapers which pass on facts about the civil war now brewing up in the Basque lands and northern coalfields.

Although the defeat of the Republicans, and of the Left, by the Fascist nationalists cannot be shown to have much affected the world war that followed, Spain was always felt to be symbolically crucial. For the elder of us it was the first experience of gathering from the papers and the 'wireless' that widespread danger and destruction was a thing that could happen in our own world, not just in the bad old days of Flodden or Waterloo or Flanders. It was *the* extreme situation. As it says in much the finest (translated) Spanish memoir of the War, *The Clash* (1944) by Arturo Barea:

We had to fight them. It was not a question of political theories. It was life against death. We had to fight against the death-bringers, the Francos, the Sanjurjos, the Molas, the Millán Astrays, who crowned their blood-drenched record, selling their country so as to be the masters of slaves and in their turn the slaves of other masters.[6]

The Astray whom Barea mentions was a Nationalist general, founder of the Spanish Foreign Legion, and one of the Nationalists' chief propagandist broadcasters. He was famous for his slogan '¡*Viva la muerte!*' – Long live death. His extraordinary clash with the Basque philosopher and Rector of Salamanca University, Unamuno, goes to the heart of much we have discussed in this book. In a ceremony at the university, Astray violently attacked Catalonia and the Basque country as 'cancers' and extolled Fascism as a 'resolute surgeon' which would 'exterminate' them. Unamuno's last public act was to make a reply which included these words:

General Millán Astray is a cripple. Let it be said without any slighting undertone. He is a war invalid. So was Cervantes. Unfortunately there are all too many cripples in Spain just now. And soon there will be even more if God does not come to our aid. It pains me to think that General Millán Astray should dictate the pattern of mass psychology. A cripple who lacks the spiritual greatness of a Cervantes is wont to seek ominous relief in causing mutilation around him.[7]

Barea's later thoughts on the war also bring out its peculiar status as an event which, for many even of the first-hand witnesses, symbolised or *stood for* rather than *was*:

> The spectator countries favoured one or other of our two fronts; their ruling classes leaned towards the camp of international Fascism, a part of their working people and intellectuals leaned more or less clearly towards international Socialism. An ideological guerrilla warfare was going on in Europe and America ... some groups may have hoped that Spain would provoke war between Soviet Russia and Germany and many were curious to see the strength of the two opposing ideologies tested, not in the field of theory but of arms.[8]

From the viewpoint of the British Left Spain helped us out of the contradiction between wishing to stop Fascism and wishing, idealistically, to have no part in the capitalist arms race:

> Spain cut the knot of emotional and intellectual contradictions in which the Left had been entangled ever since Hitler came to power. Suddenly the claims of international law, class solidarity and the desire to win the Soviet Union as an ally fitted into the same strategy. These subconscious releases no doubt played their part in swelling the mood of sympathy for the Spanish Republic which swept so swiftly through the British working class.[9]

Our argument is that these tendencies to ideologise about the war affected the quality of the art aroused by it.

This art was copious – a great many poems, including remarkable ones by Auden, John Cornford, and Brian Howard and even two good ones by Stephen Spender; masterly novels by Malraux (*Days of Hope*) and Serge (chapter 5 of *Comrade Tulayev*); two of the century's best memoirs, Barea's *Clash* and Orwell's *Homage to Catalonia*; and in the visual media, Picasso's 'Guernica', the first classic photos by the classic photographer of war, Robert Capa, and more recently an outstanding documentary film, *To Die in Madrid*. In the English-speaking world it is plain from anthologies, academic studies, and even the main historians,[10] that they think Spain acted as a major inspiration, something like the Somme and the October Revolution rolled into one. Are there good grounds for this?

The political inspiration of the Republican cause shows in the eager rush of detail near the start of *Homage to Catalonia* (1938) – a passage that vies with Gorky's *Fragments from My Diary* in its evocation of socialist *élan*:

Churches here and there were being systematically demolished by gangs of workmen. Every shop and café had an inscription saying that it had been collectivized; even the bootblacks had been collectivized and their boxes painted red and black. Waiters and shop-walkers looked you in the face and treated you as an equal. Servile and even ceremonial forms of speech had temporarily disappeared. Nobody said 'Señor' or 'Don' or even 'Usted'; everyone called everyone else 'Comrade' and 'Thou,' and said 'Salud!' instead of 'Buenos dias.' Tipping was forbidden by law; almost my first experience was receiving a lecture from an hotel manager for trying to tip a lift-boy. There were no private motor cars, they had all been commandeered, and all the trams and taxis and much of the other transport were painted red and black. The revolutionary posters were everywhere, flaming from the walls in clean reds and blues that made the few remaining advertisements look like daubs of mud. Down the Ramblas, the wide central artery of the town where crowds of people streamed constantly to and fro, the loudspeakers were bellowing revolutionary songs all day and far into the night. And it was the aspect of the crowds that was the queerest thing of all. In outward appearance it was a town in which the wealthy classes had practically ceased to exist. Except for a small number of women and foreigners there were no 'well-dressed' people at all. Practically everyone wore rough working-class clothes, or blue overalls or some variant of the militia uniform.[11]

Red was for socialism, black for anarchism: rebel politics mingled freely. That was in December 1936. By the end of the war, Communists, Trotskyites, and Anarchists had turned their guns on each other. In 'Journey Into Defeat' from *Comrade Tulayev*, Serge shows us the Old Bolshevik Kondratiev working virtually as a Soviet secret agent, supervising the kidnapping of the ardent young Trotskyite Stefan Stern. Giddy with knock-out drugs, Stern manages to accuse him:

> He spoke fiercely, violently, and he was persuasive, subtle, stubborn, without clearly knowing what he was saying; it came out of him as blood spurts out of a deep wound (the image flitted through his mind). 'What have you done, you vermin, with your faked trials? You have poisoned the most sacred possession of the proletariat, the spring of its self-confidence, which no defeat could take from us. When the Communards were stood up and shot in the old days, they felt clean, they fell proudly; but now you have dirtied them one with another, and with such dirt that the best of us cannot comprehend it ... In this country you have vitiated everything, corrupted everything, lost everything. Look, look ...' Stefan let go of the couch, the better to show them the defeat which he held out in his two bloodless hands, and he almost toppled over.[12]

Such was the end of the revolutionary cause in Spain. Orwell's Barcelona had been its start. Between them raged the war in which 400,000 died violent deaths, 240,000 finished up in prison, and by July 1939 1000 a month were being executed by firing squad.[13]

Orwell's analysis of the murderous and demoralising struggle inside the Republican ranks is justly famous for its candour. He is here at one with Serge in his effort to keep the hands, or at least the conscience, of the revolution clean. Where are we to find the likeness of the actual experiences which the political manipulators strove to control? Serge's chapter is concerned with life behind the fighting-lines. Orwell was at the front, but his style is scarcely potent enough to make you feel the sting and blast of battle. A touchstone here would be the moment in Hemingway's *A Farewell to Arms* (chapter 9) when the narrator is hit as a shell explodes near him. It is physically intense, psychologically subtle; it is palpably at the point of the experience. By comparison

Orwell has to labour to evoke the moment when the bullet went through his neck, and though his prose is adequate, in our experience his inages soon merge with many kindred passages from *Goodbye to All That*, *Memoirs of an Infantry Officer*, and so on. He is barely an artist, more a conscientious informant, and this is characteristic: 'Benjamin leapt to his feet and shouted: "Forward! Charge!" We dashed up the short steep slope on which the parapet stood. I say "dashed"; "lumbered" would be a better word; the fact is that you can't move fast when you are sodden and mudded from head to foot and weighted down with a heavy rifle and bayonet and a hundred and fifty cartridges,' and so on.[14]

Malraux in *Days of Hope* (1938) was writing as hurriedly, as near to the experience, but he is both more coherent on strategy and goes more deep into the personal experience, and this although he himself was concerned with the war in the air, not on the ground. For example, the account of the battle for Barcelona in chapter 2 of Part 1 – the storming of the regular-army positions with improvised 'armoured' cars – plunges us into combat and there we stay for the length of the novel. That sequence is a standard piece of street fighting, although the cinematic grasp of movement is excellent, but in chapter 1 of Part 2, in the run-in to the long pounding siege of the Alcazar in Toledo, there is a moment so sensuously powerful that out of its lifelikeness there comes a lasting symbol of warfare. Fascist soldiers are using a flame-thrower in the cellars of the Museum:

Now the flame-thrower had reached the threshold. Revolver in hand the Negus was standing near the door, flattening himself against the wall. As the brass nozzle peeped round the corner, he snatched at it, but let go at once; his skin was peeling off. His flowing silky hair glimmered like a blue aureole in the vivid flame-light; bullets were crackling all around him. The fascist swerved aside so as to bring his projector to bear on the Negus, whose hand was pressing on his chest. The Negus fired. The projector clanged on the stone floor, flung all the shadows up on to the roof. The fascist, an elderly officer, stood tottering above it for a moment, his face lit up from below, bathed in the livid sheen of the dancing flames. Then with the unnatural languor of a slow-motion picture, he fell alongside the Negus, his head bumping against the nozzle, which spluttered and flung it off, like a foot kicking aside an obstacle. The Negus picked up the projector and pointed it in the other direction. At once the room was plunged in darkness, and the tunnel filled with clouds of glowing smoke traversed by flying shadows. The milicianos thronged excitedly into the tunnel, following the blue flames, in a wild hubbub of shouts and gun-shots. Suddenly everything went dim. The only lights remaining were an electric torch and a single hurricane-lamp.

'They turned off the gas once they saw we'd got hold of the projector,' a voice called in the darkness. Then, after a moment, added: 'I know what I'm talking about. I was an officer in the fire-brigade.'

'Halt!' Hernandez shouted from the tunnel. 'They've a barricade across the exit.'

'You can't go native to order!' the Negus remarked to Hernandez. (The milicianos were relighting the other hurricane lamp.) 'It was touch and go,' the Negus went on. 'He had just time enough to turn the jet on me before I fired. But I was looking him in the eyes, you know. It's queer the way men are. Yes, it must be hard to bring yourself to burn a man who's looking at you!'[15]

The almost tangibly physical writing feeds its force into those last sentences, so that they epitomise as remarkably as the close of Owen's 'Strange Meeting' what it is for people to war against each other:

> I am the enemy you killed, my friend.
> I knew you in this dark; for so you frowned
> Yesterday through me as you jabbed and killed.
> I parried; but my hands were loath and cold . . .

We could infer from this difference in quality between Orwell and Malraux that the latter was more wholly embroiled in the war, and if it should be objected that the difference lies in their calibre as artists, we would reply that it is exactly the power of the finest artist to be the most wholly embroiled. It is not a simple matter of who was there and who was not. Serge was never in Spain after 1917 yet he evokes the atmosphere and

the political detail of the treachery inside the Left at least as
effectively as Orwell. Malraux learned about the fighting in Barcelona and Toledo from a distance. Picasso painted 'Guernica' in
his Paris studio and his image of fleeing townsfolk, their eyes
turned up at the sky from which bombs are about to fall, presumably derives from photos like one that Capa took in Spain in
1936.[16] This image so possessed Picasso that after 'Guernica'
he made it into those etchings of grief-stricken women in which
their own tears, sharp black lines ending in droplets, also look
like instruments piercing them.[17] Barea saw no combat (though
he had fought as a conscript in the Moroccan war in the Twenties)
yet it is in his pages that the most shockingly unforgettable imagery
of destroyed and injured people can be found. He spent the
war in Madrid, latterly as a broadcaster called the 'Unknown
Voice from Madrid'. His talks were tremendously appreciated
by ordinary people because he did not hector them but told
things like they were. On one occasion the secretary of a Workers'
Committee told him, ' "Today you've almost made new literature." '[18] Millán Astray, on the other hand, 'raved excitedly for
six nights about death and the purity of Spanish womanhood,
but could hardly be followed by his hearers.'[19] The siege of
Madrid began in August 1936 and by November bombardment
was daily. It went on for two years four months three weeks.
Towards the end of *The Clash* there is this passage:

> The street was filled with glaring sunlight and curls of slowly
> thinning smoke. Dull thuds sounded from further up Shell
> Alley. The porter informed me that our drivers were waiting
> round the corner in the Calle de la Montera, which was safer.
> I walked ahead of the women to find the cars.
>   . . . At the corner itself a gust of the familiar acrid smell
> hit me. Out of the corner of my eye I saw something odd
> and filmy sticking to the huge show window of the Gramophone
> Company. I went close to see what it was. It was moving.
>   A lump of gray mass, the size of a child's fist, was flattened
> out against the glass pane and kept on twitching. Small, quiver-
> ing drops of gray matter were spattered round it. A fine thread
> of watery blood was trickling down the pane, away from the
> gray-white lump with the tiny red veins, in which the torn
> nerves were still lashing out.

I felt nothing but stupor. I looked at the scrap of man stuck on to the shop window and watched it moving like an automaton. Still alive. A scrap of human brain.[20]

We cannot conceive of a sharper image of what weapons do to people. Barea's sensibility is totally exposed to the extreme situation, not muffled to make things bearable, not distanced or subsumed into explanation. The difference from Orwell must be partly a matter of temperament, but we suggest it is also because Orwell belonged to one of the 'spectator nations'. Contrast the two men's treatment of the sabotaged shells. Orwell writes:

The shells the Fascists were firing at this period were wretchedly bad. Although they were 150 mm. they only made a crater about six feet wide by four deep, and at least one in four failed to explode. There were the usual romantic tales of sabotage in the Fascist factories and unexploded shells in which, instead of the charge, there was found a scrap of paper saying 'Red Front,' but I never saw one. The truth was that the shells were hopelessly old; someone picked up a brass fuse-cap stamped with the date, and it was 1917. The Fascist guns were of the same make and calibre as our own, and the unexploded shells were often reconditioned and fired back. There was said to be one old shell with a nickname of its own which travelled daily to and fro, never exploding.[21]

Orwell sounds like a quizzical traveller, commenting on the quaintly backward natives. In *The Clash* Barea writes about a Fascist shell that had gone through the walls of a police barracks but failed to explode:

It was a twenty-four centimeter shell, as big as a child. After endless telephoning hither and thither, a man from the Artillery Depot arrived to dismantle the fuse; the shell would be fetched away later on. The Shock Police cleared the western half of the building, and we waited in the other court. After a short while, the artillerist emerged triumphantly, in one hand the brass fuse cap, in the other a strip of paper. The guards carried the huge, harmless shell into the court and set it up. Somebody translated the words on the paper that had been hidden in the hollow of the shell. It said in German: 'Comrades, don't be afraid, the shells I charge do not explode. – A German worker.'[22]

Orwell could not have known this. But neither had he the political will or impulsion to believe it possible. The continental writers did have this, because they were now needing to work out actual ways of resisting the bad thing. So Brecht, also a non-combatant in the thirties, wrote in a poem for his *German War Primer*:

His SS troops should not be allowed to sleep.
They should be forced to check
Whether every warhead is correctly primed.
He should be forced to check personally
Whether every checker is checking.[23]

The poetic record in English is profuse and varied, and generally thought of as something like a school of writing in itself. How near it is to the marrow of the Spanish experience can be judged if we put a sonnet from the *Left Review* by a nearly unknown writer, Brian Howard, beside either one of the 'standard' poems on Spain, say Spender's 'Port Bou' or 'Ultima Ratio Regum', or one of the best, John Cornford's 'Full Moon at Tierz: Before the Storming of Huesca' or Auden's 'Spain'. Here is Howard's 'For Those With Investments in Spain: 1937':

I ask your patience, half of them cannot read,
Your forbearance if, for a while, they cannot pay,
Forgive them, it's disgusting to watch them bleed,
I beg you to excuse, they have no time to pray.
Here is a people, you know it as well as he does,
Franco, you can see it as plain as they do,
Who are forced to fight, for the simplest rights, foes
Richer, stupider, stronger than you, or I, or they, too.
So, while the German bombs burst in their wombs,
And poor Moors are unloosed on the unhappy,
And Italian bayonets go through their towns like combs,
Spare a thought, a thought for all those Spanish tombs,
And for a people in danger, grieving in broken rooms,
For a people in danger, shooting from falling homes.

The power of the poem comes from its being in a style seemingly as far as possible from Spain and its people – the mock politeness of English gentlefolk conversing about the nasty business from a distance – yet this of all styles is suffused with an almost shaking urgency about the Spaniards' sufferings. One sentence jostles after another without a full stop, the word-order is that of unpremeditated speech, the norm of the sonnet line is stretched to breaking, and finally the rhyme-scheme is pushed to an extreme as those repeated 'm'-sounds land like a stick of bombs. Acute pain, deep fellow-feeling are evoked without one false note. The one questionable phrase might be 'bombs burst in their wombs'. Is this accurate? Is it there to force our sympathy and to enable that last row of rhymes? It turns out to be accurate. Barea writes: 'several women were lying on the ground and shrieking. One of them was dragging herself along on a belly torn to bleeding tatters ... A woman propped up on her bleeding arm stump gave a scream and let herself drop heavily. Near me was a bundle of petticoats with a leg sticking out, bent at an impossible angle over a swollen belly.'[24]

Beside such a poem, Spender's Modernist gestures and old-fashioned poeticisms look like little more than symptoms of the will to Be A Poet. The self-consciousness which makes 'Port Bou' repellent – the poet's silly feeling that the shooting, which anyway is only practice, is somehow aimed at him – in a way comes into its own in 'Thoughts During an Air Raid', because here an ignominious feeling of being too self-centred is his subject:

> Of course, the entire effort is to put myself
> Outside the ordinary range
> Of what are called statistics. A hundred are killed
> In the outer suburbs. Well, well, I carry on.
> So long as the great 'I' is propped upon
> This girdered bed which seems more like a hearse,
> In the hotel bedroom with flowering wallpaper
> Which rings in wreathes above, I can ignore
> The pressure of those names under my fingers
> Heavy and black as I rustle the paper ...[25]

Self-consciousness is the bad side of being a spectator instead of being a participant too busy getting something done to have room to regard himself (whether preening himself or disliking himself) as playing out a role. To be a spectator, or a participant who had come in from elsewhere, is a strength when it is used to take an overview of the war, to see it in history. Both Auden's 'Spain' and Cornford's 'Full Moon at Tierz' do this in different ways. 'Spain' is the most sustained piece of Marxist *thinking* in any of the creative media.[26] Its subject is not so much Spain as the human situation of being in a history which the species makes for itself. Spain takes up only five verses out of the original twenty-six.[27] It comes into the poem as the type of something larger. The poet sees evolution as a process of learning to do without mystique and to replace it by a clear-eyed understanding of material nature:

> Yesterday the assessment of insurance by cards,
> The divination of water: yesterday the invention
>   Of cartwheels and clocks, the taming of
> Horses. Yesterday the bustling world of the navigators.

Belief in benign powers dies hard, and even today people are dependent on them:

> And the poor in their fireless lodgings, dropping the sheets
> Of the evening paper: 'Our day is our loss, O show us
>   History the operator, the
> Organiser, Time the refreshing river.'

Against this the poet, from his existentialist or materialist position, argues that value cannot be found in life, we have to create it by conscious decision. Writing as a socialist, in 1937, he sees commitment to the Spanish Republic as the prime type of such a decision:

> 'What's your proposal? To build the just city? I will.
> I agree. Or is it the suicide pact, the romantic
>   Death? Very well, I accept, for
> I am your choice, your decision. Yes, I am Spain.'

And having arrived by a wonderfully supple, knowledgeable, and witty argument at the vanguard-point of history, the poem gathers to a vision of the Spanish situation which is both noble and realistic:

> Many have heard it in remote peninsulas,
> On sleepy plains, in the aberrant fisherman's islands
> > Or the corrupt heart of the city,
> Have heard and migrated like gulls or the seeds of a flower.
>
> They clung like birds to the long expresses that lurch
> Through the unjust lands, through the night, through the
> > alpine tunnel.
> > They floated over the oceans;
> They walked the passes. All presented their lives.
>
> On that arid square, that fragment nipped off from hot
> Africa, soldered so crudely to inventive Europe;
> > On that tableland scored by rivers
> Our thoughts have bodies; the menacing shapes of our fever
>
> Are precise and alive . . .

It is not surprising that Spain has no sooner materialised in the poem than it vanishes, since Auden's morale turns out to be too low, too discouraged on both the intimate and the public plane, to supply him with the energy needed for identification with great political efforts. The public comes down to 'the flat ephemeral pamphlet and the boring meeting', the intimate to the 'Fumbled and unsatisfactory embrace before hurting'. To end his poem without bathos, he has to move outwards to a series of classic epigrams, genuinely resonant, deeply defeated:

> The stars are dead. The animals will not look.
> We are left alone with our day, and the time is short, and
> > History to the defeated
> May say alas but cannot help or pardon.

Whether one likes it or not (by which we obviously mean that we do not), Auden's depressed morale gave him a truer perspective on the immediate political future than the revolutionary *élan* of Cornford, the other poet who at that time was pondering in a deep Marxist way the lines along which history was shaping.

A month after arriving in Spain and three months before being killed there, he put down in his diary a series of thoughts in lyrical form.[28] As a fervent student-Communist leader, he felt he was in at the making of history, he was not an unenchanted or even estranged observer of it like Auden. The rare quality of his main poem, 'Full Moon at Tierz: Before the Storming of Huesca', is that it brings home the reality of the grand revolutionary clichés which might have seemed worn featureless by a million reiterations, e.g. phrases from the 'Internationale' and 'Bandiera Rossa': 'The last fight let us face ... Raise the red flag triumphantly/ For Communism and for liberty.' Post-Stalinist eyes are bound to look sceptically back at a piece which seems to *assume* the rightness of Communism. 'Our Maurice Thorez held the light ... Now, with my Party, I stand quite alone' – in what sense, by September 1936, was a Communist Party General Secretary any longer ours, and not Stalin's? How could the party which expelled a Victor Serge be anybody's but the *apparatchik's*? Nevertheless Cornford's sense of imminent action, and action as the test of valid politics, gives his poem its true ring:

> All round the barren hills of Aragon
> Announce our testing has begun.
> Here what the Seventh Congress said,
> If true, if false, is live or dead,
> Speaks in the Oviedo mauser's tone.

The nearer the poem is to this notion, the better it works. It is this belief in practice, in changing the world, which holds the imagery of the opening verses together in a strong formation:

> The past, a glacier, gripped the mountain wall,
> And time was inches, dark was all.
> But here it scales the end of the range,
> The dialectic's point of change,
> Crashes in light and minutes to its fall.
>
> Time present is a cataract whose force
> Breaks down the banks even at its source
> And history forming in our hand's
> Not plasticine but roaring sands,
> Yet we must swing it to its final course.[29]

This is impressive not only because it is genuinely exalted but also because the 'big' words (past, time, history, dialectic) turn out to have been thought through to their core. Each phrase or image which holds us up, in doubt or puzzlement, presently yields a clear meaning, and often a complex one. What exactly is happening in verse 1? The 'it' of line 3 must be time. Is time, then, still the subject of the final clause, 'Crashes in light and minutes to its fall'? Yes, because the dialectic (the principle of change) is in apposition to 'the end of the range', which means the point at which the quality of life is transformed by a heaping-up of powers or forces. So it is time which, by the end of the verse, has crashed and fallen. But time cannot have ended? No: what it has done is to break into movement again, after seeming to stay still during the long freeze-up of a society before the revolution. Wherever you try the imagery, it is thus pregnant with meaning, or double meaning – 'range' at once becomes both the line of mountains which had hemmed in that deadlocked life and the scale against which change must be measured. In verse 2 the doubleness or ambiguity goes further and suggests an element of tragic doubt (whether conscious or not on Cornford's part) about how effective the revolution can be. No sooner has the changefulness of history been likened to an inspiring force than this is undercut by the metaphor of sand – age-old symbol of the hopelessly unstable or unmanageable; and this is signalled in the word that links the train of thought to the stirring positive which comes in to clinch it – '*Yet* we must swing it to its final course.' Although the whole poem ends with an outright slogan, 'Raise the red flag triumphantly', its best section, the first one, is so deep because it realises the uncertainty of even the most militant standpoint, the forever problematic quality of what is to come:

> The intersecting lines that cross both ways,
> Time future, has no image in space,
> Crooked as the road that we must tread,
> Straight as our bullets fly ahead.
> We are the future. The last fight let us face.

Auden's poem and Cornford's are akin (for all the great difference in militancy) in that both see Spain less as an actuality and more as representing something other than itself. Both men were from a spectator country and hence, as Barea put it, 'curious to see the strength of the two opposing ideologies tested, not in the field of theory but of arms.' In what he did, which was to die for his beliefs, Cornford was not a spectator, but in his imaginative view of the war he was – it is significant that his other main Spanish poem, 'A Letter from Aragon', which does plant itself firmly in veritable Spain, is much shorter than 'Full Moon at Tierz' and much less achieved. After the solid opening description,

We buried Ruiz in a new pine coffin,
But the shroud was too small and his washed feet stuck out,

it rather tails off in randomly personal touches and a peroration which feels tacked on.[30] It is another ground for our argument that Spain meant a great deal to our artists, that is unquestionable, but rather more as an idea than as an experience. It was *the* political touchstone in its time, both of their own integrity and nerve as socialists and of the validity of socialism in Europe. In the event, not much was tested in Spain, apart from the bravery of many individuals. Fascism triumphed, but this meant little for the future since Franco's rigidly practical and military form of it had little of the manic overreaching of Hitler, Mussolini, or Japan's military caste. Socialism was defeated, but this meant little for the future since an idealistic coalition of the Left was never again attempted and the Second World War was won by a purely provisional and forced alliance of Stalinists and social democrats.

The essence of the Spanish situation, therefore, lay in its extremity, rather than in whatever ideology could make of it, and it was this, the crunching and pulping of people's fields and homes and bodies, which the continental artists could feel to the full, although it took political commitment on their part and not just physical nearness. (In Sartre's *Roads to Freedom* trilogy, the chronically detached philosopher, Mathieu, observes more or less admiringly of the wholly committed Communist, Brunet, 'it was he who had been bombarded', that is, he had felt the distant atrocity as though it had hit him.[31] So it is that to get the sunk, beaten, inconsolable grief of defeat we have to go to Koestler's *Spanish Testament* and *Scum of the Earth*; to get the scorching warfare itself we must go to Malraux' *Days of Hope*; to get the first heavings of revolution and then the agony of its betrayal we must go to Serge's *Birth of Our Power* and *Comrade Tulayev*; to get the *élan* of revolution, not speechified or ideologised about but uttered with a full throat, we must go to the song of the Republican XVth Brigade, 'Viva La Quince Brigada', which evolved out of an Aragonese folksong during the Battle of the Ebro in 1938[32]; and to get the actual look of a way of life in the act of shattering we must go to Barea's memoirs or Picasso's 'Guernica'.[33]

The Times of 27 April 1937 described the bombing of Guernica as follows:

> Guernica, the most ancient town of the Basques and the centre of their cultural tradition, was completely destroyed yesterday afternoon by insurgent air-raiders. The bombardment of the open town far behind the lines occupied precisely three hours and a quarter, during which a powerful fleet of aeroplanes consisting of three German types, Junkers and Heinkel bombers and Heinkel fighters, did not cease unloading on the town bombs weighing from 1,000 lb. downwards . . . The fighters meanwhile flew low from above the centre of the town to machine-gun those of the civilians who had taken refuge in the fields. The whole of Guernica was soon in flames except the historic Casa de Juntas.[34]

Within two weeks of the bombing, Picasso, who had already been commissioned by the Republican government to paint a mural for the World Fair in Paris, had produced 'Guernica'.

The most immediately striking thing about it is the absence of colour, or, rather, Picasso's choice of black, white, and grey in which to work. Visual psychology aside – black and grey evoke gloom and despair – Picasso is using the visual expectations created by newspaper photos. In the days before colour film, reality (and especially political reality) had become what the photo-journalist recorded. By drawing unexpectedly on visual conventions other than the traditional painterly ones, Picasso gave his work far greater force than if he had used, say, Gauguinesque colour. (Red and orange flames usually look too pretty in war paintings even though they are obviously more lifelike than the seven stiff grey cut-out-looking flames at the top right-hand side of 'Guernica'.)

At the same time the newspaper theme, as we may call it, is picked up in the type-sheet body of the horse, a device which enables Picasso to do two other things. He lightly suggests the collage convention and all that it implies about modern cultural disorder, e.g. the continuous jumble of data from a great variety of sources.[35] Secondly, Picasso was drawing on one of the recurring motifs in literary Modernism, direct citation from the daily press. This happens again and again in the important Modernist works. In Dos Passos's *USA*, for example, there are sixty-eight 'Newsreels' made up mainly of cuttings from the press. We saw how Farrell used newsreel captions in *Studs Lonigan*. In *Native Son* (1940) Richard Wright simulates newpaper reports as much as two pages long. One of the finest of Communist poets, Nazim Hikmet, used actual reports in his masterpiece, 'Letters to Taranta-Babu'.[36] Part of the same trend is the shading over from fiction into documentary. Not only does imaginative writing begin to transpose social facts without altering or recreating them, but the work of reporters and other social observers begins to take on qualities of art. An outstanding case is *Let Us Now Praise Famous Men* by James Agee and Walker Evans. They had been commissioned by *Fortune* magazine to make a study in words and pictures of poor cotton farmers in Alabama. The result was not a feature article but a large book in which a way of life is treated with the inwardness and complexity that the 'standard' Modernist novelists (Joyce, Woolf) spent on individual characters. Documentary became under the historical pressures of the thirties a major genre, and Picasso seems to have been sensitive to this.

'Guernica' is rich in creative ambiguities. We mean by this that every image in it has several meanings each of which reinforces the others and so gives the whole its extraordinary power (it bears looking at indefinitely). For example, what is the exploding object over the horse's head? On one level it is an explosion, the jagged lines of force reaching outwards at the moment of ignition. But the rays have shadows, which implies solidity, and shadows which do not correspond exactly to the jagged edges, which implies movement. At the same time the jagged area could be a hole blasted in the ceiling and the central object in it a glimpse of a bomb dropping outside. Most literally it is a lamp-shade with a bulb in it, lighting up a peasant's farm, perhaps. More abstractly it resembles an eye edged with metallic lashes (recalling the eyes of Dr T. J. Meckleburg – 'the eyes of God' – which surveyed another famous waste land). And is there not a hint, not obtrusively done but recognisably there as soon as it is pointed out, of the Christian crown of thorns?

So Picasso both permits and intends many levels of meaning to inhere in his images, as Eliot does in *The Waste Land*, but he does not depend, as Eliot does, on specialised knowledge to decode his allusions, or on the reader or viewer's prior agreement with some point of view which is not made good in the work itself. What 'Guernica' requires of us is that we be observant, imaginatively open – that we release our whole selves into our response to it.

Look at the bull. His eyes, contrasted with all the other eyes in the painting, are intelligent and unafraid. Picasso has done it by giving him eyelids, a simple little line above each orbit (not the eyelids raised and sharpened by horror of the face which balloons in, in the right-hand half of the picture). The bull suggests sheer animality, brute force released into a room, an almost literal rendering of the phrase 'a bull in a china shop'. His hooves and body lower dangerously over the human faces of mother and child. His is the only presence in the painting unripped or undistorted by the terrible nameless thing that has happened there. He appears to have stepped a moment before through the opening behind him, his tail still smoking like a bomb crater or a volcano, and – such is the impact of the simultaneous profile and full-face Picasso has given him, together with the pencilled-in third eye left showing in his forehead – he seems to be surveying the scene with dangerous equanimity. His tongue and nostrils are sharp, threatening, like so much else in the painting: metallic, pointed, and dangerous to soft human flesh. His ears are like 9mm cannon shells.

The bull is Picasso's single concession to the Spanishness of the scene. He is drawing on the conventions of the bull-fight, the moment when the dangerous black killer pounds into the ring, then stops to size up his adversaries. The dotted area on the horse's body may also pick this up: it is like the padded quilts worn by the picadors' nags. But one does not need to go outside the painting to read the meanings of the bull. They are multiple, and Picasso confirmed this years later when he said, 'The bull is not fascism, but it is brutality and darkness.'[37]

The figures of the mother and child, over whom the bull stands, share in the powerfully creative distortion of the whole triangular composition in that part of the picture. The pulling and rending – downward and outward, as shown in her pointed breasts and swelling left hand – perfectly render suffering and pain. The child is obviously dead, not only because the eyes are blank but also because the nose, amazingly, has flopped back onto his forehead and his ear has revolved on its axis. His mother is hysterical with grief, her head thrown back at right angles to her body as she screams, her teeth and tongue hardening into sharp, horrible objects in her mouth. Touches recall Michelangelo's 'Pietá' – the woman's expressive left hand, the dead son, the folds of skirt on which he lies. But it is so simply done, it is in any case so natural to the scene, that it does not get in the way. Like Eliot, Picasso is willing to cite others, but creatively, and not as wilful or pretentious gestures towards things quite foreign to most of his public.

Look at the figure on the floor, beneath the madonna and the bull. It is a dead man – his left arm thrown behind his head, his right arm cut off and lying further away, clutching a sword – and a smashed statue. The shatter lines in the arms, the clean square cut at the neck, suggest this. So he is both humanity and art trampled on, both a dead person and perhaps the figure in the town square which the bombs have destroyed. Moreover, this figure contains the only weapon in the whole war painting (the spearhead coming out of the horse's belly might as well be the blade of a bricklayer's trowel). And it is a primitive weapon, useless against bombs, so that it both suggests the defence-lessness of civilians under air-raids and connects this massacre with the long history of man's inhumanity to man.

What of the horse, in many way the painting's central and most memorable image? Look at the screaming, maddened face, the eyes stupid with terror. It is the archetypal silent scream that recurs in twentieth-century art, from Munch's 'The Cry' to Francis Bacon's 'The Screaming Pope.' (One also thinks of Mother Courage's silent scream as she turns away from Swiss Cheese's corpse – a posture which Brecht's wife, Helene Weigel, who played the part, is said to have copied from a newsreel photo.[38]) The horse's body crumples, dismembers, and slowly turns transparent in the heat of the blast. He is at the centre of the painting and Picasso said that he represented the people.

On the middle right stand two observers – ourselves, if you like, for such is the size of the painting that we feel as though drawn into the thick of an action. Both figures – the one swooping in through the door, or perhaps leaning out of the window, and the woman kneeling in the foreground – have expressions of uncomprehending dismay, despair, and bewilderment, although the upper face looks more seeingly and the arm beside it is trying to thrust a lantern into the darkness beside the horse. No light comes from the lamp but at least the fingers are clenched round its paraffin-lamp as strongly as a tree-root round a stone. This female figure expresses determination to see, but the lower one is dragging to the ground, as though her own weight were crushing her. Her buttocks are bare. When Picasso was painting this figure, Penrose happened to be there and asked him what he had in mind. Without a word Picasso fetched a piece of toilet paper and held it where the thin white rectangle now is.[38] He meant the woman had been caught on the toilet and simply rushed out to see what was happening. The painter felt there was no sharper image of unpreparedness and he also wanted homely details in the midst of historically momentous actions (Brecht admired the same thing in Brueghel's painting of Jesus on the way to Calvary). He also felt free to distort in order to multiply meanings (so long as the common-or-garden original was not lost). So the lower woman's right hand has become an animal's paw with pads, and her nipples have become nuts and bolts. People are being treated as things, this image implies.

The figure on the right is the last one the eye picks out but it is very important. Behind it a fire roars – the light is so intense that the bottom line of the windowsill cannot be seen. The flames leap up over the building – flames that are also like the nails on a huge hand or the spine of a prehistoric beast. The figure – a man, with striped trousers – is reacting to the consuming fire. But how is he reacting? He is falling, drowning in flames, throwing up his mouth for air from the little square window. But he is also rising, his arms are solid, not shattered, he is not beaten down like horse, infant corpse, adult corpse,

or half-naked woman. He is a dialectical figure, embodying opposing impulses. His hands are lifted up in suffering and self-protec-
tion, yes, but also in defiance and, by the spreading angle of
his arms, as though to display the atrocity. He still bears witness,
he does not only suffer. With his capacity to communicate and
defy, he balances the bull's mindless savagery. He is the source
of the political optimism in the picture, since at this moment
of utter defeat he makes at least a signal towards future struggles.
As Picasso once said, 'No, painting is not done to decorate apartments. It is an instrument of war [against] brutality and darkness.'[40]

11. Collapse and Survival

'The whole world doesn't collapse at once.' Serge began *The Long Dusk* (1946) with this characteristic sentence, terse and unlaboured yet terribly sharp in what it implies. The most prescient writers now felt that it was touch and go for the species – that the most extreme situation conceivable might well have been reached. The French writer Michel Leiris said that in 'Guernica' Picasso 'sends us our announcement of our mourning : all that we love is going to die'.[1] Orwell's alternative title for *Nineteen Eighty-four*, which he was thinking about from the middle of the war, was *The Last Man in Europe*.[2] At about the same time Anna Seghers was writing in *The Seventh Cross*: 'if we were to be destroyed on that scale, all would perish because there would be none to come after us. The almost unprecedented in history, the most terrible thing that could happen to a nation, was now to be our fate'.[3] In what may well be the classic message to come out of the Stalinist Soviet Union, Nadezhda Mandelstam's *Hope Against Hope*, the writer constantly speaks as though for a people who have gone under for the last time, in the faint but enduring hope that there may be someone on the far side to hear her words:

> For our generation, kindness was an old-fashioned, vanished quality, and its exponents were as extinct as the mammoth. Everything we have seen in our times – the dispossession of the kulaks, class warfare, the constant 'unmasking' of people, the search for an ulterior motive behind every action – all this has taught us to be anything you like except kind.
>
> Kindness and good nature had to be sought in remote places that were deaf to the call of the age. Only the inert had kept these qualities as they had come down from their ancestors.

Everybody else had been affected by the inverted 'humanism' of the times. . . .

. . . People of M.'s generation – and of mine, for that matter – no longer had anything to live for. He would not have lived to see even the comparatively good times since Stalin's death which Akhmatova and I regard as bliss. I realized this at the end of the forties and the beginning of the fifties, when most people who had returned from the camps after the end of their sentences (including many who had fought in the war) were sent back to them again. 'M. did well to die straightaway,' said Kazarnovski, who met M. in a transit camp and then spent ten years in Kolyma. Could we ever have believed such a thing in Voronezh? We probably imagined that the worst was behind us, or, rather, like other doomed people, we tried not to peer into the future. We slowly prepared for death, lingering over every minute and relishing it, to keep the taste on our lips, because Voronezh was a miracle and only a miracle could have brought us here.[4]

What seemed to have put the species in jeopardy was both the thoroughness and the scale of the destruction, whether by the Himmler–Eichmann industrial methods – the most economical use of railroads, poison gas, and high-density accommodation – or the Allies' fusion of scientific and military methods to burn out Dresden and raze Hiroshima. The scale has been so great that, as we saw in the dispute about Dresden, people back away from admitting it. Even the excellent documentary collection called *The War 1939–1945* (1960), edited by Desmond Flower and James Reeves, is dedicated 'to the 30,000,000 dead', whereas the military historians estimate the death-roll at fifty-five million *not* counting the Far East, where loss of life was so great, since the social services there were too backward to keep an exact count.[5]

Mortality on this colossal scale was likely to call out the supreme creative efforts that result in masterpieces, and we discussed three classic novels about it in Chapter 2, 'Total War'. The remarkable thing is that the experience of the war as utterly deathly gathered itself so soon into a central dramatic symbol, in Camus' *The Plague*. He conceived of it in April 1941. This was ten months after the French parliament voted (in a proportion of seven to one) to hand over three-fifths of France to the German army and the Gestapo, and nine months before Camus joined the Resistance.[6] Under an odd heading, 'The liberating plague', he wrote: 'Happy town. People live according to different systems. The plague: abolishes all systems. But they die all the same. Doubly useless.' He then spent five years developing this idea, though some of the best details – for example, the trams full of corpses that run regularly to the dumping ground on the cliffs – were there from the start.

The notion of political violence as a *disease* endemic in the human world was there in the first novel that dealt seriously with this general theme, Conrad's *The Secret Agent* (1907). At the close, the Professor, maker of bombs for assassinations, with his cult of force and his scorn for the 'mediocrity' of people, is still at large in London, walking the streets. The novel ends: 'Nobody looked at him. He passed on unsuspected and deadly, like a pest in the street full of men.' At the same time as Camus, but independently, the deepest psychological thinker of our time, Reich, was working on 'emotional plague' as the best term for the 'widespread and violent breakthroughs of sadism and criminality' that have marked the middle years of this century.[7]

In Camus' wonderfully imaginative and concerned handling of the symbol, there is scarcely a detail that does not stand at the same time for the lethal forces that generally threaten human life and for the specific methods and circumstances of Nazi rule. The intellectuals have lived and worked inside the bureaucracy, fussing impotently at the writing of insipid books, but now they join the resistance and finally learn to write rather more trenchantly: this is the clerk, Grand. The Church justifies the evil as part of an unintelligible but necessary 'scheme of things', though its more humane members come round to working with the Resistance: this is the priest, Paneloux. The most effective person, the leader of the Resistance, is not the middle-class socialist with a bad conscience for personal reasons (Tarrou), though he is an impressively committed and feeling person, but the practical man who sees and does *what has to be done*: the doctor and narrator, Rieux. Camus himself said to an interviewer after the war: 'You ask me why I took the side of the Resistance. This is a question which has no meaning for a certain number of men, of whom I am one. It seemed to me then, and it still seems to me, that you cannot be on the side of concentration camps.'[8]

Furthermore, people of such different outlooks were able to combine effectively in face of the worst thing, to combine as they could not in normal conditions. As Camus wrote during a major discussion of *The Plague*: 'Compared to *The Outsider*, *The Plague* does represent, beyond any possible discussion, the movement from an attitude of solitary revolt to the recognition of a community whose struggles must be shared . . . towards solidarity and participation.'[9]

The more physical details remind us just as closely of the war – the Nazis and their death-camps, the Occupation, and the Resistance. The trams full of the dead which ply incessantly to the tipping-place, the mass graves with layers of corpses and layers of quicklime, and finally and most unmistakably 'that hag-ridden populace a part of which was daily fed into a furnace and went up in oily fumes'. Here are counterparts of the typical horrors which since the thirties have bitten deepest into our sensibilities. Compare the terrible joke of the death-camp inmates: 'The only way out of Auschwitz is through the chimney.'

So the novel is about France under Nazi rule, and Camus was able to claim with pride, in his letter to Roland Barthes, that 'everyone in every European country recognised' who the enemy were in the novel, and that part of it had appeared during the Occupation, in a collection of 'resistance texts'.[10] He was equally concerned to show human life as generally and by its nature under threat. In our experience younger readers, less aware of the war and Fascism, react foremost to the vision of a community surviving, barely, through an intensification of the usual mortal ills – fever, pain, bereavement. It is because this vision comes over with such unfailing physical power that the diagnosis of Nazi Fascism is then so telling. It is indeed *the worst thing*. We cannot imagine a more potent proof of the bane which Nazism was felt to be than the unrelenting sequence of morbid symptoms, crises, deaths which give the book its atmosphere. The first deaths are of rats:

At night, in passages and alleys, their shrill little death-cries could be clearly heard. In the mornings the bodies were found lining the gutters, each with a gout of blood, like a red flower, on its tapering muzzle; some were bloated and already beginning to rot, others rigid, with their whiskers still erect.

The first human death is marked by the graphic detail which is sickening, and never becomes less so, but is never overdone, never gratuitous:

> Two hours later the doctor and Mme Michel were in the ambulance bending over the sick man. Rambling words were issuing from the gaping mouth, thickly coated now with sordes. He kept on repeating, 'Them rats! Them blasted rats!' His face had gone livid, a greyish green, his lips were bloodless, his breath came in sudden gasps. His limbs spread out by the ganglions, embedded in the berth as if he were trying to bury himself in it or a voice from the depths of the earth were summoning him below, the unhappy man seemed to be stifling under some unseen pressure.[11]

Naturally, it is the cases of people for whom we care most that have the most intense effect (for example, Tarrou's long-drawn-out crisis), but it is always an effect the author earns, by precise descriptions, not by the mixture of piety and pathos which Dickens uses at the deathbed of Paul Dombey. With that famous scene, contrast Camus' presentation of the magistrate's young son, on whom Dr Castel tries his new vaccine:

> And, just then, the boy had a sudden spasm, as if something had bitten him in the stomach, and uttered a long, shrill wail. For moments that seemed endless he stayed in a queer, contorted position, his body racked by convulsive tremors; it was as if his frail frame were bending before the fierce breath of the plague, breaking under the reiterated gusts of fever. . . .
> The light on the whitewashed walls was changing from pink to yellow. The first waves of another day of heat were beating on the windows. They hardly heard Grand saying he would come back, as he turned to go. All were waiting. The child, his eyes still closed, seemed to grow a little calmer. His clawlike fingers were feebly plucking at the sides of the bed. Then they rose, scratched at the blanket over his knees, and suddenly he doubled up his limbs, bringing his thighs above his stomach, and remained quite still. For the first time he opened his eyes, and gazed at Rieux, who was standing immediately in front of him. In the small face, rigid as a mask of greyish clay,

slowly the lips parted and from them rose a long incessant scream, hardly varying with his respiration, and filling the ward with a fierce, indignant protest, so little childish that it seemed like a collective voice issuing from all the sufferers there.[12]

The victim has not had to be sainted to exact our sympathy, and his ugly symptoms (his mouth is 'fouled with the sordes of the plague') are not censored, in order to ennoble, and therefore to justify, his death. A material and social sickness is what we are concerned with, not a mysterious curse or abstract 'evil'. The boy's death gives rise to Rieux' most definite statement of what he values, said with restrained anger to the priest: '"until my dying day I shall refuse to love a scheme of things in which children are put to torture . . . Salvation's much too big a word for me. I don't aim so high. I'm concerned with man's health; and for me his health comes first."'[13]

Although the plague abates, it is because it has lost its virulence. The vaccines have not worked, the hospitals and sanitary authorities have only contained the social effects of the disease, they have not cured sufferers or destroyed the virus. This is a measure of Camus' pessimism, or if that word is too strong, or too simple a polarising of values into 'optimism' and 'pessimism', let us call it his stoicism, his refusal to fall for any of the big consolations. At the start of the novel he has stressed the 'banality' of the townsfolk's life: 'The truth is that everyone is bored, and devotes himself to cultivating habits . . . But, at least, social unrest is quite unknown amongst us.'[14] This holds good even through the plague. As Camus put it in his plan, 'Develop social criticism and revolt. That they are lacking in imagination. They settle down to an epic as they would to a picnic. They don't think on the right scale for plagues. And the remedies they think up are barely suitable for a cold in the nose.'[15] In the novel this comes out as the normality, almost the acceptance, which so soon settles in – the lack of public grief, the absence of widespread attempts to break out of quarantine. At its most specifically political or national, this can be taken as pointing to the way the French capitulated – the very word 'capitulation' has still the squashy or spineless feel it took on when we heard the news in 1940 of the military débâcle and the setting up of the Vichy régime. In the classic work on that débâcle, Sartre's *Iron in the Soul*,

there is a scorn like Camus' for the ease with which people
curl up inside defeat and replicate their usual grubbing lives even
under the Terror, e.g. the ready way in which the prisoners of
war behind the wire play cards and cook and accept the visits
of their relatives.

There are two further levels at which the grave atmosphere
of Camus' ending can be taken. He is evoking the aftermath
of a prolonged atrocity, which cannot be cancelled out by its
having ended. Here he shows his characteristic moral depth. We
are expecting some distinct relief or upbeat as the plague dies
away and quarantine ends. The author sternly precludes any such
thing:

> Far more effectively than the bands playing in the squares
> they vouched for the vast joy of liberation. These ecstatic
> couples, locked together, hardly speaking, proclaimed in the midst
> of the tumult of rejoicing, with the proud egoism and injustice
> of happy people, that the plague was over, the reign of terror
> ended. Calmly they denied, in the teeth of the evidence, that
> we had ever known a crazy world in which men were killed
> off like flies, or that precise savagery, that calculated frenzy
> of the plague, which instilled an odious freedom as to all that
> was not the Here and Now; or those charnelhouse stenches
> which stupefied whom they did not kill.[16]

This is surely the essence of what people must feel if they think
through an extreme situation that they have survived. It is not
surprising that the atmosphere of that second-last chapter of
The Plague should be so close to Simone de Beauvoir's account
of how they felt as the war ended in Algeria:

> There was an enormous crowd of people there, and a lot of
> smoke; we almost suffocated in the little overcrowded room;
> up on the platform, some beautiful Algerian girls dressed in
> white and green were singing to the accompaniment of a small
> orchestra. This gaiety was not unclouded; serious differences
> of opinion had broken out among the Algerian leaders. Even-
> tually they would be settled. But for us, the French, the situation
> in which we were leaving Algeria left no room for joy. For
> seven years we had desired this victory; it came too late to
> console us for the price it had cost.[17]

The final significance of *The Plague*, and what is meant by the chastened and severe atmosphere of its ending, is clinched by Rieux' thoughts as he looks out over the town with its fireworks and noise of celebrating. He is thinking that the fight against terror is never-ending and happiness is always in jeopardy:

> He knew what those jubilant crowds did not know but could have learned from books: that the plague bacillus never dies or disappears for good; that it can lie dormant for years and years in furniture and linen-chests; that it bides its time in bedrooms, cellars, trunks, and bookshelves; and that perhaps the day would come when, for the bane and the enlightening of men, it roused up its rats again and sent them forth to die in a happy city.[18]

The moral weight of this, the really unanswerable truth of it, is felt in the concision of the prose – the clear, deep note of it has sounded many times throughout the novel (for example, the passage near the start of Part 3 about the way in which 'even people's distress was coming to lose something of its poignancy'). Camus is dealing with conditions of being human which we have no reason to think are not permanent. The standard demurral at the novel (for example, Barthes' objection that Camus had 'replaced a struggle against men by a struggle against the impersonal microbes of a plague'[19]) can only be valid if you suppose that one day a world will emerge which has been freed for ever from exile, disease, and murderous struggles. This may come about, but the notion seems to us more wishful than reasoned. History, whether of conflict inside the socialist countries or between them and capitalist ones, gives few grounds for a utopian level of hopefulness.

Such things cannot be proved – it is a matter, in the end, of what you are inclined to believe. For our own part we take seriously, as this book has implied throughout, the creative testimony offered by writers, and what the post-war writers bear witness to on the whole is survival rather than something more decidedly thriving or positive. In the theatre, Beckett's fables have absorbed audiences as different as West End theatre-goers and long-stay prisoners in American jails, and what he typically does is to show a few representative humans managing a sort of life in the most scanty and stripped environment. The empty

Beckett stage could be the waste-ground near a shanty town; it could be anywhere, jungle or city, after the pounding, searing, and spraying of total war. Ernst Fischer has pointed suggestively to the likeness between a Beckett stage, the sparsity of the action on it, and the denuded surroundings in *One Day in the Life of Ivan Denisovich*.[20]

In poetry (not only in English) a striking feature of this last generation is how many people have written vividly about war, even when they have not been in combat themselves. Some of this work is situated in real wars – the best, in our view, is Adrian Mitchell's writing about Vietnam[21] – while others, of a more fabling kind, fuse elements from different ages to image war as chronic. Ted Hughes, though loosely thought of as a nature poet, has again and again reached his peak in poems about war, and while 'Griefs for Dead Soldiers' and 'Scapegoats and Rabies' are clearly based on ordinary shooting wars and 'A Woman Unconscious' on the Cold War, in *Crow* there are two 'legends' of a less specific kind. 'Notes for a little Play' stares ahead towards some nuclear flash which burns up the world, leaving just two sub-human mutants:

Horrors – hairy and slobbery, glossy and raw.

They sniff towards each other in the emptiness.

They fasten together. They seem to be eating each other.

But they are not eating each other.

They do not know what else to do.

They have begun to dance a strange dance.

And this is the marriage of these simple creatures –
Celebrated here, in the darkness of the sun,

Without guest or God.

This is the sheer nightmare which probably lurks in all our minds. 'Crow's Account of the Battle' is subtler: its weirdly impersonalised phrasing, which is still so specific and weighty, suggests again that helplessness which we saw in the novels of total war:

There was this terrific battle.
The noise was as much
As the limits of possible noise could take.
There were screams higher groans deeper
Than any ear could hold.
Many eardrums burst and some walls
Collapsed to escape the noise . . .
The cartridges were banging off, as planned,
The fingers were keeping things going
According to excitement and orders . . .

There was no escape except into death.
And still it went on – it outlasted
Many prayers, many a proved watch,
Many bodies in excellent trim,
Till the explosives ran out
And sheer weariness supervened
And what was left looked round at what was left.

The last stage of the poem then brings to explicitness the suggestion that the extremity of such situations has exhausted our moral sense, our ability to will a better world:

And when the smoke cleared it became clear
This had happened too often before
And was going to happen too often in future
And happened too easily
Blasting the whole world to bits
Was too like slamming a door
Too like dropping in a chair
Exhausted with rage
Too like being blown to bits yourself
Which happened too easily
With too like no consequences.

So the survivors stayed.
And the earth and the sky stayed.
Everything took the blame.

Not a leaf flinched, nobody smiled.[22]

Such a poem virtually ventures a forecast – the bad thing is 'going to happen too often in future' – as does Camus at the end of *The Plague*: 'the tale he had to tell could not be one of a final victory . . . the plague bacillus never dies or disappears for good'. When we discussed forecasts before,[23] we said that really they are observations of something present which is thought likely to repeat or intensify itself, and so it is with these poems, plays, and novels which envisage the human situation as likely to remain extreme. If Utopia comes about in 2084 or 2184, rich in abundance and rid of class, our present fears will look like medieval bogeys. But in the present and for the foreseeable future, our species remains racked by troubles.

Towards the end of the war Reich wrote 'The Emotional Plague'. Most of the symptoms he noted are still rife, for example 'authoritarian bureaucracy; imperialistic war ideologies; everything that falls under the American concept of 'racket'; antisocial criminality; pornography; profiteering; racial hatred'. The usual reaction to these, he points out, is itself plague-ridden: 'The nature of the emotional plague necessitates police force, and this is how it spreads.'[24] So long as crime-rates rise with the growth of cities, police forces and arms expenditures swell, prisons fill to bursting, and guns and bombs spread with the spread of industry, we will not break out of this pattern of aggression and retaliation. It is a tragic aspect of this pattern that the person able to diagnose the plague tends to be so close to it himself that he is infected by it and drawn into its style of attack and counter-attack. So at the end Reich writes:

> Today, five, eight, ten, fourteen years after various unexpected and incomprehensible catastrophes, this is my standpoint: *just as a bacteriologist devotes all his efforts and energies to the total elimination of infectious diseases, the medical orgonomist devotes all his efforts and energies to the unmasking and combatting of the emotional plague as a rampant disease of the people of the world . . .* we cannot believe in the fulfilment of human existence as long as biology, psychiatry, and educational science have not come to grips with the universal emotional plague, and fought it as ruthlessly as one fights plague-ridden rats.[25]

Reich knew the aggression in himself, and knew too that it could not be wished away. But, realising fully that the situation was extreme – he died of a heart attack, in prison on a trumped-up charge, his works incinerated by the Manhattan Public Health department – he could not resist what may be called the benign extreme of a messianic, one-track solution: *'it is solely the re-establishment of the natural love-life of children, adolescents, and adults which can rid the world of . . . the emotional plague in its various forms.'*[26] This may be 'health' as Rieux means the word, but to make everything pivot on a single factor sounds very much like 'salvation' as Paneloux uses it. Probably the most any of us can do is to work stoically for health in the particular place we live in. As Nigel Gray says in his poem 'The Maze' (named after the notorious internment camp in Ulster):

> I can only carry on the struggle in small ways
> and hope the roar of the world's bombers
> will not deafen me
> to the cries of children in my own street.[27]

References

1. Literature and Crisis

1. R. Palme Dutt, *World Politics 1918–1936* (1936) p. 19; *Frendz*, (December 1972) p. 19.

2. Gerhard Schoenberner, *The Yellow Star*, trans. Susan Sweet (1969 edn) pp. 51–4.

3. *The Observer* (12 December 1971).

4. *The Listener* (12 June 1969).

5. Victor Serge, *Memoirs of a Revolutionary 1901–1941* (1951), trans. and ed. Peter Sedgwick (1963; 1967) pp. 9–10.

6. Inter-Parliamentary Union of Enquiry, 1931, quoted by Dutt, *World Politics*, pp. 31–2; W. Ashworth, *Economic History of England 1870–1939* (1960) pp. 185–6; John Terraine, *The Guardian* (19 November 1968); David Irving, *The Destruction of Dresden* (1966 edn) p. 260.

7. *The Observer* (4 October 1971).

8. See George Thayer, *The War Business* (1969).

9. Edmund Wilson, *To the Finland Station* (1955 edn) p. 384.

10. Simone de Beauvoir, *Force of Circumstance*, trans. Richard Howard (1965; 1968 edn) pp. 669–70.

11. *Solzhenitsyn: A Documentary Record*, ed. Leopold Labedz (1970 edn) p. 108.

12. David Boadella, *Wilhelm Reich* (1973) pp. 63–4, 81–8.

13. Robert Jay Lifton, *Death in Life* (1971 edn) pp. 9, 11, 17; Lifton in *The Listener* (31 August 1972); Lifton, *Home from the War* (1974).

14. Nadezhda Mandelstam, *Hope Abandoned*, trans. Max Hayward (1974) pp. 224, 613.

15. Bertolt Brecht, *Poems 1913–1956*, ed. John Willett and Ralph Manheim (1976) p. 131.

16. Interview with George Theiner, the *Guardian* (12 October 1977).

2. Total War

1. Robert Graves, *Good-bye to All That* (1929) pp. 240–1.

2. Michael Holroyd, *Lytton Strachey* (1971 edn) p. 604; Scott Fitzgerald, *Letters*, ed. Andrew Turnbull (1968 edn) p. 351.

3. *1914*, 'Peace', from *Poetical Works* (1946 edn) p. 19.

4. Siegfried Sassoon, *Collected Poems* (1947 edn) p. 11; Wilfred Owen, *Collected Poems*, ed. C. Day Lewis (1964) p. 129; Isaac Rosenberg, *Collected Poems* (1949 edn) p. 87.

5. Rosenberg, *Poems*, pp. 83–4.

6. Sassoon, *Poems*, p. 68.

7. Introduction to 'M. M.'s' *Memoirs of the Foreign Legion* (1924) pp. 89–90.

8. Sassoon, *Poems*, p. 78.

9. Owen, *Poems*, p. 72.

10. John Brophy and Eric Partridge, *The Long Trail* (1965 edn) pp. 55, 67.

11. Sassoon, *Poems*, p. 75.

12. Brophy and Partridge, *Long Trail*, p. 67.

13. Owen, *Poems*, p. 48.

14. Wilfred Owen, *Collected Letters*, ed. Harold Owen and Julian Bell (1967) p. 568.

15. Graves, *Good-bye to All That*, pp. 183–6; Sassoon, *Poems*, p. 79.

16. Joan Littlewood and Theatre Workshop, *Oh What a Lovely War* (1965) p. 90.

17. Robert Roberts, *The Classic Slum* (1971; 1973 edn) pp. 210–11.

18. *The Cruel Wars*, ed. Karl Dallas (1973) p. 213.

19. *Ibid.* p. 38.

20. *Ibid.* p. 122.

21. *Ibid.* p. 156.

22. These are all sung by Ewan MacColl on *Bundook Ballads* (1965), the second song, Hamish Henderson's 'Fareweel to Sicily', is in *101 Scottish Songs*, ed. Norman Buchan Glasgow (1962) pp. 116–17.

23. A first sampling is available in the special issue of *Fireweed* called *Phoenix Country*, ed. Nigel Gray Lancaster (1976). It includes work from Vietnam, America, and Britain.

24. Our sampling is indebted to two anthologies which we have used to fill out our own knowledge of the field: *Components of the Scene*, ed. Ronald Blythe (1966) and *The Terrible Rain*, ed. Brian Gardner (1966).

25. *Components of the Scene*, p. 171.

26. Owen, *Poems*, p. 50.

27. Keith Douglas, *Collected Poems* (1951) p. 40.

28. Keith Douglas, *From Alamein to Zem Zem* (1969) edn) pp. 23, 127–8, 140.

29. *Components of the Scene*, pp. 161, 210.

30. A. J. P. Taylor, *English History 1914–1945* (1970 edn) p. 533.

31. 'September Journal', *The Golden Horizon*, ed. Cyril Connolly (1953) p. 4.

32. *The Golden Horizon*, p. 2.

33. *Components of the Scene*, p. 170.

34. *The Golden Horizon*, p. 11.

35. Douglas, *From Alamein to Zem Zem*, pp. 5–6.

36. E. M. Forster, *Two Cheers for Democracy* (1965 ed.) p. 76.

37. Angus Calder, *The People's War* (1971 edn) p. 38.

38. John Masters, *Fourteen Eighteen* (1970 edn) plates on pp. 91, 93.

39. Peter Weiss, *The Investigation* (1965), trans. Alexander Gross (1966), pp. 10, 40.

40. We have put 'Sholokhov' in inverted commas to show our agreement with the new Russian work which strongly suggests that this modern masterpiece of epic was written, not by Sholokhov, but by the Cossack novelist F. D. Kryukov: see *Times Literary Supplement* (4 October 1974).

41. Norman Mailer, *The Naked and the Dead* (1947; 1964 edn) pp. 130–1.

42. ———, *Miami and the Siege of Chicago* (1969 edn) p. 212.

43. Bruno Apitz, *Naked Among Wolves*, trans. Edith Anderson (Berlin, 1960) pp. 183–5; A. Anatoli, *Babi-Yar* (1970), trans. David Floyd (1972 edn) pp. 109–11.

44. 'Mankind always sets himself only such tasks as he can solve': Marx, Preface to *A Contribution to the Critique of Political Economy*: Marx and Engels, *Selected Works* (Moscow, 1958) vol. I, p. 363.

45. P. E. Schramm, *Hitler: the Man and the Military Leader* (1972) p. 37; Günther Wallraff, 'A Square Deal' in *Fireweed*, 12 (1978), p. 74; a similar idiom is credited to Stalin by Victor Serge, *The Case of Comrade Tulayev* (1968 edn) p. 168.

46. *The Naked and the Dead*, p. 151.

47. Richard West, *Victory in Vietnam* (1974) p. 20.

48. *The Goebbels Diaries*, trans. and ed. Louis P. Lochner (1948) p. 38; Hans Peter Bleuel, *Strength Through Joy* (1973) p. 200; Erwin Leiser, *A Pictorial History of Nazi Germany* (1962) p. 140.

49. Compare the imagery of white space in the sequences showing Stalin in the Kremlin: Serge, *Comrade Tulayev*, pp. 165–72.

50. Tolstoy, *War and Peace*, Book X, chs 33–8.

51. *The Naked and the Dead*, pp. 476–8.

52. Wilhelm Reich, *The Mass Psychology of Fascism*, 3rd edn, trans. Vincent R. Carfagno (New York, 1970) pp. 31–2.

53. R. D. Laing, 'The Obvious' in *The Dialectics of Liberation*, ed. David Cooper (1968) pp. 29, 32.

54. *The Naked and the Dead*, p. 606.

55. Mary McCarthy, *Vietnam* (1968 edn) pp. 71–5.

56. *New Scientist* (30 March 1972); *The Guardian* (27 April 1972).

57. Thayer, *The War Business*, pp. 10, 301.

58. Jules Henry, 'Social and Psychological Preparation for War', *Dialectics of Liberation*, pp. 63–4.

59. William H. Whyte, *The Organisation Man* (1960 edn) pp. 159, 161, 279.

60. *The Observer* (29 August 1976).

61. See plates 1 and 2.

62. Irving, *Destruction of Dresden*, p. 260.

63. Kurt Vonnegut, *Welcome to the Monkey House* (1972 edn) p. 11.

64. ———, *Slaughterhouse-Five* (1969; 1972 edn) pp. 9-10, 14.

65. See below, p. 88.

66. *Slaughterhouse-Five*, pp. 52, 58.

67. David Harris, 'Ask a Marine', *Rolling Stone* (New York, 19 July 1973).

68. *Slaughterhouse-Five*, pp. 118–9, 142.

69. *Ibid*, p. 54.

70. Irving, *Destruction of Dresden*, pp. 175, 181–2, 203, 206, 215.

71. *Ibid*, pp. 203–4.

72. *Ibid*, pp. 103, 153, 190, 220, 234–6.

73. *Ibid*, pp. 125–6, 98.

74. Robert Jungk, *Brighter Than a Thousand Suns* (1960 edn) pp. 188, 190 n.2, 192; Lifton, *Death in Life*, p. 24.

75. Peter Calvocoressi and Guy Wint, *Total War* (1974 edn) pp. 872–3.

76. The peacetime situation has been no better. According to Margaret Gowing's history of British nuclear weapons policy, *Independence and Deterrence* (1974), the full Cabinet was not told of the decision to make nuclear weapons; throughout the Labour Governments of 1945–51 there was no Commons debate on atomic energy; and expenditure of £100 million on nuclear weapons was kept from Parliament.

77. *Slaughterhouse-Five*, p. 64.

3. The Russian Revolution and Stalinism

1. Marx and Engels, *Selected Correspondence* (1941 ed.) pp. 509–10.

2. Marx, *Die Moralisierende Kritik und die Kritische Moral*, quoted (and trans.) by Tony Cliff in *Russia: a Marxist Analysis* (1970 edn) p. 104.

3. E. J. Hobsbawm, *The Age of Revolution* (1962) p. 237.

4. Quoted by Isaac Deutscher, *Stalin* (1961 edn) pp. 19–20; Victor Serge, *Year One of the Russian Revolution* (1930; 1972 edn) p. 28.

5. Serge, *Memoirs of a Revolutionary*, p. 2 and n.

6. Tony Cliff, *Russia: A Marxist Analysis* pp. 102–3.

7. Friedrich Engels, *The Peasant War in Germany* (Moscow, 1956 edn) pp. 138–9.

8. V. I. Lenin, *Selected Works*, vol. VIII (Moscow, 1957) p. 37.

9. *Ibid*, vol. III (Moscow, 1971 edn) p. 626.

10. *Ibid.*, vol. III (Moscow, 1971 edn) p. 626.

11. Victor Serge, *From Lenin to Stalin* (1937; New York, 1973) pp. 43–4.

12. Konstantin Fedin, *The Conflagration* (Moscow, 1962) p. 185.

13. Deutscher, *Stalin*, p. 365.

14. Nadezhda Mandelstam, *Hope Against Hope*, trans. Max Hayward (1971) pp. 239, 332; *Hope Abandoned*, pp. 151, 248.

15. Serge, 'The Writer's Conscience', *Marxists on Literature*, ed. David Craig (1975) p. 439.

16. Konstantin Fedin, *No Ordinary Summer* (Moscow, 1950) vol. II, pp. 717–18.

17. Deutscher, *Stalin*, pp. 211–16.

18. *Ibid*, p. 211.

19. Konstantin Fedin, Preface to *Early Joys* (Moscow, 1967 edn) pp. 18, 24–5.

20. Fedin, *Early Joys*, pp. 136—8.

21. ———, *No Ordinary Summer*, vol. II, pp. 575, 656, 681–2.

22. ———, *The Conflagration*, p. 264.

23. *No Ordinary Summer*, vol. I, p. 313.

24. *Ibid*, vol. II, pp. 558–9.

25. *Early Joys*, p. 39.

26. *No Ordinary Summer*, vol. I, p. 236.

27. *Ibid*, vol. I, pp. 305–6.

28. *Ibid*, vol. II, p. 47.

29. *Ibid*, vol. II, pp. 405, 409.

30. *The Conflagration*,

31. Cliff, *Russia*, pp. 54–7.

32. *Ibid*, p. 58.

33. Quoted by Raya Dunayevskaya in *Marxism and Freedom* (1958) p. 202.

34. Cliff, *Russia*, p. 300.

35. *Ibid*, pp. 78–9.

36. *Ibid*, p. 80.

37. Zhores Medvedev, *Ten Years After Ivan Denisovich* (1973) pp. 16–44. His work and his brother Roy's is, in our opinion, the best source on this period, since the Medvedevs are non-Stalinist Russian Communists – Serge's heirs.

38. Fedin, *The Conflagration*, p. 314.

39. *Ibid*, p. 292.

40. Compare Kondratiev's dismissal to the Eastern Siberian Gold Trust

in Serge's *The Case of Comrade Tulayev* (1948; trans. Willard R. Trask, 1951) ch. 8.

41. Fedin, *The Conflagration*, p. 335.
42. *Ibid*, p. 322.
43. *Ibid*, pp. 308, 291.
44. Serge, *Comrade Tulayev*, p. 48.
45. Fedin, *The Conflagration*, p. 353.
46. *Ibid*, pp. 381–2, 294.
47. Quoted by Trotsky in *The Revolution Betrayed* (New York, 1972) p. 94.
48. Fedin, *The Conflagration*, p. 292.
49. *Ibid*, pp. 29, 274, 280.
50. *Ibid*, pp. 281–283, 277.
51. *Ibid*, pp. 57–8.
52. *The Sunday Times* (3 March 1974).
53. David Burg and George Feifer, *Solzhenitsyn* (1973 edn) pp. 142, 218.
54. Medvedev, *Ten Years After Ivan Denisovich*, p. 157; Burg and Feifer, *Solzhenitsyn*, p. 216.
55. *Soviet Literature* (Moscow, 1963) No. 2, 5.
56. Alexander Solzhenitsyn, *One Day in the Life of Ivan Denisovich*, trans. Ralph Parker (1963 edn) p. 143.
57. Solzhenitsyn, *The First Circle*, trans. Michael Guybon (1968) p. 536.
58. *The First Circle*, pp. 548, 534.
59. *Ivan Denisovich*, p. 32.
60. Medvedev, *Ten Years After Ivan Denisovich*, p. 156.
61. Burg and Feifer, *Solzhenitsyn*, p. 212.
62. Mandelstam, *Hope Abandoned*, p. 414.
63. Serge, *Memoirs*, p. 298 ff.
64. *The First Circle*, p. 581.
65. *Comrade Tulayev*, pp. 233–4.
66. Burg and Feifer, *Solzhenitsyn*, p. 161.
67. *Comrade Tulayev*, p. 202; *The First Circle*, p. 231; Solzhenitsyn, *The Gulag Archipelago* (1974 edn) vol. I, pp. 439–40.
68. *The First Circle*, pp. 280–1; Medvedev, *Ten Years After Ivan Denisovich*, p. 154; *Comrade Tulayev*, pp. 154, 277.
69. *The Guardian* (6 April 1974).
70. Leon Trotsky, *1905* (1973 edn) p. 49.
71. Medvedev, *Ten Years After Ivan Denisovich*, p. 158.
72. *Force of Circumstance*, p. 387.
73. Serge, *Memoirs*, pp. 322, 372.
74. *Comrade Tulayev*, pp. 165–72.
75. *Ibid*, p. 174.
76. *Ibid*, p. 259.

77. Osip Mandelstam, *Selected Poems*, trans. Clarence Brown and W. S. Merwin (1973) pp. 69–70.

78. *The First Circle*, p. 91.

79. *Comrade Tulayev*, pp. 180, 183, 120, 184, 197–8.

80. Solzhenitsyn, *Cancer Ward*, trans. by N. Bethell and D. Burg (1971 edn) pp. 205–7.

81. Mandelstam, *Hope Abandoned*, p. 157.

82. Serge, *Memoirs*, pp. 125–32.

83. *Memoirs*, pp. 125–7.

84. Ignazio Silone, *Fontamara*, trans. Gwenda David and Eric Mosbacher (1934; 1975 edn) p. 188.

85. Silone, *Bread and Wine*, trans. Gwenda David and Eric Mosbacher (1937; New York, 1946 edn) pp. 309–10. We have quoted from the earlier version of the novel, since Silone rewrote it, taking away much of its political edge and many powerful scenes, when he returned to Italy after the war. He also renamed it *Wine and Bread*: this is the version most recently published in Britain (Panther) – under the original title!

86. Serge, *Memoirs*, pp. 128–9.

4. *Decadence and Crack-up*

1. 'Echoes of the Jazz Age', *The Bodley Head Scott Fitzgerald*, vol. II (1959) p. 18.

2. Robert Graves and Alan Hodge, *The Long Weekend* (1961 edn) p. 324.

3. Arnold Bennett, *Journals* (1954 edn) pp. 301–2.

4. Michael Phillips, 'Landfall', *The Listener* (21 November 1974).

5. *The Bodley Head Scott Fitzgerald*, vol. II, p. 11.

6. Reich, *Mass Psychology of Fascism*, p. 32.

7. *The Tales of D. H. Lawrence* (1934) p. 612.

8. James Klugmann, 'Basis and Superstructure', *Essays on Social Realism and the British Cultural Tradition* (n.d.) p. 15.

9. Lawrence, *Tales*, pp. 565, 568, 640.

10. Sybille Bedford, *Aldous Huxley, I, 1894–1939* (1973) p. 266.

11. Christopher Isherwood, *The Lion and the Shadows: An Education in the Twenties* (1938) p. 265.

12. Victoria Sackville-West, *Passenger to Teheran* (1926) p. 74.

13. Evelyn Waugh, *When the Going Was Good* (1951 edn) pp. 236–7.

14. *When the Going Was Good*, pp. 254, 272.

15. *Passenger to Teheran*, pp. 170–1.

16. *When the Going Was Good*, pp. 8, 187.

17. Graham Greene, *Journey Without Maps* (1936; 1971 edn) pp. 17–19.

18. Leonard Woolf, *Growing* (1961) pp. 51–3, 211–2.

19. Woolf, *Downhill All the Way* (1967) pp. 9, 40, 48.

20. Noreen Branson and Margot Heinemann, *Britain in the Nineteen Thirties* (1971) pp. 145–6.

21. F. Scott Fitzgerald, *The Great Gatsby* (1926; 1950 edn) pp. 11–13, 19.

22. See also his remark in his notebooks that 'there were citizens travelling in luxury in 1928 and 1929 who, in the distortion of their new condition, had the human value of Pekinese, bivalves, cretins, goats.' (Edmund Wilson (ed), *The Crack-up and Other Pieces* (New York, 1945) p. 21.)

23. *The Great Gatsby*, pp. 68–9.

24. *Ibid*, p. 168.

25. L. H. Myers, *The 'Clio'* (1925; 1945 edn) pp. 5, 15, 17.

26. *The 'Clio'*, pp. 123–9.

27. *Ibid*, pp. 34, 120, 131.

28. Woolf, *Growing*, pp. 212–13.

29. We owe this point to Dr D. C. R. A. Goonetilleke of the Vidyodaya University, Ceylon. See also his article 'Colonial Neurosis: Kipling and Forster', *Ariel* (Calgary, 1974) vol. v, no. 4.

30. Aldous Huxley, *Beyond the Mexique Bay* (1934; 1949 edn) pp. 8–9.

31. Waugh, *When the Going Was Good*, p. 204.

32. Sackville-West, *Passenger to Teheran*, p. 103.

33. Harold Nicolson, *Diaries and Letters 1930–1939*, ed. Nigel Nicolson (1969 edn) pp. 89, 92.

34. *Passenger to Teheran*, pp. 74–5.

35. Greene, *Journey Without Maps*, p. 89.

36. *Journey Without Maps*, p. 121.

37. *Ibid*, p. 79.

38. V. G. Kiernan, *The Lords of Human Kind* (1972 edn) p. 336.

39. Woolf, *Downhill All the Way*, p. 189.

40. Huxley, *Beyond the Mexique Bay*, pp. 175–80.

41. Alan Bullock, *Hitler: A Study in Tyranny* (1962 edn) pp. 66, 339; William L. Shirer, *The Rise and Fall of the Third Reich* (1964 edn) pp. 63–4, 299; Richard Grunberger, *A Social History of the Third Reich* (1974 edn) pp. 548–9.

5. *The Nullity of the Slump*

1. George Orwell, *The Road to Wigan Pier* (1937; 1959 ed) pp. 76–7; Allen Hutt, *The Condition of the Working Class in Britain* (1933) p. 181.

2. Maurice Dobb, *Studies in the Development of Capitalism* (1946) p. 331.

3. Orwell, *The Road to Wigan Pier*, p. 19; *Collected Essays, Journalism, and Letters* (1970) vol. I, p. 217.

4. Dos Passos, *USA* (New York, 1937) vol. III, p. 136.

5. Orwell, *The Road to Wigan Pier*, p. 20; *Nineteen Eighty-four* (1949) pp. 25–6, 78.

6. Harold Macmillan, quoted in Branson and Heinemann, *Britain in the Nineteen Thirties*, p. 6; Taylor, *English History 1914–1945*, p. 340; L. C. B. Seaman, *Post-Victorian Britain, 1902–1951* (1966) p. 232.

7. Orwell, *Essays*, vol. I, pp. 585–6.

8. H. L. Beales and R. S. Lambert (eds), *Memoirs of the Unemployed*, (1934) pp. 280–1, 287, 24.

9. Orwell, *Essays*, vol. I, p. 207.

10. *Memoirs of the Unemployed*, pp. 13, 25.

11. J. McLaren-Ross, *Memoirs of the Forties* (1965) p. 25.

12. We are indebted to Colin Pickthall for the loan of this book.

13. *Memoirs of the Unemployed*, pp. 93–4, 217–18.

14. Robert Tressell, *The Ragged Trousered Philanthropists* (1914; 1955 edn) p. 630; Upton Sinclair, *The Jungle* (1906; 1965 edn) p. 412.

15. Lewis Grassic Gibbon, *A Scots Quair* (1950 edn) vol. III, pp. 143–4.

16. David Craig, *The Real Foundations*: Literature and Social Change (1973) pp. 145–9.

17. Eric Hobsbawm, *Industry and Empire* (1968) p. 5.

18. Dutt, *World Politics 1918–1936*, p. 46; Allen Hutt, *The Post-War History of the British Working Class* (New York, 1938) pp. 10–14.

19. Wal Hannington, *A Short History of the Unemployed* (1938) pp. 64–7.

20. Walter Greenwood, *Love on the Dole*, ch. 10; *There Was a Time* (1967) ch. 38.

21. Dobb, *Development of Capitalism*, pp. 326–7 and n. 1, pp. 344–6; Arthur Schlesinger, 'The First Hundred Days of the New Deal', *The Aspirin Age*, ed. Isabel Leighton (1964 edn) p. 286.

22. Howard Fast, 'An Occurrence at Bethlehem Steel', *The Aspirin Age*, pp. 394–408; Dobb, *Development of Capitalism*, pp. 353–7.

23. *Harlan Miners Speak: Report on Terrorism in the Kentucky Coal Fields* (New York, 1932) p. 31.

24. Edmund Wilson, *The Shores of Light* (New York, 1952) p. 435.

25. James T. Farrell, 'Some Observations on Literature and Society', *Reflections at Fifty* (1956) p. 184.

6. *Social Tragedy*

1. Arthur Miller, *Collected Plays* (1958) p. 49; Dennis Welland, *Arthur Miller* (1961) pp. 4–5.

2. We owe these and later factual points on Farrell to Peter R. Sheal, who took our course in 'Literature and Society, 1910–1945' at the University of Lancaster in 1967–8.

3. Reich, *Character Analysis* (1973 edn) ch. 16; and see below, p. 286.

4. See also Farrell, *Reflections at Fifty*, pp. 183–7.

5. Farrell, *The Young Manhood of Studs Lonigan* (1936 edn) pp. 465–8.

6. *Studs Lonigan*, pp. 429–31.

7. *Ibid*, p. 405.

8. *Ibid*, p. 499.

9. *Ibid*, pp. 507–12.

10. Review in *Scrutiny* (Cambridge, 1937) vol. v, p. 424.

11. Farrell, *Reflections at Fifty*, pp. 188–223.

12. *The Guardian* (16 December 1974).

13. Steinbeck, *The Grapes of Wrath* (1950 edn) pp. 260–1, 320; see also pp. 138, 219.

14. *Ibid*, p. 182.

15. *Ibid*, pp. 36–7.

16. *Ibid*.

17. *Harlan Miners Speak*, p. 289.

18. Dorothea Lange and Paul Schuster Taylor, *An American Exodus: a record of Human Erosion in the 'Thirties* (1969 edn) p. 134.

19. *Chi wai-chih*, quoted in Huang Sung-k'ang, *Lu Hsun and the New Culture Movement of Modern China* (Amsterdam, 1957) p. 65; 'Silent China', *Selected Writings of Lu Xun*, ed. Gladys Yang (1973) pp. 163–4.

20. Gibbon, *A Scots Quair*, vol. i, p. 193.

21. G. S. Pryde, *Scotland from 1603 to the Present Day* (1962) pp. 232–3.

22. William Wordsworth, *Letters*, ed. Philip Wayne (1954) p. 40.

23. Pryde, *Scotland from 1603*, pp. 293–4, 296.

24. Gibbon, *A Scots Quair*, vol. i, p. 33.

25. *Ibid*, vol. ii, p. 138.

26. 'A Note on Nostalgia', *Scrutiny* (Cambridge, 1932) vol. i, p. 16.

27. *A Scots Quair*, vol. iii, p. 144.

28. Grunberger, *Social History of the Third Reich*, p. 152.

29. *The Price of a Head*, trans. Eva Wulff, Anna Seghers, *Two Novelettes* (Berlin, 1960) pp. 113–14.

30. *The Price of a Head*, pp. 245–7.

31. R. A. C. Parker, *Europe, 1914–1945* (1969) p. 225; Karl Dietrich Bracher, *The German Dictatorship* (1970) p. 147; plus additional figures from Peter Mensing, University of the Rühr at Bochum.

32. Reich, *Mass Psychology of Fascism*, pp. 49–50.

33. *Ibid*, pp. 60–2.

34. *The Price of a Head*, p. 293.

35. *Mass Psychology of Fascism*, p. 66.

36. *Fontamara*, pp. 29–31.

37. *Ibid*, pp. 82–3.
38. *Ibid*, pp. 53–4, 140–5.
39. *Ibid*, p. 32.
40. *The Observer* (14 November 1973).
41. 'Report of an Investigation into the Peasant Movement in Hunan', esp. section 'Vanguard of the Revolution', *Selected Works*, vol. I (Peking, 1953) p. 32.
42. Antonio Gramsci, *The Modern Prince and Other Writings* (1957) pp. 42–3, 29.
43. Christopher Hibbert, *Mussolini* (1965 edn) p. 74.
44. *Fontamara*, p. 173.
45. Gramsci, *Modern prince*, p. 35; Silone, *Emergency Exit* (1969) p. 61.

7. *Thwarted Revolutionaries*

1. Seghers, *Two Novelettes*, pp. 108–9.
2. 'Sholokhov', *The Don Flows Home to the Sea*, trans. Stephen Garry (1970 edn), pp. 827–8.
3. Victor Serge, *Birth of Our Power* (1931; 1970 edn) p. 231.
4. Serge, *Case of Comrade Tulayev*, p. 362.
5. Arthur Koestler, *Scum of the Earth* (1941; 1955 edn) pp. 114–7.
6. Orwell, *Essays*, vol. III, pp. 270–2.
7. 'Some Thoughts on Our New Literature', *Marxists on Literature*, ed. Craig, pp. 395–6.
8. Georg Lukács, 'Tolstoy and the Development of Realism', *Marxists on Literature*, p. 315.
9. *Man's Estate*, trans. Alastair Macdonald (1961 edn), pp. 5–7.
10. *Ibid*, p. 95.
11. *Ibid*, p. 97.
12. *Ibid*, pp. 96–7.
13. *Ibid*, pp. 86–7.
14. *Ibid*, p. 91.
15. Jean Lacouture, *André Malraux* (1975) pp. 134, 147.
16. *Ibid*, p. 89; Malraux, *Days of Contempt*, trans. Haakon M. Chevalier (1936) pp. 13–14.
17. F. R. Leavis, 'Literature and Society', *The Common Pursuit* (1952) p. 185.
18. Christopher Caudwell, *Illusion and Reality* (1946 edn) p. 125.
19. *Man's Estate*, p. 62.
20. *Ibid*, p. 270.
21. *Ibid*, p. 168.
22. Serge, *From Lenin to Stalin*, pp. 45–6.

23. Pavel Vladimirov, *The Special Region of China 1942–5*, quoted in *The Observer* (30 September 1973).

24. Edgar Snow, *Red Star Over China* (1937) pp. 161–2.

25. *Man's Estate*, pp. 129–30.

26. *Ibid*, pp. 304–5.

27. *Ibid*, p. 310.

28. Brecht, 'Theatre for Pleasure or Theatre for Instruction', *Marxists on Literature*, pp. 417–8.

29. Lacouture, *André Malraux*, pp. 172, 183–4.

30. *Man's Estate*, p. 311.

31. *Ibid*, p. 319.

32. There are several translations of this poem in print. We have used the one in *Fireweed* (1976) no. 5, pp. 59–60.

8. The Literature of Unfreedom

1. Sinclair, *The Jungle*, pp. 198–9.

2. Franz Kafka, *In the Penal Settlement*, trans. Ernst Kaiser and Eithne Wilkins (1949) p. 215.

3. Victor Serge, *Men in Prison*, trans. Richard Greeman (1972 edn) pp. 45–6.

4. *The Collected Short Prose of James Agee*, ed. Robert Fitzgerald (1972) pp. 50, 214–17.

5. Simone de Beauvoir, *The Prime of Life*, trans. Peter Green (1965 edn) p. 554.

6. D. J. Dallin and B. I. Nicolaevsky, *Forced Labour in the Soviet Union* (1948), quoted by Robert Conquest, *The Great Terror* (1971 edn) pp. 9, 454 and n.2.

7. Conquest, *The Great Terror*, pp. 493, 495.

8. Anna Akhmatova, *Selected Poems*, trans. Richard McKane (1969) pp. 10, 90, 95, 97, 99, 101, 105.

9. *Izvestia*, (18 August 1963); Conquest, *The Great Terror*, p. 495.

10. Angela Davis, *If They Come in the Morning* (1971) p. 30.

11. *The Militant*, 5 July 1974.

12. Zhores and Roy Medvedev, *A Question of Madness* (1971).

13. See esp. Erich Fromm, *The Fear of Freedom* (1942, 1966) and Isaiah Berlin, *Two Concepts of Liberty* (1958).

14. Reich, *Mass Psychology of Fascism*, pp. 18–19.

15. Bettelheim, *The Informed Heart* (1970 edn) p. 138.

16. Huw Beynon, *Working for Ford* (1973) pp. 114, 118, 121.

17. *The Informed Heart*, pp. 223–4; compare the treatment of workers drawn from the death camps in the Krupp works during the war: Wallraff, 'A Square Deal', *Fireweed*, no. 12, pp. 73–5.

18. Beynon, *Working for Ford*, pp. 75–6.

19. Primo Levi, *Survival in Auschwitz* (1958) p. 120.

20. *Ibid*, p. 80; *The Jungle*, p. 214.

21. Emile Zola, *Thérèse Raquin* (2nd edn, Paris, 1868).

22. Tennyson, *Works* (1897) p. 464.

23. E. M. Forster, *Howards End* (1941 edn) p. 44.

24. H. G. Wells, *The History of Mr Polly* (1946 edn) pp. 7, 9.

25. Brecht, *Poems 1913–1956*, pp. 23, 524.

26. Evgenya Ginzburg, *Into the Whirlwind*, trans. Paul Stevenson and Manya Harari (1968 edn) pp. 288–9.

9. *Artists and the Ominous*

1. *USA*, vol. III, pp. 461–4.

2. *Ibid*, vol. III, p. 432; Brecht, *Selected Poems*, trans. H. R. Hays (New York, 1959), pp. 121–3. The central passage seems to us better translated than in *Poems 1913–1956*, p. 216.

3. Anna Seghers, *The Seventh Cross*, trans. James A. Galston (Boston, 1942) pp. 140–1.

4. *Ibid*, pp. 287–8.

5. *Selected Works of Lu Hsun*, trans. Yang Hsien-yi and Gladys Yang, vol. III (Peking, 1959) pp. 212–13.

6. See below, p. 302, n. 28.

7. Auden, *Collected Shorter Poems 1930–1944* (1950), pp. 51–2.

8. *Ibid*, p. 64.

9. *Ibid*, pp. 111–12; Jean-Paul Sartre, *What Is Literature?* (1947; 1967 edn) p. 157.

10. John Berger, *The Success and Failure of Picasso* (1965) p. 123.

11. 'Guernica' is discussed in detail in the chapter on the Spanish Civil War: see below, pp. 271–5.

12. Lewis Mumford, *The Condition of Man* (1963 edn), plate XIII, facing p. 374.

13. Mumford, *The Culture of Cities* (1940) ch. 3; *The City in History* (1966) ch. 15.

14. Shirer, *Rise and Fall of the Third Reich*, pp. 1152–4.

15. See Plates 3–4.

16. See Plate 5.

17. Craig, *The Real Foundations*, pp. 87–9, 184–7, 195–207.

18. *Reminiscences of Marx and Engels* (Moscow, n.d.) p. 59.

19. Berger, *Success and Failure of Picasso*, pp. 146–9; Mumford, *Condition of Man*, caption to plate XIV.

20. This painting and four others discussed in the next few pages are reproduced in black and white in *Fireweed* (1976) no. 12, pp. 5–9.

21. See Plate 6.

22. See above, Ch. 4, p. 137.

23. 'Ballad of the "Jew's Whore", Marie Sanders', *Tales from the Calendar* (1949; 1961 edn (trans Yvonne Kapp and Michael Hamburger) pp. 26–7.

24. Wilhelm Boeck and Jaime Sabartés, *Picasso* (1955) p. 400.

25. Lowry, *Under the Volcano* (1963 edn) p. 112.

26. *Ibid*, pp. 154, 157.

27. *Ibid*, pp. 235–6.

28. *Ibid*, p. 370.

29. *Ibid*, p. 311.

30. *Ibid*, pp. 357–73; 375–6.

10. Spain: Life Against Death

1. *The Observer* (30 June 1975).

2. See above, ch. 2, pp. 54, 61–2.

3. Hugh Thomas, *The Spanish Civil War* (1965 edn) pp. 416–17.

4. *Ibid*, pp. 537 ff.

5. Edgell Rickword, 'To the Wife of a Non-Interventionist Statesman', *Left Review* (March 1938); quoted from Edward Lucie-Smith (ed.), *The Penguin Book of Satirical Verse* (1967) p. 271.

6. Arturo Barea, *The Forging of a Rebel*, trans. Ilsa Barea (1972) pp. 624–5.

7. Thomas, *Spanish Civil War*, p. 349 and n. 1, pp. 443–4.

8. Barea, *Forging of a Rebel*, pp. 670–1.

9. Michael Foot, *Aneurin Bevan*, vol. I (1966 edn) p. 189.

10. Thomas, *Spanish Civil War*, pp. 190–1.

11. George Orwell, *Homage to Catalonia* (1951 edn), p. 3.

12. Serge, *Case of Comrade Tulayev*, pp. 158–9.

13. Thomas, *Spanish Civil War*, pp. 760–1, 790.

14. Orwell, *Homage to Catalonia*, pp. 198–9; 96–7.

15. Malraux, *Days of Hope*, trans. Stuart Gilbert and Alastair Macdonald (1968 edn) pp. 113–14.

16. See Cornell Capa (ed.), *The Concerned Photographer* (New York, 1968), seventh photo by Capa.

17. Boeck and Sabartes, *Picasso*, p. 237; Berger, *Success and Failure of Picasso*, p. 168.

18. Barea, *Forging of a Rebel*, pp. 680–1, 695.

19. Thomas, *Spanish Civil War*, p. 349 n. 1.

20. Barea, *Forging of a Rebel*, p. 659.

21. Orwell, *Homage to Catalonia*, p. 76.

22. Barea, *Forging of a Rebel*, p. 596.

23. From *Deutsche Kriegsfibel: Gesammelte Werke*, 9, *Gedichte*, 2 (Frankfurt, 1967) p. 640, trans. Peter Mensing and Keith Evans, *Fireweed* (1977) no. 8, p. 10.

24. Barea, *Forging of a Rebel*, p. 551.

25. Robin Skelton, *Poetry of the Thirties* (1964) p. 150.

26. This refers to work in English. Hugh MacDiarmid's major poems from 1931–5 are the comparable work from Scotland (for quotation and commentary, see Craig, *The Real Foundations*, pp. 239–47) and kindred work in other languages would include, in Spanish, Neruda's 'The People' and 'The Invisible Man' (translations by Alastair Reid in *Fireweed*, no. 1 (1975) pp. 14–18, and no. 5 (1976) pp. 17–23.

27. Cut to twenty-three in the course of Auden's final jettisoning of the poem as 'trash which he is ashamed to have written'. The cut verses include one of the most sanguine and politically positive, which we judge to be artistically quite all right –

> The beautiful roar of the chorus under the dome;
> Tomorrow the exchanging of tips on the breeding of terriers,
> The eager election of chairmen
> By the sudden forest of hands. But today the struggle.
>
> (Skelton, *Poetry of the Thirties*, 41, 136)

28. Peter Stansky and William Abrahams, *Journey to the Frontier* (1966) pp. 346–51.

29. Skelton, *Poetry of the Thirties*, p. 137.

30. *Ibid*, pp. 150–1.

31. Sartre, *The Age of Reason*, trans. Eric Sutton (1963 edn) p. 121.

32. Sung in Spanish by the Ian Campbell Group on *Songs of Protest* (1962), side 1, track 1.

33. See Plate 7.

34. Berger, *Success and Failure of Picasso*, p. 164.

35. See John Berger, *Ways of Seeing* (1972) pp. 151–3.

36. *Selected Poems*, trans. Tanya Babars (1967) pp. 60, 64–5.

37. Roland Penrose, *Picasso* (1971 edn) p. 311, n. 11.

38. Ronald Gray, *Brecht* (1961) p. 100.

39. Penrose, *Picasso*, p. 315.

40. Alfred H. Barr, *Picasso: Fifty Years of His Art* (New York, 1946) p. 250.

11. Collapse and Survival

1. Penrose, *Picasso*, p. 317.
2. Orwell, *Collected Essays*, vol. IV, p. 507.
3. Seghers, *The Seventh Cross*, p. 140.
4. Mandelstam, *Hope Against Hope*, pp. 159, 171–2,
5. John Terraine, *The Guardian* (19 November 1968).
6. Albert Camus, *Selected Essays and Notebooks*, ed. and trans. Philip Thody (1970) pp. 225–6; Conor Cruise O'Brien, *Camus* (1970) p. 33.
7. Reich, *Character Analysis*, p. 504; and see below, pp. 286–7.
8. O'Brien, *Camus*, p. 33.
9. Camus, *Essays and Notebooks*, p. 220; for Malraux' similar 'conversion', see above, p. 199.
10. *Ibid*, p. 220.
11. Camus, *The Plague*, trans. Stuart Gilbert (1960 edn) pp. 15, 21.
12. *Ibid*, pp. 175–6.
13. *Ibid*, p. 178.
14. *Ibid*, pp. 5, 7.
15. *Essays and Notebooks*, p. 228.
16. *The Plague*, p. 242.
17. Simone de Beauvoir, *Force of Circumstance*, p. 658.
18. *The Plague*, p. 252.
19. *Essays and Notebooks*, p. 307.
20. Ernst Fischer, *Art Against Ideology* (1969) pp. 25–34.
21. Brought together as 'Peppermints and Daisychains' in *Phoenix Country*, pp. 30–6.
22. Ted Hughes, *Crow: From the Life and Songs of the Crow* (1970 edn) pp. 72, 21–2.
23. See above, pp. 242–5.
24. Reich, *Character Analysis*, pp. 505, 508.
25. *Character Analysis*, pp. 538–9.
26. *Character Analysis*, p. 539.
27. Nigel Gray, *Come Close* (1978), p. 68.

Index

Abrahams, P. 9
Aeschylus 212
Africa 126, 134–6
Agee, J. 213, 271
Akhmatova, Anna 216–17, 277
Alexander III, Tsar 69–70
Algeria 282
anarchists 236
Anatoli, A. 36, 42
Anderson, S. 152
anonymous soldiers' poetry 13, 17–24, 26
Apitz, B. 36, 41–2, 193, 214
Aragon, L. 27
armed conflicts, post-1945 3, 51
arms trade 51
Asia 121, 124, 126–7, 131–3
Astray, M. 255–6, 261
atomic bombs 7, 36, 62–4, 277, 284
Auden, W. H. 141, 150, 240–2, 256, 263, 265–8
Austin, E. 219–20
Austria 7

Babel, I. 8, 9, 211
Bacon, F. 273
Bangash, Mohammad Aszal 183
Barea, A. 255–6, 261–4, 269–70
Barthes, R. 279, 283
Basque freedom movement 253, 255
Beauvoir, Simone de 4, 111, 214, 282
Behan, B. 211, 213
Bettelheim, B. 6–7, 211, 214, 223, 225
Beynon, Huw 224–5
Birrell, A. 14
Borodin, A. P. 203
Borkenau, F. 191
Bosch, H. 247
Brecht, B. 8, 150, 207–9, 211, 232–3, 236–7, 247–8, 263, 273–4
Brierley, W. 142–5

Britain 134, 141
    alienated labour in 224–5
    depression of thirties 138–46
    race riots 118–19
    repression 148–50
    social tragedy 168–73, 184
BBC 12
Brooke, R. 15
Brueghel 247, 274
Bukharin 189
Buñuel, L. 128
Burgess 154

Camus, A. 27, 131, 193, 277–83, 286
Capa, R. 257
capitalism 206–7, 222, 226
    alienated labour under 224–7
Cary, Joyce 142, 193
cattle-trucks, human transport
    in 56–7
Caudwell, C. 199
censorship 222
Chamberlain, N. 117–18
Ch'en Tu-hsiu 203
Cherwell, Lord 62
Chiang Kai-shek 202–4
children in war 1–2, 33–4, 280–1
China 191–2, 195–8, 239
Chon Shu-jen 8
Churchill, Sir W. 62–3
civilisation, collapse of 119–30, 136
    and survival 276–87
classes, social, in industry and
    war 42–6, 50
comedy 37, 41
communism 189–91, 200, 203, 215, 218, 267, 269; see also Soviet
    Union; Stalinism
concentration camps 6–7, 36–7, 41–2, 193, 213, 215, 223, 225–7, 238–40, 277, 279, 282

Conrad, J. 123, 126, 133, 135, 198, 278
Cooper, D. 221
Cornford, J. 256, 263, 265–9
Craig, D. 33
Crane, S. 228, 231–2
Crimean war 21–2, 24
crisis, literature of 1–11
Cummings, E. E. 37

Daily Mail 13, 15
Dali, S. 244
Dallas, K. 21
Darwin, C. 231
Davidson, J. 146
Davis, Angela 218
decadence of the twenties 117–26
Delacroix, F. V. E. 243
depression:
  economic and psycho-social 34–5, 138, 140, 159
  industrial action in 148–9
  literature of 141–62, 168–78
  paintings of 245–8
Deutscher, I. 65, 68, 73
di Chirico, G. 243–4
Dickens, C. 46, 146, 183, 280
Disraeli, B. 205
Dix, Otto 245–6
Dos Passos, J. 14, 26, 43, 139, 152, 166, 235, 248, 271
Dostoevsky 212
Douglas, K. 25, 28–30
Dreiser, T. 152, 231, 226,
Dresden 54–5, 58–62, 277
  painters 245
Dryden, J. 121
Dunayevskaya, Raya 84

Eastern Europe, art in 10
Eisenhower, D. D. 61
Eisenstein, S. M. 88–9
Eliot, G. 150, 201, 227
Eliot, T. S. 32–3, 119–20, 123, 125, 140, 199, 273
Eluard, P. 27
emigrants, post-war 124
Engels, F. 66, 71
Evans, W. 271

Fanon, F. 193
fantasy 37

Farrell, J. T. 141, 152–62, 271
fascism 43, 45, 53, 119, 121, 129, 134, 136, 178–86, 191, 244, 254–6, 269
fascist prisons 213
Fedin, K. 10, 72–83, 86–91, 246
Fischer, E. 284
Flaubert, G. 228
Flower, D. 277
forecasting 242–6, 248, 254
Forster, E. M. 34, 131, 193, 230–1
France:
  occupied 214, 277–9
  poetry of 27
  revolution 67–8, 121, 243
Frank, Hans 45
freedom, concept of 221–2
Freud, S. 211

Gaskell, Elizabeth 150
Germany:
  depression in 173–8
  post–1918 decadence 123–4
  see also Nazism
Gibbon, L. G. 141, 147, 149, 166, 167, 168–73, 178
Ginzburg, E. 6, 213, 215, 233–4
Gissing, G. R. 150
Goebbels, J. 45
Gorky, M. 69, 167, 229, 231, 257
Graebe, F. 1
Gramsci, A. 185, 211
Graves, R. 13, 35
Gray, N. 287
Greene, G. 6, 126, 134, 142, 193, 240
Greenwood, W. 142, 149–50
Grosz, G. 245
Groves, General 63
Grundig, Hans *and* Lea 245–8

Harding, D. W. 171, 172
Hardy, T. 14, 169, 231–2
Harris, Sir A. T. 61–2
Heilpern, J. 1
Heller, J. 37, 52–3
Hemingway, E. M. 26, 258
Hersey, J. 36
Hikmet, N. 271
Himmler, H. 45
Hiroshima 7, 36, 277
Hirszfeld, L. 1
Hitler, A. 34, 136–7, 177, 226, 236, 245
Howard, B. 256, 263–4

Hughes, T. 284
Hungary 193-4
Huxley, A. 123, 133, 136-7
Huxley, J. 50

Indo-China 206
industry, war as special case of 42-6,
   50, 52
Ireland 22
   Northern 1-2, 149, 218, 287
irradiation of brain 220-1
Irving, D. 54
Isherwood, C. 123-4, 142
Italy, fascist 178-86

James, H. 227-9
Japanese 243
Jews 213, 240, 247
Jones, T. 55
Joyce, J. 153, 271
Jungk, R. 63-4

Kafka, F. 211
Keats, J. 5
Kesey, K. 221
Keyes, S. 25, 28
Khrushchev, N. 86, 215, 216-17
Kibalchich, Victor 8
Kipling, R. 133
Koestler, A. 5, 8, 10-11, 189, 191,
   211, 213, 270
Korean war 1, 26
Kronstadt rising 113-15
Kundera, M. 10
Kuomintang 196-7, 201-3

labour:
   alienated 224-7
   camps 215-18, 277
   division of 42-4
   repression of 148-52
La Guma, A. 9
Laermans, E. 245-6
Laing, R. D. 50, 221
Lange, Dorothea 166
Latin America 129-33, 136
Lawrence, D. H. 14, 16, 120-3, 198,
   243
League of Nations 53
Leahy, Admiral W. D. 63
Leavis, F. R. 199
Leavis, Q. D. 161
Leiris, M. 276
Lenin, V. I. 4. 7, 65, 68-72, 75, 91, 245

Levi, P. 214, 226-7
Lewis, A. 25, 30
Lewis, C. D. 32
Lifton, R. J. 7
literature, *see* crisis; depression;
   massacres; unfreedom; World War
   II
Lloyd George, D. 140
lobotomy 220
London, J. 226, 231
Lowry, M. 248-52
Ludendorff, E. von 1
Lu Hsun 6, 8, 166-7, 192, 239-40
Lukács, G. 194

MacArthur, General 63
MacDiarmid, H. 141
Macdonald (US journalist) 118
Mailer, N. 22, 37-52
Malraux, A. 191, 193, 195-208,
   211-13, 256, 259-61, 270
Manchester Guardian 13
Mandelstam, N. 6, 73, 99-100, 113,
   211, 215, 276-7
Mann, T. 211
Mao Tse-tung 167, 203
Marchenko, A. 211, 213
Marx, K. 42, 66, 193, 222
Marxism 104, 234, 265
massacres 64, 202
   literature of 36-7, 54-5, 58-62
   and music 3-4, 244
Meckleburg, T. J. 272
Medvedev, Roy 216
Medvedev, Zh. 93, 98-9, 103-4, 216,
   221
Melekhov, G. 38
mental hospitals 221
Mexico 248-52
Michelangelo 273
middle class 35, 68, 70-1, 128
Milgram, S. 50
Miller, A. 153, 214
Mitchell, A. 284
Molotov, Y. M. 83
mothers 20
Mphahlele, E. 9
Muggeridge, M. 140
Mumford, L. 243-4
Munch, E. 273
Mussolini, B. 185
Myers, L. H. 129-32, 193

naturalism 228-33

Nazism 45, 168, 176–7, 207, 213, 223, 225–7, 240–3, 246–8, 254, 278–9; *see also* concentration camps; Hitler
Newman, O. 244
newspaper reports, use of 271, 274
Nicolson, H. 134
Nkasa, N. 9
Nkosi, L. 9
Norstad, General 62
Northern Ireland 149, 218, 287
children in 1–2

Orwell, G. 139–42, 150, 152, 191, 248, 256–63, 276
Owen, W. 5, 15, 17, 19, 25, 28, 260
Oxenham, J. 14

painters 243–8, 256, 261, 270–5
Pakistan 183–4
Parker, R. 93
Parker, T. 213
patriotism 13, 32, 34–5
peasants' struggle 183–6
pen-names 8
Penrose, R. 274
personality change operations 221
Phillips, M. 119
Picasso, P. 243, 246–7, 256, 261, 270–6
planners, war 3, 23–4, 46, 62–4
poetry 13–32
glorifying war 14–15, 17, 23
realist 14–32
political prisoners 218–21
political restraints 223
political struggle in folk-myth 8
politicians' speeches 32
Pope, A. 120–1
Portal, Air Chief Marshal 62
Pound, Ezra 123
prison 210–20, 229
writers in 211, 287
prisoners, political 218–21
private property 219
propaganda 50–1
psychiatry, unfreedom and 221

racism 9, 118–20
Radvanyi, Netty 8
realism 30, 38, 227–9
in poetry 14–32
Reed, H. 25

Reeves, J. 277
Reich, W. 7, 50, 119, 155, 177, 211, 276, 286–7
religion 13, 14–15
repression 136, 253
in Britain 148–50
Soviet 72, 85–6, 90, 108, 167, 213, 215–18, 277; *see also* Soviet Union; Stalinism
in USA 150–2, 160, 235–6
of writers 8–9
revolution 2, 7, 65, 67
betrayed 65, 114–16
French 67–8, 121, 243
Mexican 248
Russian 65–74, 80–1, 121
revolutionaries:
in Britain 141
in China 194–204
in France 189–91
in Germany 236–9, 245–6
in Spain 253–8, 266–9
Rosenberg, I. 15–16, 35
Rousseau, J.-J. 243
Royal Air Force 61–2
Russia 8, 66, 68
Civil War 74, 81, 113–14, 200
industrialisation 68–9
revolution 65–74, 80–1, 121; *see also* Soviet Union

Sackville-West, Victoria 124–5, 133–4
Salvemini, G. 191
Sartre, J.-P. 27, 56, 192, 211, 214, 242, 269, 281
Sassoon, S. 12, 15–18, 25, 35, 38
satire 37
Schulz, W. 190
Scotland 168–73
Scott Fitzgerald, F. 117–19, 128–9, 132
Seghers, Anna 8, 146, 150, 168, 173–8, 185, 187, 189, 201, 211, 213, 237, 276
Serge, V. 2–3, 6, 65, 72, 74, 86, 91, 191, 207–8, 211–12, 215, 237, 267
Birth of Our Power 188, 270
Case of Comrade Tulayev, The 10–11, 100–16, 189, 256, 258, 270
Long Dusk, The 8, 276
sexuality, repressed 47, 49, 177–8
Shahn, B. 248

Shakespeare, W. 208
Shelley, P. B. 212, 227
Sholokhov, M. 72–3, 187–8
Sillitoe, A. 187, 217
Silone, I. 6, 8, 114–15, 150, 168,
    178–87, 191, 201, 211
Sinclair, Upton 146–7, 162, 167,
    210–11, 226–7, 231
slump of thirties 118, 246–8; *see also*
    depression
sociology 6, 155–6
Solzhenitsyn, A. 5, 6, 10, 38, 72, 86,
    91–100, 102–5, 110–12, 211, 215–16
South Africa 9
Soviet Union 10, 74–116, 167, 221
    bureaucracy in 202
    Communist Party 83, 85–8, 115–16
    labour camps 215–18, 277
    Old Guard 85–91
    purges 85–6, 90, 108, 213
    revolutionary refugees from 189–90
    see also repression; Russia; Stalinism
Spaatz, USAF Chief 61
Spain 253
    Civil War 243, 246–7, 253–75
Spender, S. 31–2, 256, 263–4
Squire, J. C. 14
Stagg, F. 218
Stalin, J. 65, 72–5, 83–5, 91–2, 105,
    111, 202–3, 222
Stalinism 86, 89–90, 97–116, 190–1,
    213, 233, 269
Stalinolatry 74–5, 86, 106
Steinbeck, J. 6, 141, 152, 162–6, 168,
    201
Steiner, G. 41
Sutherland, G. 246
swastika 137
Swinburne, A. C. 159
Szasz, T. 221

Taylor, A. J. P. 54
Taylor, P. S. 166
Tennyson, Alfred Lord 229–32
Terkel, S. 224
terror 42, 282
terrorism:
    anti-officer 44
    as fable 5
Teush, V. 99
Theatre Workshop 6, 12
Thomas, E. 35
Thrasher, F. M. 154

Times, The 13, 270
Tolstoy, L. 38, 46, 96, 229
tradition 223
Tranquilli, Secondo 8
trench poets 12, 17, 21, 35
Tressell, R. 146–7, 162, 167
Trotsky, L. 71, 75, 90, 189, 237
Truman, President 63
Tvardovsky 93, 217–18

unemployment 138, 141–6, 149–51,
    162
unfreedom:
    concept of 221–4
    psychiatry and 221
    depression in 139, 150, 159–62
    militarisation 51–2
    poetry of 26–7
    political prisoners in 218–21
    repression in 150–2, 160, 235–6
    social tragedy in 152–62

values, breakdown of 118
Vercors 27
Vietnam war 1–3, 7, 27, 61, 284
    anti-officer terrorism 44n
Vittorini, E. 8, 211
Vizetelly, H. R. 229
Vonnegut, K. 36–7, 53–62, 64
Vyshinsky, A. 215

war:
    casualties 3, 6, 35, 54
    glorification of 12–14
    children in 1–2, 33–4, 280–1
    escalation of 61–2
    morale after 117–23
    mothers' attitudes to 20
    planners 3, 23–4, 46, 62–4
    as special case of industry 42–6, 50,
        52
    total 12–64
    see also poetry and specific wars
War Illustrated 19
Waugh, E. 124–5, 130, 133, 142
weapons, modern 3
Weigel, Helene 273–4
Weiss, P. 36–7
Weissberg, A. 213
Wells, H. G. 118, 231–2
West, R. 2
wilderness, appeal of 125–6, 131–5
Wilson, E. 152

Wolfe, General 23–4
Woolf, L. 126–7, 132–3, 136
Woolf, Virginia 127–8, 198, 271
Wordsworth, W. 169
World War I:
  casualties 1, 3–13, 35–6
  children in 1
  poetry of 14–21, 25, 35
  racism after 118–20
  total war in 12–29
World War II 77, 242
  anticipated 248

  casualties 1, 12–13, 35–6, 54, 277
  children in 1
  dress rehearsal in Spain 253–4
  poetry of 25–32
  prose literature of 30, 38–64
  total war in 12, 30–64
Wright, R. 271

Yeats, W. B. 119, 121–2, 240

Zola, E. 167, 226, 228–9, 231